Automate Everyday Tasks in Jira

A practical, no-code approach for Jira admins and power users to automate everyday processes

Gareth Cantrell

BIRMINGHAM—MUMBAI

Automate Everyday Tasks in Jira

Copyright © 2021 Packt Publishing

Group Product Manager: Aaron Lazar
Publishing Product Manager: Richa Tripathi
Senior Editor: Storm Mann
Content Development Editor: Nithya Sadanandan
Technical Editor: Rashmi Choudhari
Copy Editor: Safis Editing
Project Coordinator: Francy Puthiry
Proofreader: Safis Editing
Indexer: Pratik Shirodkar
Production Designer: Aparna Bhagat

First published: January 2021

Production reference: 1200121

Published by Packt Publishing Ltd.
Livery Place
35 Livery Street
Birmingham
B3 2PB, UK.

ISBN 978-1-80056-286-8

www.packt.com

`Packt.com`

Subscribe to our online digital library for full access to over 7,000 books and videos, as well as industry leading tools to help you plan your personal development and advance your career. For more information, please visit our website.

Why subscribe?

- Spend less time learning and more time coding with practical eBooks and videos from over 4,000 industry professionals

- Improve your learning with Skill Plans built especially for you

- Get a free eBook or video every month

- Fully searchable for easy access to vital information

- Copy and paste, print, and bookmark content

Did you know that Packt offers eBook versions of every book published, with PDF and ePub files available? You can upgrade to the eBook version at `packt.com` and, as a print book customer, you are entitled to a discount on the eBook copy. Get in touch with us at `customercare@packtpub.com` for more details.

At `www.packt.com`, you can also read a collection of free technical articles, sign up for a range of free newsletters, and receive exclusive discounts and offers on Packt books and eBooks.

Contributors

About the author

Gareth Cantrell is currently working at Square Enix as an ITSM Solution Architect. He has a software engineering background, having spent at least 15 years of his 25-year career developing various software solutions for clients.

For the past 10 years, Gareth has been involved in designing, implementing, and integrating solutions with Jira and other Atlassian tools, most of which involve automation to varying degrees.

He has worked on projects including end-to-end ITSM solutions with Jira/Slack and other third-party tools, Agile and DevOps implementations in Jira, and integrations with various CI/CD tools.

About the reviewers

Grant Andrew Finnemore qualified as an electrical engineer in the 1990s, but his passion is for building software, focusing on business empowerment. He also readily imparts his knowledge and experience.

Grant owns, and is the CEO of, a boutique software company – GuruHut. This company has been in operation since 2000, and has a reputation for quality and delivery. In 2014, Obsidian Systems took an interest, and together they became an Atlassian Platinum Partner.

Grant is married to Ania. Fast-forward 20 years and they manage a household comprising 4 young children – Liam, Rory, Sean, and Ewan, and 3 energetic labradors. When not working, he is often to be found on his bicycle, either riding the hills around home or virtually.

This is Grant's second book. The first was entitled *Views from the Southern Cross*.

I'd like to express my thanks to the diligent staff at Packt who guided my input to this project – not always an easy task. My sincere gratitude to the author, who I had the pleasure of working with at GuruHut, and who roped me into this project. Finally, to my wife and family for their support over so many years – thank you. I'm so much better for having you all in my life.

Ravi Sagar is an Atlassian consultant, Drupal expert, and author of several Jira books. He currently works for Adaptavist, an Atlassian partner company headquartered in London. In 2010, Ravi founded Sparxsys Solutions Pvt. Ltd., a start-up company that provides consultancy and training services on Atlassian tools and Drupal.

In his spare time, he loves blogging and publishes free online courses on his website, `ravisagar.in`, covering Jira, Drupal, Linux, Emacs, Org Mode, and programming. He also has a popular YouTube channel, Ravi Sagar, where he produces free content on these topics with a focus on ScriptRunner for Jira and Automation.

I would like to thank my wife, Shelly, who has always stood by me and helped me achieve my goals, and my daughter, Raavya, for allowing me to spend time reviewing this book. Finally, I also wish to thank my parents for their endless support.

Packt is searching for authors like you

If you're interested in becoming an author for Packt, please visit authors. packtpub.com and apply today. We have worked with thousands of developers and tech professionals, just like you, to help them share their insight with the global tech community. You can make a general application, apply for a specific hot topic that we are recruiting an author for, or submit your own idea.

Table of Contents

Section 2: Beyond the Basics

3
Enhancing Rules with Smart Values

4
Sending Automated Notifications

5
Working with External Systems

Section 3: Advanced Use Cases with Automation

6
Automating Jira Service Management

7

Automating Jira Software Projects

8

Integrating with DevOps Tools

9

Best Practices

10

Troubleshooting Tips and Techniques

11

Beyond Automation: an Introduction to Scripting

Other Books You May Enjoy

Index

Preface

Jira started life as a tool for developers to track bugs in their software and, over the years, has evolved into a powerful project management platform, allowing organizations to plan, manage, and track work across multiple teams and across software, service management, and business projects.

Over time, this has enabled teams to keep on top of their projects; however, it comes at a price of administrative overhead, with users having to constantly perform simple and repetitive tasks in order to ensure that Jira issues stay relevant to the work being performed.

In late 2019, Atlassian acquired Automation for Jira, an app that allows users to automate tasks in Jira without needing to write any code. This has since been incorporated into Jira Cloud as a native feature, while still being offered as an optional add-on for users of server-based Jira products.

This book is a hands-on guide for power users and Jira administrators to automate daily, repetitive, and tedious tasks using a no-code approach with the Jira family, including Jira Software, Jira Service Management, and Jira Core.

Who this book is for

This book is for Jira administrators and project managers who want to learn about the automation capabilities provided in Jira. Familiarity with Jira and a working knowledge of Jira administration concepts, including workflows and project configurations, is required.

What this book covers

Chapter 1, Key Concepts of Automation, introduces you to the key concepts of automation rules in Jira. We will explore the basic building blocks of rules and what a typical rule looks like. By the end of this chapter, you will understand how automation rules work, and how to create your first rule.

Chapter 2, Automating Jira Issues, explores how conditions are used to narrow the scope of automation rules and how to target and work with related issues such as sub-tasks and linked issues. We will also learn how to edit and transition issues and how to use the advanced field editor. Finally, you will learn how to schedule tasks at defined intervals, all with the help of working examples presented for each topic.

Chapter 3, Enhancing Rules with Smart Values, talks about smart values and how they enable you to add significantly more power and complexity to your automations. We will learn how to manipulate and format text strings, dates and times, and lists of values, and finally, the powerful math expressions that are available.

Chapter 4, Sending Automated Notifications, explains how to use automation to send notifications using automation rules. You will learn how to send email notifications to customers as well as how to integrate into external chat systems including Slack and Microsoft Teams with the help of practical use cases covered in each topic.

Chapter 5, Working with External Systems, explains how to use automation rules to send requests to external systems and how to work with the data returned from those systems. We will also learn how automation rules can be used to create incoming webhooks to receive requests from external systems and how to process the data received.

Chapter 6, Automating Jira Service Management, explains how to use automation rules to triage and automatically route incoming requests to Service Management projects. We will also learn how to monitor SLA compliance for service requests and, finally, how we can fully automate common tasks end to end.

Chapter 7, Automating Jira Software Projects, explores a number of automations targeted at Jira Software projects in particular. You will be taken through some practical examples of automating typically repetitive tasks that developers encounter in their everyday work, such as keeping versions in sync between multiple projects, and ensuring that the correct sub-tasks are created for tasks and stories.

Chapter 8, Integrating with DevOps tools, explains how to use automation to integrate with tools such as GitHub and Bitbucket. We will discover how to hook into events within these tools to automatically transition related issues on your Scrum board and notify the relevant parties of the updates. We'll also look at how you could kick off a deployment in your build tool when your Sprint is completed.

Chapter 9, Best Practices, introduces you to some best practices to follow when authoring your automation rules. In particular, we will explore how to plan and organize rules and look at the best ways to ensure that your rules do not have a negative impact on performance.

Chapter 10, Troubleshooting Tips and Techniques, focuses on troubleshooting techniques. We will explore techniques for debugging rules and solving common issues. We will also look at service limits and how you can monitor and maintain them, and finally, we'll examine automation performance insights and how you can use them to fine-tune your rules.

Chapter 11, Beyond Automation; an Introduction to Scripting, takes an introductory look at one of the most popular scripting add-ons for Jira and compares it with automation rules using a prior example so we can examine the differences between no-code automation rules and scripting in both Jira Cloud and Jira Server.

To get the most out of this book

You will need to have as a minimum a free Atlassian account with access to both Jira Software and Jira Service Management on Jira Cloud. Alternatively, you will need to install the latest version of Jira Server/Jira Data Center and Automation for Jira. All examples have been tested against both Jira Cloud and Jira Server:

Software/hardware covered in the book	OS requirements
Jira Cloud	Not applicable
Jira Server (latest version)	Windows, macOS X, and Linux (any)
Automation for Jira (if using Jira Server)	Not applicable
ScriptRunner for Jira	Not applicable
Confluence Cloud	Not applicable
Bitbucket Cloud	Not applicable
GitHub	Not applicable
Jenkins	Windows, macOS X, and Linux (any)

If you are using the digital version of this book, we advise you to type the code yourself or access the code via the GitHub repository (link available in the next section). Doing so will help you avoid any potential errors related to the copying and pasting of code.

If you haven't already done so, you should sign up to the Atlassian Community at `https://community.atlassian.com`. This is a community of Atlassian users from all over the world where you can ask questions or join discussions and get answers to many of the questions you may have regarding any Atlassian-related topic, including automation.

Download the example code files

You can download the example code files for this book from GitHub at https://github.com/PacktPublishing/Automate-Everyday-Tasks-in-Jira. In case there's an update to the code, it will be updated on the existing GitHub repository.

We also have other code bundles from our rich catalog of books and videos available at https://github.com/PacktPublishing/. Check them out!

Code in Action

Code in Action videos for this book can be viewed at http://bit.ly/3spH12T.

Download the color images

We also provide a PDF file that has color images of the screenshots/diagrams used in this book. You can download it here: https://static.packt-cdn.com/downloads/9781800562868_ColorImages.pdf.

Conventions used

There are a number of text conventions used throughout this book.

Code in text: Indicates code words in text, database table names, folder names, filenames, file extensions, pathnames, dummy URLs, user input, and Twitter handles. Here is an example: "Set the **Due date** field to {{now.withDayOfMonth(15)}} and click **Save**."

A block of code is set as follows:

```
{
    "summary": "some summary text",
    "bugDescription": "some descriptive text",
    "softwareVersion": "version string"
}
```

When we wish to draw your attention to a particular part of a code block, the relevant lines or items are set in bold:

```
{
    "type": "page",
    "title": "Version {{version.name.jsonEncode}}",
    "space": {
```

Any command-line input or output is written as follows:

```
$displayName = "Service Desk Autobot"; $objectId =
(Get-AzureADServicePrincipal -SearchString $displayName).
ObjectId
```

```
$roleName = "Company Administrator"; $role =
Get-AzureADDirectoryRole | Where-Object {$_.DisplayName -eq
$roleName}
```

Bold: Indicates a new term, an important word, or words that you see on screen. For example, words in menus or dialog boxes appear in the text like this. Here is an example: "Select **New action** and then **Send email** and complete the fields as follows before clicking **Save**."

> **Tips or important notes**
> Appear like this.

Get in touch

Feedback from our readers is always welcome.

General feedback: If you have questions about any aspect of this book, mention the book title in the subject of your message and email us at customercare@packtpub.com.

Errata: Although we have taken every care to ensure the accuracy of our content, mistakes do happen. If you have found a mistake in this book, we would be grateful if you would report this to us. Please visit www.packtpub.com/support/errata, selecting your book, clicking on the Errata Submission Form link, and entering the details.

Piracy: If you come across any illegal copies of our works in any form on the internet, we would be grateful if you would provide us with the location address or website name. Please contact us at copyright@packt.com with a link to the material.

If you are interested in becoming an author: If there is a topic that you have expertise in, and you are interested in either writing or contributing to a book, please visit authors.packtpub.com.

Reviews

Please leave a review. Once you have read and used this book, why not leave a review on the site that you purchased it from? Potential readers can then see and use your unbiased opinion to make purchase decisions, we at Packt can understand what you think about our products, and our authors can see your feedback on their book. Thank you!

For more information about Packt, please visit `packt.com`.

Section 1: Getting Started – the Basics

In this section, you will be introduced to automation rules and learn about the best practices around defining and managing rules.

This section consists of the following chapters:

- *Chapter 1, Key Concepts of Automation*
- *Chapter 2, Automating Jira Issues*

1
Key Concepts of Automation

Atlassian Jira is a popular workflow management system that allows teams to track their work in various scenarios, the most common of these being software projects, followed closely by service desks. Over time, most teams come to realize that there are many repetitive and time-consuming tasks that need to be performed to ensure project tasks and requests are tracked accurately and in a timely manner.

Since Atlassian recently acquired **Automation for Jira** and incorporated it as a native feature in Jira Cloud, it is now even easier to create complex and powerful automation rules using an intuitive *if-this-then-that* approach without having to write any code. Automation for Jira is still available as an add-on app for Jira Server and Jira Data Center and we'll cover both use cases where they diverge in this book.

If, like me, you find yourself saying *I'm sure there is a way we can automate this somehow* when confronted with yet another monotonous and time-consuming task in Jira, then you've picked up the right book.

In this chapter, we are going to cover the following main topics:

- Getting started with rules
- Working with triggers
- Working with conditions

- Working with actions
- Creating your first rule

By the end of this chapter, you will have a good understanding of the key concepts of automation rules in Jira and how the various components of rules work together to enable you to write rules that will help you to automate any repetitive and other time-consuming tasks in Jira so that you can focus on what really matters: getting things done!

Technical requirements

The requirements for this chapter are as follows:

- **Jira Cloud environment**: If you don't already have access to Jira, you can create a free Jira Cloud account at `https://www.atlassian.com/software/jira/free` and ensure that you have both Jira Software and Jira Service Management selected; or
- **Jira Server environment**: If you are using Jira Server (available from `https://www.atlassian.com/software/jira/download`), ensure that you have licenses for both Jira Software and Jira Service Management. In addition, you will also need to ensure that you install the *Automation for Jira* app available from the Atlassian Marketplace.

In both instances, you will need to have at least Project Administrator access to a Jira project.

You can download the latest code samples for this chapter from this book's official GitHub repository at `https://github.com/PacktPublishing/Automate-Everyday-Tasks-in-Jira`.

The Code in Action videos for this chapter are available at `https://bit.ly/38POLVA`

Getting started with rules

To understand automations, we need to first take a look at some of the basic concepts associated with them, the foremost of which is the rule.

In this section, we will examine the following concepts:

- The definition of a rule
- Rule scopes
- Owners and actors
- Audit log

These will give us a foundation on which to build in the following chapters, so without further ado, let's get started.

What is a rule?

A rule, in its basic form, is a list of steps required to be executed in a specific order to achieve a desired outcome that is both repeatable and auditable.

By this, we mean that a rule should have the exact same outcome each and every time it is executed, and we should be able to examine the actions applied by the rule chronologically.

Specifically, a rule in Jira allows you to perform actions against issues based on criteria that you set.

Every rule is comprised of three basic components:

- **Triggers**: The entry point for a rule.
- **Conditions**: These refine the criteria of the rule.
- **Actions**: These perform the actual tasks.

In addition to these, a rule also contains some other basic information:

- The rule name
- The rule description
- The rule scope
- The rule owner and actor
- Options to notify the rule owner in the case of rule failures
- Options to allow other rules to trigger this rule
- The rule audit log

Together, these form the building blocks of automation rules. By combining these basic components, you are able to create rules that can be used to automate many time-consuming and repetitive tasks.

The following screenshot shows an outline of the basic components of a rule in Jira:

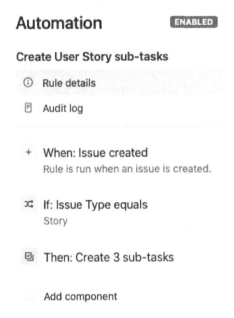

Figure 1.1 – Visualizing the basic components of a rule

We will cover each of these components in more detail in this and the following chapter.

Understanding scopes

Rules in Jira have can be applied in one of four **scopes**:

- Global rules
- Multi-project rules
- Project type-specific rules
- Project-specific rules

The following table shows how these rule scopes are defined and which Jira permission is required in order to create and manage a rule that is applied in that scope:

Scope	Description	Permission
Global	Rule is applicable to issues in all projects	Global admin
Multiple project	Rule is applicable to issues in selected projects	Global admin
Project type-specific	Rule is applicable to issues in the selected project types (Jira Cloud only)	Global admin
Project-specific	Rule is applicable to issues in only one project	Project admin Global admin

Figure 1.2 – Rule scope permissions

As we can see, most of the rule scopes require you to have Jira Global admin permissions in order to manage them, and this is expected, as these rules span multiple projects and cannot therefore rely on project-specific permissions.

Project rules, on the other hand, can be created and managed by project administrators in addition to Jira global administrators.

Having this distinction allows Jira administrators to delegate the project-specific automations and gives project administrators more flexibility in managing their own project rules, whilst Jira Global admins can focus on automation rules that can be applied across a much wider audience.

Rules can also be moved between the global and project scopes by Jira administrators. If, for example, it is determined that a project-specific rule could be reused across multiple projects, a Jira administrator can adjust the scope of the rule. The reverse is also true. If a particular global rule is only ever utilized by a single project, a Jira administrator can adjust the scope to that specific project and by doing so, transfer administration of the rule to the project administrators.

Owners and actors

Every rule requires both an owner and an actor.

The **owner** of the rule is generally the user who created the rule and is responsible for maintaining the rule. The rule owner will also receive email notifications from Jira if the rule fails while executing.

The rule **actor** is the user the rule will execute as. This user must have the correct permissions in the project for both the trigger and any actions the rule will perform. For example, if you create a rule that needs to add a comment to an issue, the rule actor will need to have the *Add Comments* permission in the project.

> **Important note**
>
> In Jira Cloud, the default rule actor is always the *Automation app user* and will belong to the *atlassian-addons-project-access* project role. This project role is assigned every permission in a project and can be changed in the **Project settings | Permissions** section. Removing permissions from this role could potentially cause add-ons not to work correctly, so it is generally advised not to change these permissions.

Audit log

Every rule has its own **audit log**, which tracks the execution of a rule chronologically and allows you to examine the outcome as well as the actions applied to the affected items for each execution.

This functionality is not only necessary to be able to track the outcomes of a rule execution; it also gives us the ability to be able to debug rules when things don't go as planned.

We will examine the role of the audit log in debugging rules in more detail in *Chapter 10, Troubleshooting Tips and Techniques,* when we will explore techniques for debugging rules and solving common issues.

Working with triggers

The starting point for every rule is a **trigger**. A trigger defines how the rule will activate and will generally listen for events in Jira, such as when an issue is created or when values in fields within an issue change.

In this section, we will begin by looking at Jira events as this will help you to understand *when* and *why* rules are triggered, after which we'll explore the available rule triggers, *what* each of them are, and *how* they can be used.

Understanding Jira events

To better understand how triggers work, it is worth taking a brief look at how events in Jira work as these are the driving force behind most of the triggers available in the automation rules.

Jira, like many applications, incorporates an event-driven architecture. In essence, this means that every time an action is performed within Jira, an event is fired that allows interested components to listen to and perform additional actions based on those events.

There are two main types of events that affect issues in Jira. The first of these are workflow events. These events are fired when an issue is created and any time an issue is transitioned to a new status in its underlying workflow, and are responsible for causing the **Issue created** and **Issue transitioned** triggers in an automation rule to fire.

The second type of event is issue events and these are responsible for the majority of the remainder of the issue triggers and are fired whenever a user (or app) makes a non-workflow-related change to an issue, such as updating a field or linking two issues together.

Rule triggers

Jira automation provides us with a number of triggers that we can use to kick off the execution of our rules.

These triggers are grouped into categories to make it easier to identify which type of trigger you will need when creating your rule, and these categories are as follows:

- Issue triggers
- DevOps triggers
- Scheduled triggers
- Integration triggers

We will take a look at each category in turn and the available triggers in each.

Issue triggers

As we mentioned in the *Understanding Jira events* section, the majority of triggers relate to events occurring on issues, such as when an issue is created or edited.

Most of the triggers are self-explanatory and single purpose. However, there are some that can be further configured to make the trigger more specific without needing to use additional conditions.

Let's take a look at the issue triggers available at the time of writing and what each one does:

- **Field value changed**: This rule will run when the value of a field changes. You configure this trigger by selecting the fields you want to monitor or by using a regular expression that matches the field names you want to monitor. You can also optionally narrow which issue operations will trigger the rule.

- **Issue assigned**: This rule will run when the assignee of the issue changes.

- **Issue commented**: This rule will run every time a new comment is added to an issue. Note though that this does not include when comments are edited or deleted.

- **Issue created**: This rule will execute every time an issue is created. This trigger listens for the issue-created event that is always fired as the first step in a workflow.

- **Issue deleted**: This rule will run when an issue is deleted.

- **Issue link deleted**: This rule will run when an issue is unlinked from another issue. You can optionally configure this trigger to only execute for specific link types.

- **Issue linked**: This rule will execute when an issue is linked to another issue. Like the issue link deleted trigger, you can optionally configure which issue link type the trigger will execute for.

- **Issue moved**: This rule will execute when an issue is moved from one project to another. You can optionally specify that the trigger only executes if an issue is moved from a specific project.

- **Issue transitioned**: This rule will execute every time an issue transitions through the workflow from one status to another. You can optionally configure this trigger to listen for a specific transition or multiple transitions to or from a specific status.

- **Issue updated**: This will trigger the rule when details on an issue are updated, except when changes are made by linking, assigning, or logging work on an issue.

- **SLA threshold breached**: This rule will get triggered for issues in a Service Management project when the SLA threshold has breached or is about to breach. You can configure which SLA to monitor as well as the time before or after it has breached.

- **Work logged**: This rule will run when a worklog is created, updated, or deleted.

There are a few specialized issue triggers worth taking note of and these are the following:

- **Manual trigger**: This trigger is not dependent on any underlying events. Instead, triggers of this type are presented to the user in the Issue view and require the user to manually activate them.

- **Multiple issue events**: This trigger allows you to listen to more than one event for an issue. For example, this is useful when you need to perform the same automation when a ticket is both created and updated, rather than having to create a separate rule for each event.

- **Sprint and Version triggers**: These triggers are not directly associated with underlying issues, and instead they allow you to perform actions against the related issues when something happens to the containing Sprint or when the versions pertaining to a project are created or changed.

- **Service limit breached**: This is a specialized trigger that allows you to monitor and manage your automation rules themselves.

DevOps triggers

DevOps triggers are specific to Jira Cloud and allow you to create rules that are linked to events in your connected development tools, such as Bitbucket and GitHub.

Let's take a quick look at these triggers and what they do:

- **Branch created**: This rule will run when a branch in a connected source repository is created.

- **Build failed**: This rule will be executed when a build in a connected build tool fails. You can optionally configure this to trigger on specific build names, branches, or tags.

- **Build status changed**: This rule will be run when the build status in a connected build tool changes, for example, from failed to success, or vice versa. This can optionally also be configured to trigger on specific build names, branches, or tags.

- **Build successful**: Similar to the previous triggers, this will cause the rule to execute when a build in a connected build tool is successful. This can also optionally be configured to listen for specific build names, branches, or tags.

- **Commit created**: This rule will run when a commit is created in a connected source repository.

- **Deployment failed**: This rule will execute when a deployment against a specified environment fails.

- **Deployment status changed**: This rule will run when the deployment against a specified environment changes status from failed to success, or vice versa.

- **Deployment successful**: This rule will run when the deployment against a specified environment is successful.

- **Pull request created**: This rule will execute when a pull request in a connected source repository is created.

- **Pull request declined**: This rule will execute when a pull request in a connected source repository is declined.

- **Pull request merged**: This rule will execute when a pull request in a connected source repository is merged.

> **Important note**
> DevOps triggers are not available in Jira Server, although these triggers can be emulated using the *Incoming webhook integration* trigger.

We will explore these triggers in more detail in *Chapter 8, Integrating with DevOps tools*.

Scheduled triggers

Scheduled triggers allow you to configure rules that run at defined intervals. These can be simple fixed-rate intervals or more complex schedules.

Scheduled triggers are perfect for automating clean-up processes or to create recurring tasks that need to be actioned and we'll look at these in more detail in *Chapter 2, Automating Jira Issues*.

Integration triggers

The final type of trigger is the incoming webhook. This trigger provides a way for third-party applications to trigger automation rules.

An incoming webhook trigger can specify the exact issues to act on or even provide real-time data that you can use to update issues.

Chapter 5, Working with External Systems, is dedicated to exploring the ways in which we can integrate our automation rules with external systems.

Working with conditions

Once a rule has been triggered and in order for it to continue to run, it will need to meet the criteria that you have specified.

Conditions, therefore, narrow the scope of a rule and if a condition fails, the rule will stop running and no actions following that condition will be performed.

Automation provides a number of conditions that can be applied to a rule, most of which can be applied either in isolation or chained together to form more complex conditions.

The set of conditions available to automation rules is as follows:

- **Advanced compare condition**: This condition allows us to compare two values using smart values, functions, and regular expressions. This condition gives more flexibility for when the `Issue` fields condition is not sufficient.

- **If/else block**: This condition allows us to perform alternate actions depending on whether the conditions in each block match and you can have as many conditions as you need.

- **Issue attachments**: This condition checks whether attachments exist for an issue.

- **Issue fields condition**: This condition checks an issue field against a particular criterion that you can specify.

- **JQL condition**: This condition allows you to check an issue against any valid JQL query.

- **Related issues condition**: This condition allows you to check whether related issues exist for the triggered issue and whether they match a specific JQL query.

- **User condition**: This condition allows you to compare a user to a set of criteria.

We will cover conditions in more detail in *Chapter 2, Automating Jira Issues.*

Working with actions

The final building block in the rule chain is **actions**. Actions are the components that allow you to make changes within your projects and can perform many tasks, including editing issues, sending notifications, creating tasks, and much more.

Like conditions, a rule chain can include multiple actions in the chain, allowing you to perform more than one task in a single rule; for example, editing an issue field followed immediately by sending a notification via email.

Rule actions are grouped in categories in order to make it easier to identify the type of action you want your rule to perform.

Let's take a look at the categories and then we'll examine the actions in each category:

- Issue actions
- Notifications
- Jira Service Management
- Software
- Advanced

Issue actions

Actions in the **Issue actions** category allow you to make changes to existing issues as well as create new issues. Let's look at the available actions in this category, and what each of them do:

- **Assign issue**: This action assigns the issue to a user. This can be to a specific user or by using a method such as balanced workload, round-robin, or randomly when using a list of users.

- **Clone issue**: This action creates a new issue, in the same project or in a different project, copying across all possible fields. It is not a true clone and will therefore not copy across links, attachments, or comments.

- **Comment on issue**: This action allows you to add a comment to the issue, optionally specifying the visibility in Service Management projects.

- **Create issue**: This action creates a new issue in the project, or selected project for global rules, and allows you to select which fields to configure and their corresponding values.

- **Create sub-tasks**: This action creates sub-tasks on the issue and sets the summary to the specified value. If you select to add additional fields, this action will be converted to a **Create issue** action with the issue type set to **sub-task**.

- **Delete comment**: This action can only be used with triggers that involve adding a comment and can only be used to delete the comment that triggered the rule. It cannot be used to delete any other comment.

- **Delete issue**: This action causes the current issue that is in context to be deleted.

- **Delete issue links**: This action allows you to delete any issue links on an issue. You can specify certain types of links to delete or specific issues.

- **Edit issue**: This action lets you edit the fields on the issue by choosing the fields and setting their corresponding values.

- **Link issues**: Using this action will allow you to link an issue to another issue by selecting the link type and the issue to link.
- **Log work**: This action allows you to log time worked against an issue using either actual dates and times, or by using smart value functions.
- **Manage watchers**: Use this action to specify users to add or remove as watchers on the issue.
- **Transition issue**: This action allows you to transition an issue from one status to another through the assigned workflow. You can additionally select fields and their associated values to be updated during the transition, providing these fields are present on the issue transition screen.

Notifications

Actions in this category allow you to send **notifications** via various channels as well as give you the ability to send data to other external systems. The actions in this category are as follows:

- **Send email**: This action sends an email when the rule executes.
- **Send Microsoft Teams message**. This action allows you to send a message to notify a team in Microsoft Teams when the rule is run.
- **Send Slack message**: This action allows you to send a message to a Slack channel or specific Slack user when the rule is run.
- **Send Twilio notification**: Use this action to send an SMS message using Twilio when the rule is executed.
- **Send web request**: This action allows you to send a request to any third-party system that can accept web requests. You can also configure this action to accept response data from the external system that can be used in subsequent actions.

Jira Service Management

These actions allow you perform tasks specific to **Service Management** projects and are as follows:

- **Add Service project customer**: This action allows you to add customers to your Service Management project.
- **Approve/Decline request**: You can use this action to approve or decline a request in a Service Management project.
- **Create service request**: This action allows you to create a service request in a Service Management project. It is similar in function to the **Create issue** action, but adds the ability to select the request type and customer.

Software

Software actions allow you to manipulate the **software** versions within a Software project and are limited to the following actions:

- **Create version**: This action allows you to create new versions within the project. It will not create a version if one with the same name already exists.

- **Release version**: This action releases the next unreleased version in the project using the version's release date. Alternatively, you can configure which unreleased version to release and optionally override the release date.

- **Unrelease version**: This action allows you to unrelease a version.

Advanced

The final category is the **advanced** actions. These actions allow you to do things such as creating variables for use in later rule components, log information to the audit log, and more. Let's take a look at these now:

- **Create variable**: This action allows you to create a smart variable for use in other actions and conditions within this rule, and is only available in Jira Cloud.

- **Delete attachments**: This action allows you to delete attachments from an issue using regular expressions against the attachment filenames.

- **Log action**: Use this action to log a message to the rule's audit log. This action is particularly useful in debugging rules.

- **Lookup issues**: This action allows you to use JQL to search up to 100 other issues and include the results list in other actions in this rule.

- **Re-fetch issue data**: This action refreshes the smart values with the latest issue data. This is especially useful in multi-action rules where subsequent actions rely on previously updated data.

- **Set entity property**: You can use this action to set entity properties on issues, projects, and users. These are hidden key/value stores that are used by certain apps.

Creating your first rule

Now that we've covered the key concepts, let's take a look at creating your first automation rule.

Before we dive into the actual rule, we'll take a brief look at the rule editor user interface and its layout.

The rule editor

The following screenshot represents the **automation rule editor**. As you can see, it is presented in a structured format that makes working with rules straightforward and intuitive:

Figure 1.3 – The automation rule editor

Let's take a look at the main components that we have numbered in the preceding screenshot:

1. **Rule-chain view**: In this panel, you can see the name of the rule, along with the components that make up the rule, in the order in which they will be processed during execution. This is also where you can access the rule's main details and its bespoke audit log. You can also drag and drop components in this panel to reorder them.

2. **Components**: You can add new components anywhere in the rule chain by clicking on the **Add components** link that appears when you move your mouse pointer between any existing components.

3. **Rule details view**: The rule details view allows you to edit the main rule details, view the rule's audit log, and edit the component configurations as applicable.

Creating a rule to assign the highest priority to VIP users' issues

This brings us to our first automation rule. In many organizations, issues raised by VIP users such as managers or executives need to be assigned the highest priority so that they get the attention of the team members immediately.

As this is our first rule, we'll show you step by step, with associated screenshots, how to author an automation rule in Jira so you can see how the rule editor enables us to quickly create a rule intuitively.

> Tip
> The location of the automation rules configurations differs slightly between Jira Cloud and Jira Server.
>
> In Jira Cloud projects, automation rules can be found under the **Automation** tab in **Project Settings**, whilst in Jira Server, they can be found under the **Project automation** tab.

For this rule, we are going to use a Service Management project. To follow along with this rule, you will need to have a user group defined, called **VIP**, to which the appropriate users are assigned.

Firstly, in your Service Management project, navigate to **Project settings**, click on the **Automation** tab, and then click the **Create Rule** button in the upper-right corner:

1. After you've decided to create a new rule, the first thing you're presented with is the option to choose your trigger.

   For this rule, click on the **Issue created** trigger and then click **Save**, as shown in the following screenshot:

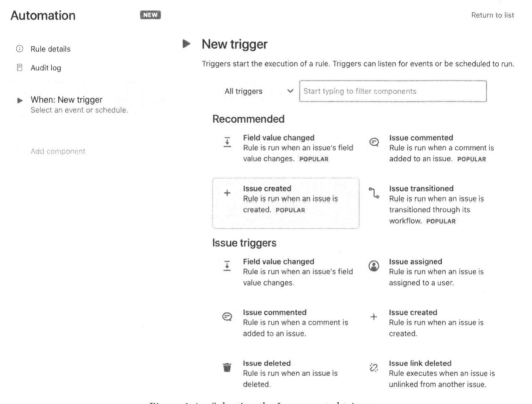

Figure 1.4 – Selecting the Issue created trigger

2. Next we are going to add in a condition that checks whether the user who reported the issue is a member of the *VIP* user group.

    In the following screen, select **New condition**, followed by the **JQL condition** component:

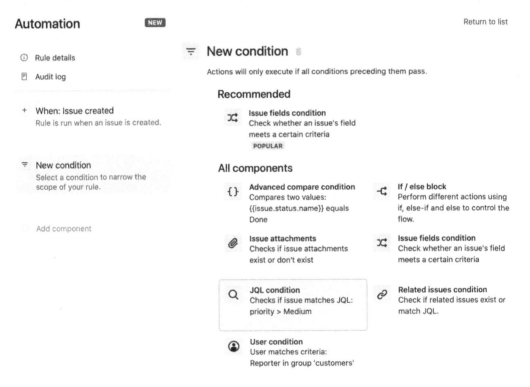

Figure 1.5 – Adding the JQL condition component

3. The JQL condition component requires further configuration in the form of a JQL query. In the component's configuration screen, enter the following JQL query, then click the **Validate query** link to ensure the query is valid, and finally, click the **Save** button:

```
reporter in membersOf("VIP")
```

Your rule should look similar to the following screenshot:

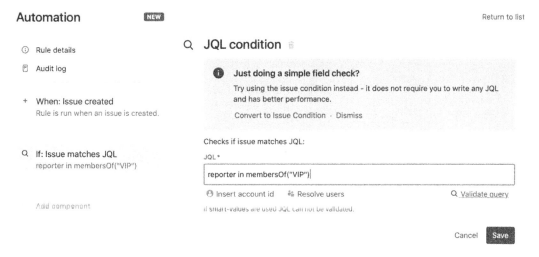

Figure 1.6 – Configuring the JQL condition component

4. Next, we need to insert the action to perform. In this case, we need to use the **Edit issue** action in order to set the **Priority** field to **highest**.

    Go ahead and click on **New action**, followed by **Edit issue**:

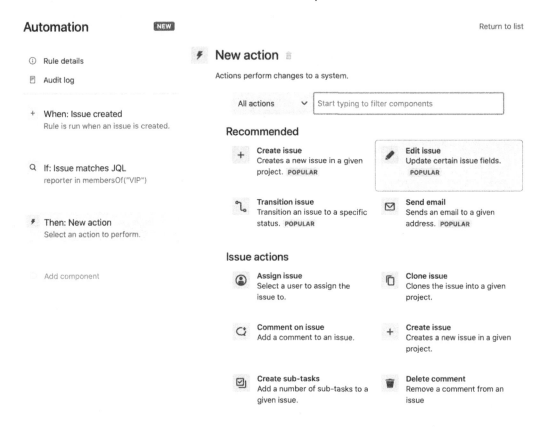

Figure 1.7 – Selecting the Edit issue action

5. Like the **JQL condition** component, the **Edit issue** component also requires further configuration and we now need to choose the fields we wish to update.

    You can set multiple fields in this action. However, for this rule, we are only going to set the **Priority** field. Start by typing the field name, and then click on the checkbox once you've narrowed your selection:

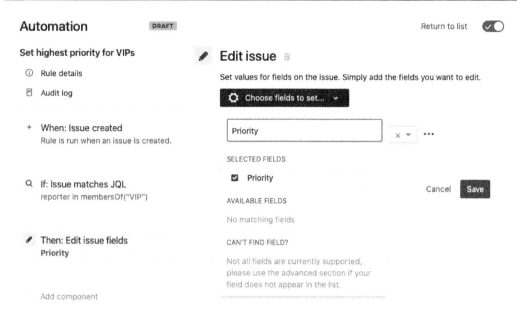

Figure 1.8 – Selecting the Priority field

6. Now that you've selected the **Priority** field, click out of the **Choose fields to set** option so that you can access the field values list where you will be presented with a dropdown of available options. Select the value **Highest**, and then click on **Save**:

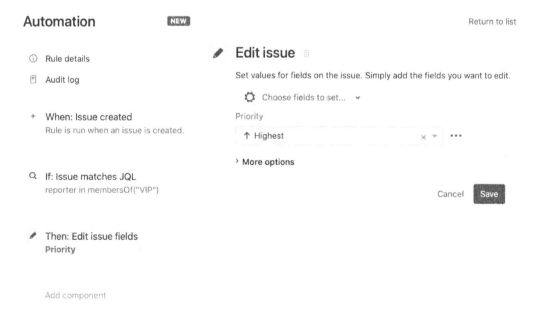

Figure 1.9 – Setting the value of the Priority field

7. We have now configured our first rule. All that remains is to give our new rule a name, turn it on, and give it a description.

    In the following screen, set the rule name as follows and then click **Turn it on** to publish the rule:

    ```
    Set highest priority for VIPs
    ```

    The completed rule components should look similar to the following screenshot:

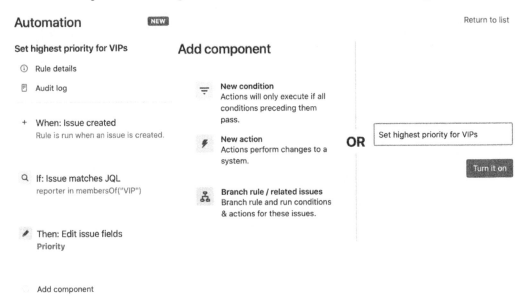

Figure 1.10 – Giving the rule a name and turning it on

8. Finally, let's give our rule a description and ensure we're happy with the general rule details. Click on **Rule details** in the **Rule-chain** view on the left, enter the following description, and then click **Save**:

    ```
    Ensure issues created by members of the VIP group are
    assigned the highest priority.
    ```

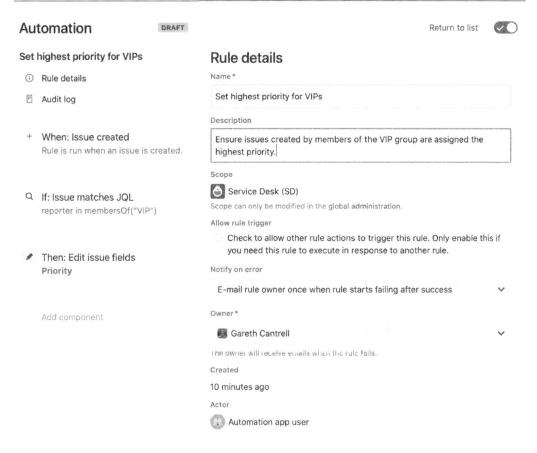

Figure 1.11 – Adding a description to your rule

9. You may have noticed that when you entered the description, the lozenge at the top of the **Rule-chain** view changed from **Enabled** to **Draft**.

   This alerts you to the fact that changes have been made to the rule, but not yet published. If you do not wish these changes to be published, either click on the **Cancel** button at the bottom of the **Rule** details panel or click the **Return to list** link in the top-right corner of the **Details** panel.

For now, click on **Publish changes**:

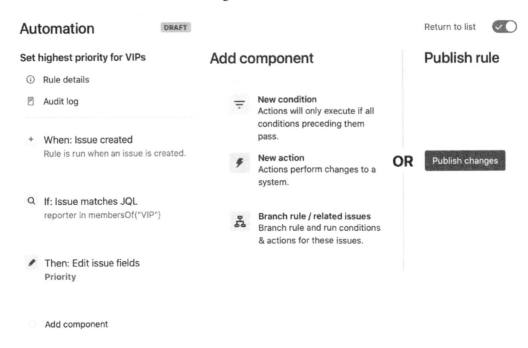

Figure 1.12 – Publishing your rule changes

Your rule will now appear in the rule list against your Service Management project and every time an issue is created by a user in the VIP user group, the priority will automatically update to **Highest**.

To test this rule, add yourself to the VIP group and create a new service request in your Service Management project. Make sure the priority is set to something other than **Highest**. Once you have created the issue, navigate to it and examine the activity in the **History** tab. You should see the priority change from what you selected to **Highest**, and the activity should be logged against the rule actor.

You have now learned how to create and publish an automation rule in Jira without writing any code.

Summary

In this chapter, you have learned about the key concepts of automation rules in Jira and the basic building blocks of rules, including triggers, conditions, and actions. We also covered rule types and the differences between rule owners and actors and finally, we saw how to combine all of these concepts into our first automation rule.

As you have learned in this chapter, we have a lot of powerful and flexible components at our disposal that will, in turn, help us to create powerful automation rules to automate everyday tasks in Jira without the need to write any code. In the following chapters, we will be exploring these components in more detail and with the help of practical examples that you can use to kick-start your own rules.

In the following chapter, we will learn how to use these components to work with issues in Jira. We'll explore all the conditions we introduced in this chapter, how to work with related issues, and how we can use some of the action components available to edit and transition issues before looking at how we can run rules on a scheduled basis.

2
Automating Jira Issues

In the previous chapter, we introduced you to some of the key concepts of automation rules in Jira and looked at the basic building blocks of rules. To really get to grips with automation rules, we need to understand how we can use those building blocks to automate issues within Jira, and this is what this chapter is all about.

Here, we will learn how the various conditions work and when to use each of them. We will also cover how we can work with related issues, such as sub-tasks, linked issues, and stories within Epics. Importantly, you will learn how to use issue actions to make changes to your issue fields.

We will also cover how to use the advanced field editing function for those rare occasions when the standard field editors are not sufficient and finally, we will look at how to transition issues through their workflows and how to create scheduled rules.

We are going to cover the following main topics:

- Understanding conditions
- Working with branch rules and related issues
- Editing issue fields
- Advanced field editing

- Transitioning issues
- Scheduling tasks

By the end of this chapter you should have a solid understanding of how you can use automation conditions and actions within your rules to effectively work with issues in Jira.

Technical requirements

The requirements for this chapter are as follows:

- **Jira Cloud environment**: If you don't already have access to Jira, you can create a free Jira Cloud account at `https://www.atlassian.com/software/jira/free` and ensure that you have both Jira Software and Jira Service Management selected; or

- **Jira Server environment**: If you are using Jira Server (available from `https://www.atlassian.com/software/jira/download`), ensure that you have licenses for both Jira Software and Jira Service Management. In addition, you will also need to ensure that you install the *Automation for Jira* app, available from the Atlassian Marketplace.

In both instances, you will need to have at least project administrator access to a Service Management project and a Scrum Software project in order to be able to follow the examples in this chapter. For the examples in this chapter, we have used the IT Service Management project template to create the Service Management project, and the Scrum Software project template to create the Software project.

You can download the latest code samples for this chapter from this book's official GitHub repository at `https://github.com/PacktPublishing/Automate-Everyday-Tasks-in-Jira`. The Code in Action videos for this chapter are available at `https://bit.ly/2XPMdR7`.

Understanding conditions

Conditions give us the ability to make our rules much more powerful and flexible as they enable us to both narrow the scope of our rules and, in the case of **if/else** blocks, alter the control flow of the rule.

In this section, we will look at each of the conditions that we introduced in *Chapter 1, Key Concepts of Automation*, in more detail, exploring what each of them can do and how we can make use of them in automation rules.

Let's start by taking a look at the **Issue fields condition**.

The Issue fields condition

The Issue fields condition is the simplest of the conditions. It allows you to test most Jira fields against certain criteria without requiring the use of smart values or **JQL** (short for **Jira Query Language**).

You can use it to compare a field against a value or set of values, and it can also be used to test the field against another field in either the same issue or certain related issues, such as a parent issue, an epic issue, a destination issue, or the issue that triggered the rule.

In addition, these conditions can be chained together to form more complex conditions by using an additive operation.

> **Tip**
> The Issue fields condition should be used ahead of any of the other conditions wherever possible, as it is not only simpler to configure, but it also has performance benefits over conditions such as the JQL and Advanced compare conditions.

Let's now take a look at how we can use this condition in a rule.

Creating a rule to generate sub-tasks for a story task

In this example, we'll assume a development team has a requirement that every user story requires the following three sub-tasks to be created at the same time that the user story is created:

- Develop the feature
- Perform QA tasks
- Document the feature

We'll create a rule that adds these sub-tasks when a user story is created to demonstrate the Issue fields condition:

1. If you're using Jira Cloud, navigate to **Project settings** and click on the **Automation** tab of your Software project, or, for Jira Server, navigate to **Project settings**, click on the **Project automation** tab, and then click on **Create rule**.

2. Select **Issue created** as the trigger and then click **Save**.

3. Next, select **New condition** and then select **Issue fields condition**.

4. Set **Field** to **Issue Type**, **Condition** to **equals**, and finally, set **Value** to **Story**, and then click **Save**.

5. Finally, select **New action** and then the **Create sub-tasks** action. Click the **Add another sub-task** button until you have three rows.

    Add the following three descriptions in the **Summary** column and then click **Save**:

    ```
    Develop feature
    ```

    ```
    Perform QA tasks
    ```

    ```
    Document feature
    ```

    Your rule should appear as follows:

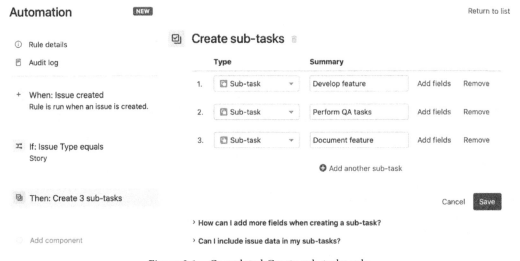

Figure 2.1 – Completed Create sub-tasks rule

6. Finally, name the rule `Create story sub-tasks` and click **Turn it on** to save and enable the rule as seen in the following screenshot:

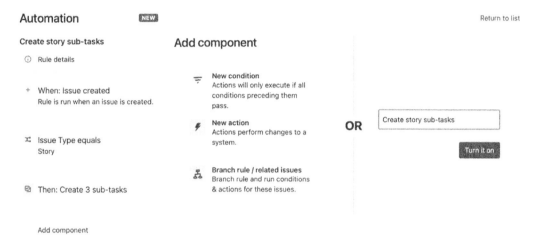

Figure 2.2 – Naming and enabling the automation rule

In this section, we have seen how we can use the Issue fields condition to create a decision point in a rule by simply selecting what we would like to evaluate from the available list of fields, conditions, and values.

In the next section, we'll look at the JQL condition and how we can use this in our automation rules.

JQL condition

The **JQL condition** allows you to test an issue against any valid JQL query. In addition to standard JQL, smart values can also be used in the query. We will cover smart values in more detail in *Chapter 3, Enhancing Rules with Smart Values*.

Let's see how we can make use of the JQL condition in an example rule.

Creating a rule to create a high-priority incident reminder

In this example, we want to ensure that the assigned team member updates a high-priority incident if it is about to breach and the reporter has not been informed of the progress of the incident within the last 15 minutes:

1. In your Service Management project, navigate to **Project settings**, click on the **Automation** tab, and then click the **Create rule** button.

2. We want to check when the Time to resolution SLA is about to breach within the next 30 minutes, so we select the **SLA threshold breached** trigger. Select **Time to resolution SLA** and then select the **will breach in the next** option, ensuring 30 minutes is selected, and then click **Save**.

3. Next, select **New condition**, followed by **JQL condition**. Enter the following **JQL** query and click **Validate query** to ensure that it is correct:

    ```
    type = Incident AND priority in (Highest, High) AND
    updated >= "-15m"
    ```

    The following screenshot demonstrates how your rule should look at this point:

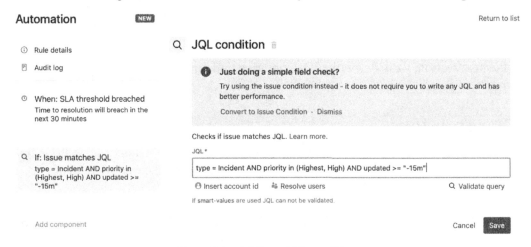

Figure 2.3 – Adding a JQL condition

4. We want the rule to notify the assignee by email, so select **New action**, then the **Send email** action, and then select **Assignee** in the **To** field.

    Set the **Subject** field to the following:

    ```
    Issue {{issue.key}} is about to breach without update
    ```

Now, set the **Content** field to the following:

```
The issue {{issue.key}} - {{issue.summary}} is about to
breach in 30 minutes and requires an update.


Please add a comment to the above issue or update it as
required.


Many thanks,

Jira Automation
```

Your rule should now look similar to the following screenshot:

Figure 2.4 – The High priority incident reminder rule

5. Finally, click **Save**, name the rule High priority incident reminder, and then click **Turn it on** to save and enable the rule.

In this section, we have seen how we can use any valid JQL query as a condition in our rules.

In the next section, we'll look at how we can use the User condition in automation rules.

User condition

The **User condition** allows you to check whether a particular type of user exists, and whether they are in a particular role or group or are a certain type of user. This condition also allows you to add multiple criteria in a single condition and you can specify whether *all* criteria should match or only *one* of the criteria specified is sufficient.

Where this condition really shines though is in a Service Management project, where a customer can be a reporter, a request participant, or a member of a customer organization, and the User condition provides us with a criterion, *User is a customer*, to check a user against all of these conditions in a single operation. In addition, we can also check whether a user belongs to a particular organization and apply specific actions accordingly.

Let's now look at how we can use this condition in a rule.

Creating a rule to add a relationship manager to customer requests

In this rule, we want to add the customer relationship manager as a watcher to any issues raised by users in our Service Management project from our more important customers. You will need to create the following organizations in your Service Management project and also create a few customers in each:

- Kate Price looks after *ACME* and *The Widget Co*
- Pete Kramer looks after *Rain Forest Books*

> **Tip**
> To add users to Jira so as to follow this example, you will need to supply each user with a unique email address. If your mail server supports email sub-addressing or tags, such as Gmail or Outlook 365, you can use this feature to create unique email addresses that get delivered to your own email. For example, if your email address is *your.name@yourcompany.com*, using the email address *your.name+kateprice@yourcompany.com* will be both unique and deliver emails to your inbox with the email tag *kateprice*.

Let's create our rule:

1. In your Service Management project, navigate to **Project settings**, click the **Automation** tab, and then click on **Create rule**.

2. Select **Issue created** as the trigger and then click **Save**.

3. Now, select **New condition**, followed by **User condition**.

    Complete the fields as follows and then click **Save**:

    User: `Reporter`

    Check to perform: `is in organization`

    Criteria: `ACME, The Widget Co`

    Your condition should look as per the following screenshot:

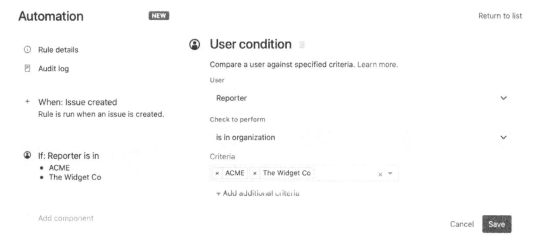

Figure 2.5 – User condition for a reporter in an organization

4. Select **New Action**, followed by **Manage watchers**, select **Kate Price** in the **Add these watchers** field, and then click **Save**.

5. Add **New condition** and select **User condition**.

    Complete the fields as follows and then click **Save**:

    User: `Reporter`

    Check to perform: `is in organization`

    Criteria: `Rain Forest Books`

6. Select **New Action**, followed by **Manage watchers**, select **Pete Kramer** in the **Add these watchers** field, and then click **Save**. Your rule should look like the following screenshot:

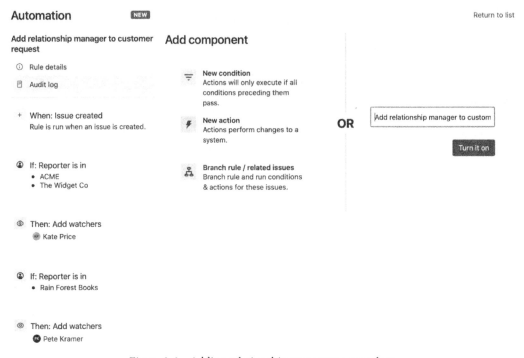

Figure 2.6 – Adding relationship managers as watchers

7. Finally, name your rule `Add relationship manager to customer request` and then click **Turn it on** to save and enable the rule.

In this section, we looked at how the User condition allows us to validate the existence of a user and whether a user belongs to a particular group, role, or organization.

Next, we'll take a look at the Related issues condition and how we can use this to test for issues related to the trigger issue.

Related issues condition

The **Related issues** condition allows you to check the state of issues related to the current issue in the rule context, be that the issue that triggered the rule, or each issue in a branch rule.

With this condition, you can check whether the related issues exist, whether all of them match a given JQL condition, or even whether only some of the related issues match the condition.

Let's take a look at an example rule that uses the **Related issues** condition.

Creating a rule to close parent bug or story tasks when all sub-tasks are complete

When an issue has sub-tasks, we need to autoclose the main issue when all the sub-tasks attain **Done** status. We'll need to use the Related issues condition to achieve this as follows:

1. In your Software project, navigate to **Project settings**, click on the **Automation** tab (or the **Project automation** tab if you're using Jira Server), and then click on **Create rule**.

2. Select the **Issue transitioned** trigger and then select **Done** in the **To** status field and click **Save**.

3. Then, select **New condition**, followed by **Issue fields condition**.

    Complete the fields as follows and then click **Save**:

    Field: Issue Type

    Condition: equals

    Value: Sub-task

4. Next, select **Branch rule / related issues** and then select **Parent** as **Type of related issue**.

5. Now select **New condition** and then **Related issues condition**.

    Complete the fields as follows and then click **Save**:

    Related issues: Sub-tasks

    Condition: All match specified JQL

    Matching JQL: status = Done

Your rule should now look similar to the following screenshot:

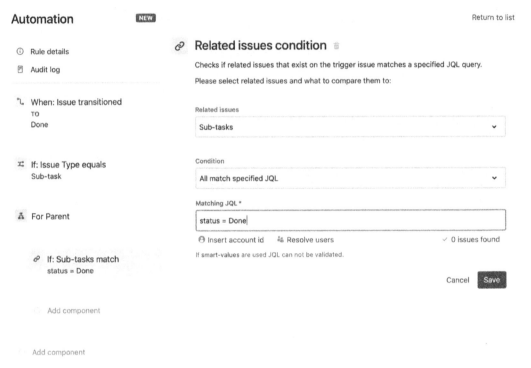

Figure 2.7 – Configuring the Related issues condition

6. Then, select **New action** followed by **Transition issue**. In this case, the parent issue, either **Bug** or **Story**, shares the same final status as the sub-tasks, so we can leave **Destination status** as **Copy from trigger issue**.

7. Click **Save**, name your rule `Close parent when sub-tasks complete`, and then click **Turn it on** to save and enable the rule.

> **Tip**
>
> When a rule needs to work with related issues in other projects, it needs to be able to execute in those projects that contain the related issues and the rule should therefore be either a global or multi-project rule.
>
> This means that only Jira global administrators will be able create and manage these rules.

In this section, we have seen how to use the Related issues condition to perform actions against issues related to the issue that triggered the automation rule.

In the next section, we'll take a look at the Advanced compare condition.

Advanced compare condition

For most rules, the Issue fields condition will be adequate; however, there will be times when you need that extra bit of flexibility when writing rules and this is where the **Advanced compare condition** comes in. This condition allows you to use compare smart values, functions and regular expressions against smart values or functions!

We will be looking at smart values and functions in detail in *Chapter 3*, *Enhancing Rules with Smart Values*, so for now, let's take a look at a rule that uses this condition.

Let's take a look at how we use the Advanced compare condition in an example rule.

Creating a rule to reopen an issue when the reporter creates a comment

In most cases, when a customer creates a request, the service desk team, or indeed an automation rule, will resolve the request without further input from the customer. In some cases, however, the request may not have been resolved to the customer's satisfaction and instead of creating a new request, we want to be able to reopen the original request when a new comment is added by the customer who opened the request.

Let's see how we can leverage the Advanced compare condition to achieve this:

1. In your Service Management project, navigate to **Project settings**, click the **Automation** tab, and then click on **Create rule**.

2. Then, select the **Issue commented** trigger and click **Save**.

3. Next, select **New condition** and then **Advanced compare condition**.

   Complete the fields as follows and then click **Save**:

   First value: `{{comment.author.accountId}}`

   Condition: `equals`

   Second value: `{{issue.reporter.accountId}}`

Your condition should look like the following screenshot:

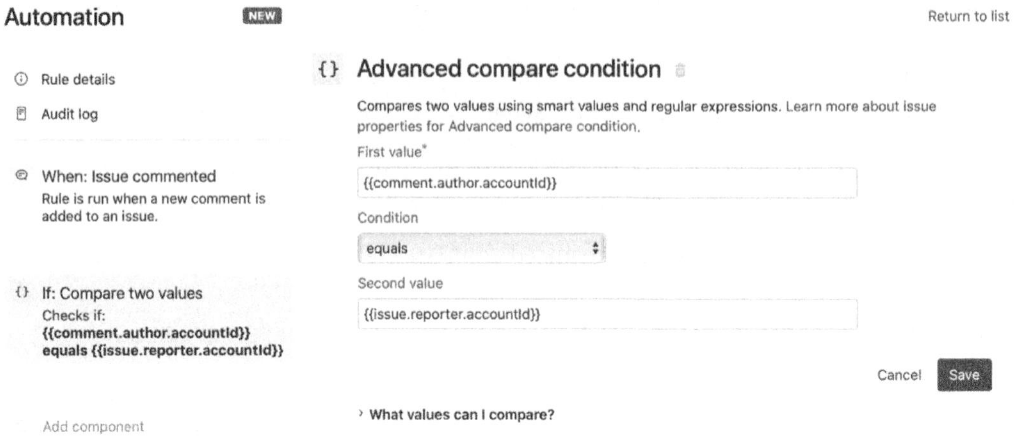

Figure 2.8 – Configuring the Advanced compare condition

> **Tip**
> The **accountId** field for users is only applicable to Jira Cloud. If you are using Jira Server or Jira Data Center, you will need to use *{{comment.author}}* and *{{issue.reporter}}* instead.

4. Then, select **New Condition** followed by **Issue fields condition**.

    Complete the fields as follows and then click **Save**:

    Field: Status

    Condition: equals

    Value: Resolved

5. Now select **New action**, then **Transition issue**, and then set the **Destination status** field to **In Progress** and click **Save**.

6. Finally, name your rule Re-open ticket on reporter comment and click **Turn it on** to save and enable the rule.

In this section, we looked at when we should use the Advanced compare condition and how it allows us to compare items using smart values.

In the following section, we'll explore the **if/else** block and how we can use it to perform alternate actions based on different conditions.

If/else block

The if/else statement is arguably the most powerful condition in the automation toolbox. It allows us to perform alternate actions based on whether the specified conditions match.

Let's take a look at how we can use the **if/else** block in an example rule.

Creating a rule to define an incident priority matrix

The correct prioritization of an incident is critical in determining the relative importance of an issue. Relying on users to select the correct priority of incidents results, more often than not, in a large number of incidents being incorrectly prioritized.

It is more common practice to define the priority of incidents based on their impact and urgency instead. The following table shows a typical priority matrix based on the impact and urgency selected and we'll use this to help define our automation rule.

		Impact		
		High	Medium	Low
Urgency	High	Highest	High	Medium
	Medium	High	Medium	Low
	Low	Medium	Low	Lowest

Figure 2.9 – Incident priority matrix

We are going to create our rule in a Service Management project created using the IT Service Management template. We have adjusted the custom fields, **Impact** and **Urgency**, with the options shown in the preceding incident priority matrix. You will also need to add these two fields to the **Request** form for the Incident Request types in your Service Management project.

Using the preceding matrix as a reference, let's create our rule:

1. In your Service Management project, navigate to **Project settings**, click on the **Automation** tab, and then click on **Create rule**.

2. We want this rule to trigger when the issue is created and also if any changes are made to either the **Impact** or **Urgency** fields, so we'll select the **Field value changed** trigger and then select the **Impact** and **Urgency** fields in the **Fields to monitor for changes** dropdown. We also want to trigger this rule only when an incident is created or edited, so we'll only select those two operations in the **For** dropdown and save our changes, as shown in the following screenshot:

Figure 2.10 – Incident priority matrix trigger

3. Next, we'll add a **New condition** field and select **If/else** block.

    In the **If** block, we are going to configure our first criterion to test for the highest priority, when both **Impact** and **Urgency** are set to **High**.

4. Select **Add conditions…**, then **Issue fields condition**, set **Field** to **Impact**, **Condition** to **Equals**, select **High** in the **Value** field, and then repeat the exact same steps for the **Urgency** field.

    Your rule should now look similar to the following screenshot:

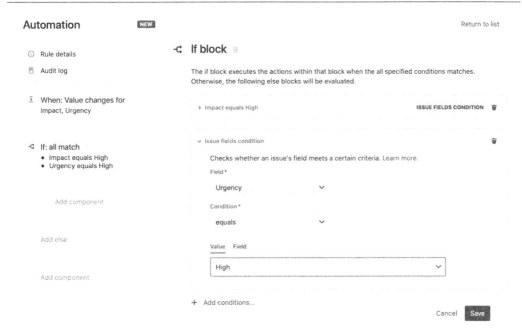

Figure 2.11 – Configuring the If block

5.   Now, we need to add the action to perform when the preceding condition is met, so select **New action**, followed by **Edit issue**, find the **Priority** field in the **Choose fields to set…** dropdown, set **Value** to **Highest**, and then click **Save**.

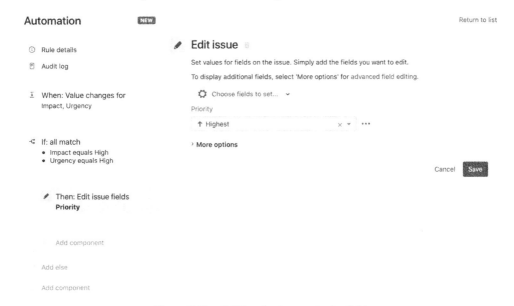

Figure 2.12 – Editing the issue priority field

6. Let's build out the rest of the matrix. Click on **Add else** in the **Rule-chain** view and then on **Add conditions**, followed by **Issue fields condition**. Set **Field** to **Impact**, **Condition** to **Equals**, and **Value** to **High**. Repeat for the **Urgency** field, setting **Value** to **Medium**, and then click **Save**.

7. We need to add the action to perform when the **else** block condition is satisfied, so click on **New action**, followed by **Edit issue**. Then, set the **Priority** field to **High** in line with the preceding matrix:

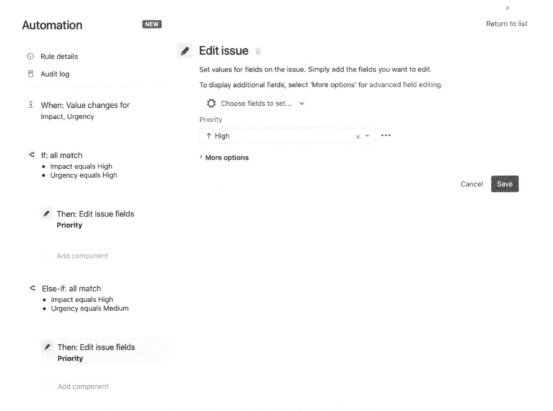

Figure 2.13 – Adding the first Else-if block

8. Repeat *steps* 6 and 7 for the remaining priorities in the incident priority matrix shown previously. You should end up with one **If** block followed by eight **Else-if** blocks corresponding to each intersection of **Impact** and **Urgency** in the priority matrix.

9. Finally, name the rule **Incident priority matrix**, and click **Turn it on** to save and enable it.

In this section, we have seen how we can use conditions to ensure we target the correct issues in our rule, and we have also learned how to control the flow of a rule using the powerful **If/else** block.

Next, we'll take a look at branch rules and how to work with related issues.

Working with branch rules and related issues

It is not often that issues exist in isolation. In fact, in many cases, there are always other issues that relate to any given issue. This could be in the form of sub-tasks, stories linked to a larger epic, or issues linked to other issues using relationships such as blocked, duplicated, and more.

You will therefore often come across situations when creating automation rules where you need to perform actions against not only the issue that triggered the rule, but also against issues related to the source issue.

This is where the **Branch** rule component and its companion condition, the **Related issues** condition, prove most useful, allowing you to create rules that can work across complex issue relationships.

Branch rule/related issues

When we use the Branch rule component to perform actions against a related issue or list of issues, the rule no longer executes in a linear fashion, instead expanding into multiple sub-branches representing each related issue. When using smart values, which we will discuss in more detail in the next chapter, the smart value *{{issue}}* refers to the related issue in the current sub-branch, and not the issue that triggered the rule, which can be found instead using the smart value *{{triggerIssue}}*.

> **Important note**
>
> Branches on *multiple issues* run in separate processes in parallel and there is therefore no guarantee that any one branch will finish execution before the next.
>
> Additionally, the main branch will continue to execute before the sub-branches start.
>
> If you have only a single related issue, the main branch will block until the sub-branch has completed its execution.

Let's now see how we can use the Branch rule/related issues component in an example rule.

Creating a rule to keep an Epic task in sync with its user story tasks

A common requirement in development projects is for Epic to transition to **In Progress** when the first story it contains transitions to In Progress. This is a perfect scenario for the Branch rules component. Let's see how we can do this:

1. In your Software project, navigate to **Project settings**, click on the **Automation** tab (or the **Project automation** tab if you're using Jira Server), and then click on **Create rule**.

2. Select the **Issue transitioned** trigger and then click **Save**.

3. Leave the **From status** field blank and select **In Progress** in the **To status** field and then click **Save**.

4. Next, select **New condition**, followed by **Related issues condition**.

    Complete the fields as follows and then click **Save**:

    Related issues: Epic

    Condition: Matches specified JQL

    Matching JQL: status != "In Progress"

5. Now select **Branch rule / related issues** and set the **Type of related issues** field to **Epic (Parent)** and click **Save**.

6. Finally, select **New action**, followed by **Transition issue**, choose **In Progress** as **Destination status**, and then click **Save**.

    Your rule should now look as per the following screenshot:

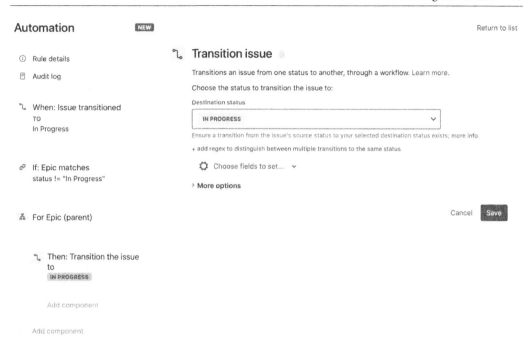

Figure 2.14 – Moving Epic to In Progress when the story changes

7. As always, the final step is to name your rule `Sync Epic status to stories` and then click **Turn it on** to save and enable the rule.

We have learned in this section how we can make use of the Branch rules component to create powerful rules enabling us to target issues related to the issue that triggered the rule.

In the next section, we will look at editing issue fields in more detail.

Editing issue fields

In the majority of your automation rules, you will be editing information in issues. In this section, we are going to cover some of the more common actions you will need to understand when creating your rules, including assignments, commenting on issues, linking issues to other issues and, of course, editing fields within issues.

Assigning issues

One of the more tedious tasks usually encountered in Jira is having team members track a queue of unassigned issues and take ownership of these issues. The other common approach is to have someone such as a team lead go through these issues and apportion them off to members of the team based on certain criteria.

We can instead use automation to handle these tasks for us, and the following list is a few of the capabilities we have at our disposal when it comes to assigning issues:

- Assigning based on current workload
- Assigning in a round-robin fashion
- Assigning to a previous assignee or commenter
- Assigning from a related issue or JQL query

Let's take a look at how we can use this in a rule.

Creating a rule to autoassign incoming bugs to developers

In this rule, we are going to assign any incoming issue of the bug type to the development team based on how much work each team member currently has, as long as the issue does not already have an assigned user. The development team are all members of the developer role in the project:

1. In your Software project, navigate to **Project settings**, click on the **Automation** tab (or the **Project automation** tab if you're using Jira Server), and then click on **Create rule**.

2. Select the **Issue created** trigger and then click **Save**.

3. Next we need to ensure that we only assign issues of the bug type. Select **New condition** and then choose **Issue fields condition**. Set the **Field** to **Issue Type**, **Condition** to **Equals**, **Value** to **Bug**, and then click **Save**.

4. Now we need to execute assignment of the new issue. Do this by selecting **New action** and then choosing **Assign issue**.

5. In the **Assign the issue to** field, select **User** in a role. Then, select **Balanced workload** in the **Method to choose assignee** field.

   Because we don't want to reassign any issues that already have an assignee set, we need to add a further restriction using JQL. Type the following query in the **JQL to restrict issues** field:

   ```
   assignee = Unassigned
   ```

And finally, set **Role** to **Developers** and then click **Save**:

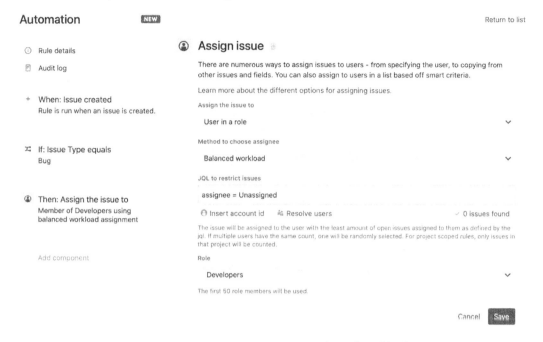

Figure 2.15 – Assigning users using Balanced workload

6. In the final screen, name the rule `Auto assign incoming bugs` and then click **Turn it on** to save and enable the rule.

> **Note**
>
> If you are using Jira Server, you must ensure that the rule actor has the **Assign Issues** permission in order to assign issues to users. In Jira Cloud, the default permissions are designed to ensure that users in the *atlassian-addons-project-access* role, such as *Automation app user*, have the necessary permissions to edit and assign issues and you should only need to adjust this if you have made changes to the default permissions.

In this section, we have seen how to use the **Assign issues** action to assign issues to users using various scenarios, including based on individual workload, round-robin, randomly, or by using input from related issues or queries.

In the next section, we'll look at how to use the **Edit issue** fields action to update issues.

Edit issue fields

The ability to edit fields within an issue is one of the main objectives of automation rules and a number of rule actions provide this functionality, these being the following:

- Cloning an issue
- Editing an issue
- Transitioning an issue

The field editors are very flexible and allow you to clear values from fields, set new values, and even copy values from other fields within the current issue, a parent issue, trigger issue, epic issue, or destination issue.

In addition, you are able to edit multiple fields in a single action and most fields support smart values and functions.

Let's look at a rule to see how to use this action in practice.

Creating a rule to align user story due dates and fix versions

In this example, when starting a sprint, we will update all the stories within that sprint, set the due date to the end date of the sprint, and set the fix version to the next unreleased version in the project:

1. In your Scrum Software project, navigate to **Project settings**, click on the **Automation** tab (or the **Project automation** tab if you're using Jira Server), and then click on **Create rule**.

2. Select **Sprint started**, choose your Scrum board from the **Boards** available and then click **Save**.

3. Next, select the **Branch rules / related issues** component and, in the **Type of related issues** field, select **Issues** in the sprint.

4. Then, select **New action** followed by **Edit issue**. In the **Choose fields to set** dropdown, select the **Due date** and **Fix versions** fields.

   Complete the **Due date** and **Fix versions** fields as follows and then click **Save**:

   Due date: `{{sprint.endDate}}`

Fix versions: `Next unreleased version`

> TIP
>
> We have used a smart value for the **Due date** field in this example and you can find the list of smart values which can be used in a rule at `https://support.atlassian.com/jira-software-cloud/docs/smart-values-general`. We will cover smart values and smart value functions in more detail in *Chapter 3, Enhancing Rules with Smart Values*.

Your rule should look like the following screenshot:

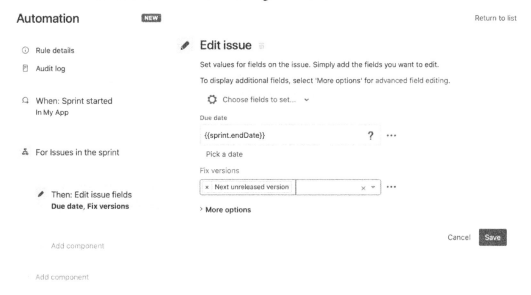

Figure 2.16 – Editing issue fields

5. Finally, name your rule `Align story version and dates to sprint` and click **Turn it on** to save and enable the rule.

In this section, we covered some of the more common actions you will be using when creating automation rules. We learned how you can use the different algorithms to assign issues to team members in a more intelligent fashion, and we also learned how we can use actions to make modifications to issue fields.

In certain cases, we may need more flexibility to edit issues and, in the next section, we will explore how to use the available advanced field editing functionality to achieve this.

Advanced field editing

Not all fields in Jira are created equal, and more especially in the case of custom fields provided by third-party apps. In these cases, where it is not possible to update the fields using the default functionality provided by the actions, an **advanced field editor** is provided that we can utilize to apply the field updates we require.

In this section, we will take a look at the advanced field editor and how we can use it to take advantage of those situations when we cannot use the standard field editors.

The advanced field editor

The advanced field editor is present in a number of actions under the **More options** section and allows you to specify the fields to edit using a JSON object using the format specified in Jira's REST API.

The actions that allow advanced field editing are as follows:

- Cloning an issue
- Creating an issue
- Creating a Service Management request
- Editing an issue
- Transitioning an issue

Before we look at how to use the advanced field editor, we'll first need to understand how the JSON object required by the field editor is structured.

Understanding the JSON object

There are two attributes that we can use in the JSON object:

- **update**: You can use any of the supported field operations, such as add, set or remove, in the update attribute. It is most useful for fields with multiple values where you want to add values to, or remove values from, the existing set of values.
- **fields**: This attribute is a shortcut for calling the update attribute with the set operation.

The fields you can use in the advanced editor within either the **update** or **fields** attribute depends on whether you're using the advanced editor when creating a new issue or editing an existing one, and these fields can be found by using one of the following REST API calls:

- *createmeta:*
  ```
  https://<yourjira.domain.com>/rest/api/latest/issue/
  createmeta?projectKeys={projectKey}&expand=projects.
  issuetypes.fields or
  ```

- *editmeta*:
  ```
  https://<yourjira.domain.com>/rest/api/latest/{issueKey}/
  editmeta
  ```

The response from these calls will return a JSON object listing all the fields available when creating or editing the issue, including the possible operations and values for each. You can read more about finding fields using the REST API in the official documentation available at `https://support.atlassian.com/jira-software-cloud/docs/advanced-field-editing-json/`.

Important note
These API calls return a list of fields on the corresponding create or edit screen configured for the project and issue type. If you cannot find a field in the returned JSON, you will need to add it to the corresponding screen first.

Let's now take a look at how we could use the advanced field editor in a rule.

Creating a rule to demonstrate the advanced field editor

To demonstrate how to use the advanced field editing functionality, we are going to use a somewhat contrived situation.

For this rule, we'll look for the word *printer* in the summary or description field and then add the **Printers** component to the **Component** field, add a new label, and update the description field. Let's begin:

1. In your Service Management project, navigate to **Project settings**, click the **Automation** tab, and then click on **Create rule**.

2. Add the **Issue created** trigger and click **Save**.

3. Add a new **Issue fields condition**, set **Issue Type** equal to **Service Request**, and then click **Save**.

4.   Add a new **JQL condition** with **JQL**:

```
summary ~ printer OR description ~ printer
```

5.   Add an **Edit issue** action, expand the **More options** section, and then set
Additional fields to the following JSON:

```
{
    "update": {
      "labels": [
        {
          "add": "label-printer"
        }
      ]
    },
    "fields": {
      "description": "{{issue.description}}\n\nUpdated by
        Automation Rule",
      "components": [
        {
          "name": "Printers"
        }
      ]
    }
}
```

TIP

The JSON structure used in the advanced field editor is based on the Jira
REST API which you can learn more about at `https://developer.`
`atlassian.com/cloud/jira/platform/rest` for Jira Cloud
and at `https://developer.atlassian.com/server/jira/`
`platform/rest-apis` for Jira Server and Jira Data Center.

---

6. Your rule should look similar to the following screenshot:

Figure 2.17 – Advanced field editing rule

7. Finally, click **Save**, name the rule `Advanced field editing example`, and then click **Turn it on** to save and enable the rule.

In this section, we have learned how to use the advanced field editor to update issue fields when the default field editors are not sufficient. We have also learned how to leverage the REST API to understand which fields are available and how to correctly format the JSON data in the advanced editor.

In the following section, we will look at how to transition an issue through a workflow using automation.

Transitioning issues

Jira, whether you're working in a Software, Service Management or Business project, is all about being able to track the progress of an issue through a particular workflow. The ability to automate the **transitioning** of an issue through the various statuses in the workflow is therefore key to completing the loop in terms of working with issues.

In this section, we are going to learn how we can use automation to react to state transitions of an issue through its workflow, as well as how we can transition an issue through subsequent statuses within its workflow.

Transitions and workflows

As we have mentioned, we can use automation to transition an issue through a workflow and, to be able to achieve this, your rules must be aligned to that issue type's particular workflow.

If we take a look at the following workflow, which represents a service request in a Jira Service Management project, we could automate the transition from **In Progress** to **Pending**; however, as there is no direct transition from **In Progress** to **Closed**, any automation rule attempting to perform this transition would result in the rule failing and an error being recorded in the audit log:

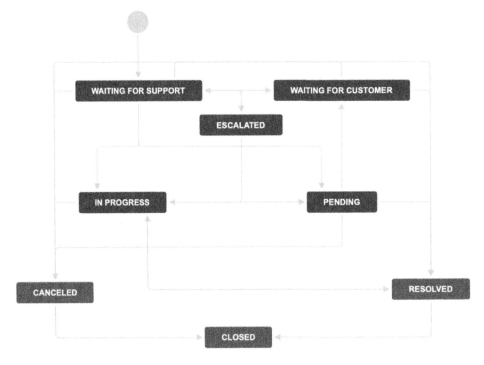

Figure 2.18 – A service request workflow

As you can see from the workflow representation in the preceding diagram, automation rules can only transition issues through a workflow where a transition already exists between two statuses in that workflow.

> **Important note**
>
> Another point to consider is that the rule actor must have permission
> to perform the particular transition. If, for example, you have a condition
> on the workflow transition that restricts it to certain users or groups, you
> will need to adjust the condition to allow the rule actor to also be allowed
> to perform the transition.

Let's look at how we can transition issues through their workflow in an automation rule.

Creating a rule to automatically escalate requests to the correct team

Let's assume a service desk team is usually inundated with requests, so, in order to free up some of their time, we want to automatically escalate any requests that we know are infrastructure-related to a member of the infrastructure team. We'll use the workflow in *Figure 2.17* as a guide:

1. In your Service Management project, navigate to **Project settings**, click the **Automation** tab, and then click on **Create rule**.

2. Select the **Issue transitioned** trigger. Because we want this rule to trigger any time an issue lands in the service management queue, we can leave the **From** status field blank and `Waiting for support` in the **To** status field, and finally click **Save**.

3. Next, we select **New condition** followed by **Issue fields condition**.

    Set the fields as follows and then click **Save**:

    Field: `Components`

    Condition: `contains any of`

    Value: `Cloud Storage Services, Data Center Services, Office Network`

4. Now select **New action**, then **Transition issue**, and set **Destination status** to **Escalated**.

    At this point, we could choose to set the **Assignee** field to a particular user; however, we want to distribute any tasks evenly across the infrastructure team, so click **Save**.

Your rule should now look similar to the following screenshot:

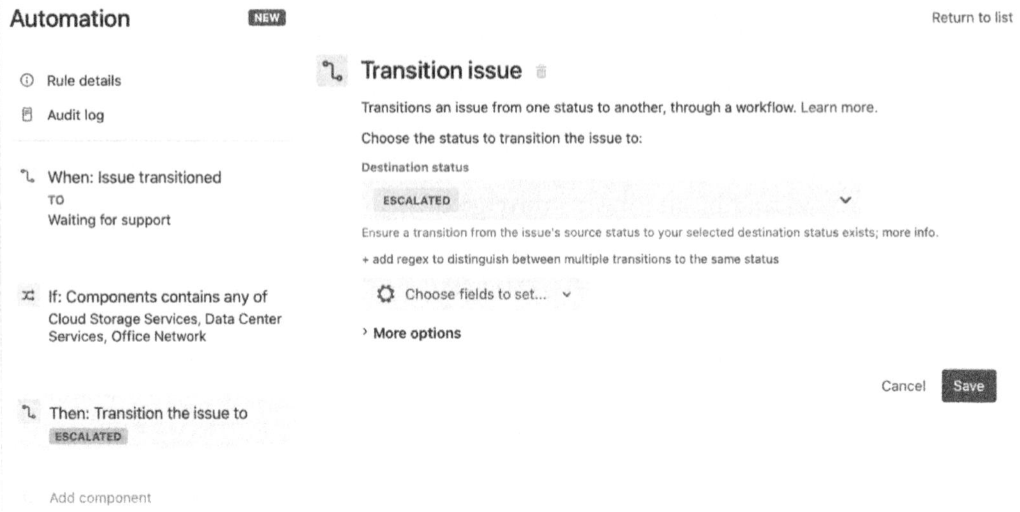

Figure 2.19 – Transitioning an issue to ESCALATED

5. Let's add the assignment next. Select **New action** AND then **Assign issue**.

    Complete the fields as follows and then click **Save**:

    Assign the issue to: `User in a group`

    Method to choose assignee: `Round-robin`

    Group: `Infrastructure Team`

6. Finally, name your rule `Auto-escalate requests` and click **Turn it on** to save and enable the rule.

In this section, you have learned how to create rules to respond to state transitions of an issue, as well as how you can automatically transition an issue to the next status in its workflow.

In the final section of this chapter, we will look at how you can use automations to schedule recurring tasks.

Scheduling tasks

One of the first things people think about when you mention automation is the ability to create issues on a scheduled basis, and with automation in Jira, this is a relatively straightforward task to achieve. In conjunction with the rest of the components we have already discussed, this gives you great flexibility in terms of what you can achieve.

In this section, we will look at how you can use the **Scheduled** trigger to perform a variety of tasks that need to be performed at defined intervals.

Scheduled trigger

The **Scheduled trigger** allows us to run rules at specified intervals. We can use either a fixed rate interval in our rule, or we can use a **cron** expression to create a more complex schedule.

Fixed rate intervals are pretty straightforward; you specify how often the rule should trigger in minutes, hours, or days, and the automation engine will initiate execution of the rule based on the interval.

> **Important note**
>
> When you use a fixed rate interval of hours or days, the automation engine will consider the starting time of the interval to be the time you saved or updated the rule. For example, if you have a schedule running daily and you save the rule at 09:21, it will run at 09:21 every day until you edit and save the rule at a different time.

Cron expressions give you greater flexibility over when your rule will trigger. Using cron expressions allows you to define schedules such as kicking off the rule every Monday and Friday at 8:30 a.m. You can find much more detailed information on creating cron expressions in Jira at `https://support.atlassian.com/jira-software-cloud/docs/construct-cron-expressions-for-a-filter-subscription/`.

> **Tip**
>
> Writing cron expressions is not always intuitive or straightforward. I'd recommend that you use a site such as CronMaker (`https://www.cronmaker.com`) to help you build cron expressions that are compatible with Jira automation. Note that Jira cron expressions have a **seconds** field, whereas some cron expression generators only support resolution down to minutes.

Let's first take a look at how we can use a fixed rate interval in a scheduled rule.

Creating a rule to close out stale issues

In this example, we'll look at how we can resolve any requests that have been waiting for customer feedback for longer than 5 days:

1. In your Service Management project, navigate to **Project settings**, click on the **Automation** tab, and then click on **Create rule**.

2. Select the **Scheduled** trigger, set the rule to run every **1 Days**, check the **Run a JQL search** checkbox, input the following **JQL** query, and then click **Save**:

    ```
    status = "Waiting for customer" AND updated > -5d
    ```

    Your rule should look like the following screenshot:

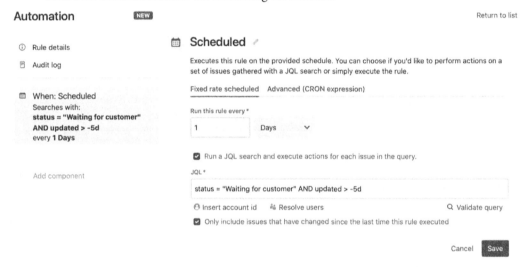

Figure 2.20 – Scheduling a fixed rate rule

3. Next, we'll add a comment to the issue that will fire a notification to the customer that we're auto-closing their request, so we'll select **New action** and then **Comment on issue** and add the following Comment before clicking on **Save**:

    ```
    Dear {{issue.reporter.displayName}},

    We haven't heard from you for a while, so we're closing
    this issue.

    If you feel this is incorrect, please reply to this
    message and we'll re-open this request for you.

    Kind regards,

    The Service Team
    ```

4. Then we'll transition the issue to **Resolved**. Select **New action, Transition issue**, and set the **Destination status** field to **Resolved**.

5. Finally, click **Save**, name the rule `Auto-resolve stale issues`, and then click **Turn it on** to save and enable the rule.

Now that we've seen how the fixed rate interval works, let's take a look at how to use a cron expression to create a more precise schedule.

Creating a rule to generate recurring start-of-week tasks

Next, let's look at how we can use the Scheduled trigger to create weekly tasks for the Service Management every Monday morning. We will create a single main task to track this and add sub-tasks as required to this main task. The due date for this task should be within 1 day:

1. In your Service Management project, navigate to **Project settings**, click the **Automation** tab, and then click on **Create rule**.

2. Select the **Scheduled** trigger, add the following cron expression under the **Advanced (CRON expression)** tab, leave the **JQL** search field unchecked, and then click **Save**:

```
0  0  9  ?  *  MON  *
```

Your trigger should look like the following screenshot:

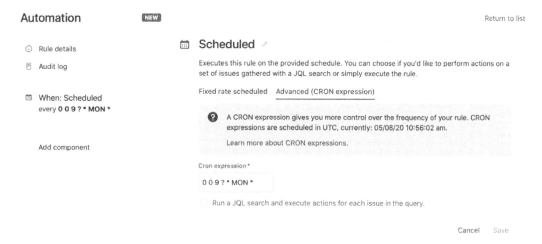

Figure 2.21 – Setting a scheduled trigger with a cron expression

3. Select **New action**, followed by **Create issue**. Choose **Fields to set** and then select **Due date**.

    Complete the fields as follows and click **Save**:

    Issue type: Task

    Summary: Start of week checks

    Due date: {{now.plusDays(1)}}

4. Next, select **Branch rule / related issues** and **All created issues** as **Type of related issue** and then click **Save**.

5. Finally, click **New action**, **Create sub-tasks**, and add as many sub-tasks as required for the actions you want to check. For this example, we'll add two sub-tasks: **Check weekend access logs** and **Other tasks**.

    Your rule should look similar to the following:

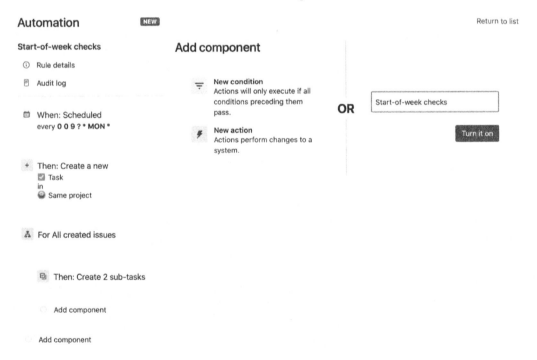

Figure 2.22 – Creating a scheduled weekly task

6. Finally, click **Save**, name your rule Start-of-week checks, and click **Turn it on** to save and enable the rule.

In this section, we have seen how to use the Scheduled trigger to automate both the creation of tasks on a regular basis as well as how we can leverage scheduling to perform maintenance tasks at defined intervals.

Summary

In this chapter, you have learned how we can use automation rules to work with issues in Jira. We have explored rule conditions in more detail and how you can use these to accurately target issues in your rules.

Next, we introduced branch rules and learned how to author rules that target not only the issue that triggered a rule, but also its related issues, and then we introduced the most common actions involved in making changes to your issues.

We then learned how to use the advanced field editor for those situations where the standard rule actions are not sufficient and also learned how to transition issues through their workflows automatically.

Finally, we looked at how to use the scheduling capability of rules to perform tasks on a regular basis using both fixed rate scheduling and cron expressions for finer control over our schedules.

These skills form the basis of working with issues in automation rules and we'll be using all of them throughout the rest of this book.

In the next chapter, we'll be learning about smart values and smart value functions and how we can use these to take your automation rules to the next level.

Section 2: Beyond the Basics

In this section, we will explore automation in more detail with practical use cases. We will also cover advanced concepts such as smart values and how to use automation to integrate with external systems.

This section comprises the following chapters:

- *Chapter 3, Enhancing Rules with Smart Values*
- *Chapter 4, Sending Automated Notifications*
- *Chapter 5, Working with External Systems*

3
Enhancing Rules with Smart Values

The visual rule editor, which we explored in *Chapter 1*, *Key Concepts of Automation*, makes the creation of complex automation rules really easy and requires no knowledge of the Jira API or any specialist scripting knowledge in order to get started.

While this approach will work for a large number of use cases, there will always be cases where you will need direct access to issue data and the ability to perform more complex functions against this data. This is where smart values come to the rescue.

This chapter will introduce you to smart values. You will learn how to find smart values, how smart functions work, and how you can introduce your own smart values into automation rules. You will also get an overview of how to manipulate dates, lists of data, text values, and how to perform numeric calculations using math expressions.

In this chapter, we'll cover the following topics:

- Understanding smart values
- Using smart value date functions
- Using smart value text functions
- Using smart value list functions
- Using smart value math expressions and functions

By the end of this chapter, you will have learned how you can use smart values and functions to manipulate dates, text strings, and lists, as well as how to use math expressions and functions to perform calculations involving numerical values.

Technical requirements

The requirements for this chapter are as follows:

- **Jira Cloud environment**: If you don't already have access to Jira, you can create a free Jira Cloud account at `https://www.atlassian.com/software/jira/free` and ensure that you have both Jira Software and Jira Service Management selected.

- **Jira Server environment**: If you are using Jira Server (available from `https://www.atlassian.com/software/jira/download`), ensure you have licenses for both Jira Software and Jira Service Management. In addition, you will also need to ensure that you install the *Automation for Jira* app, available from the Atlassian Marketplace.

In both instances, you will need to have at least project administrator access to a Service Management project and a Scrum Software project to be able to follow the examples in this chapter. For the examples in this chapter, we have used the *IT Service Management project template* to create the Service Management project, and the *Scrum Software project template* to create the Software project.

You can download the latest code samples for this chapter from this book's official GitHub repository at `https://github.com/PacktPublishing/Automate-Everyday-Tasks-in-Jira`. The Code in Action videos for this chapter are available at `https://bit.ly/39Hk44d`.

Understanding smart values

Smart values allow you to access and manipulate almost all issue data in the context of an automation rule. In addition to allowing you to access the issue data, smart values also provide advanced functionality in the form of functions that allow you to perform complex operations on the issue data.

In this section, we'll explore what smart values are available to you and how to recognize and use them in rules. We will also introduce you to smart value functions and explain how you can create your own smart values for use in your rules.

Let's begin by taking a look at where we can find smart values and how to use them.

Finding and using smart values

Smart values are generally set in the rule context by the trigger that initiated execution of the rule. In addition, certain actions, such as the **Send web request** action, can also introduce smart values into the rule context.

Each of the smart values made available by these triggers are data structures that contain fields. These can either be simple field types, such as text or numbers, or more complex data structures that, in turn, contain other fields.

For example, a trigger such as **Issue updated** will set the smart value {{issue}} to the current Jira issue in the rule context. This smart value is a data structure that represents an issue in Jira and contains both simple and complex fields.

Examples of simple fields would be {{issue.summary}} and {{issue.key}}, which allow you to access the summary and key of the issue, respectively. An example of a complex field, a field that itself is a data object, would be {{issue.assignee}}, as it itself contains further fields, which allow you to access the assignee's display name, email address, and accountId fields in the case of **Jira Cloud** or *key* in **Jira Server** or **Jira Data Center**. These would be represented as follows: {{issue.assignee.displayName}}, {{issue.assignee.emailAddress}}, {{issue.assignee.accountId}}, and {{issue.assignee.key}}, respectively.

> **Tip**
>
> To access a custom field in a smart value, you can either use the custom field's name or its ID. For example, if you had a custom field named My Custom Field with an ID value of 10000, you could access it in a smart value as either {{issue.My Custom Field}}, {{issue.my custom field}}, or {{issue.customfield_10000}}. You can find the custom field ID by editing the custom field from the **Custom Fields** admin section and copying the ID from the resulting URL. However, you should only use this approach if, for some reason, you have multiple custom fields with the same name.

In the following table, we can see the smart values made available by each automation trigger that you can use in subsequent rule components:

Trigger	Smart Value(s)
Field value changed	{{fieldChange}}
Issue assigned	{{assignee}}
Issue commented	{{comment}}
Issue created/deleted/moved/transitioned/updated **SLA threshold breached** **Manual trigger** **Multiple issue events** **Scheduled**	{{issue}}
Issue linked **Issue link deleted**	{{destinationIssue}} {{linkType}}
Work logged	{{worklog}}
Sprint created/started/completed	{{sprint}}
Version created/updated/released	{{version}}
Service limit breached	{{breachedSummary}} {{breachedRules}}
Incoming webhook	{{webhookData}}
***Branch created**	{{branch}}
***Build failed/status changed/successful**	{{build}}
***Commit created**	{{commit}}
***Deployment failed/status changed/successful**	{{deployment}}
***Pull request created/declined/merged**	{{pullRequest}}

* These triggers and smart values are only applicable to Jira Cloud

Figure 3.1 - Smart values available by trigger

The preceding table shows the main smart value for each trigger and, for the majority of cases, you can find the fields available for each of these smart values listed at `https://support.atlassian.com/jira-software-cloud/docs/smart-values-general` for Jira Cloud, or `https://confluence.atlassian.com/display/AUTOMATION/Smart+values` for Jira Server and Jira Data Center.

Smart values are based on the Mustache templating system (`https://mustache.github.io`). To use smart values (or tags, as they are referred to in Mustache), you surround keys using double curly braces (or mustaches). Using this format signifies to the rule engine that it needs to treat the given value as a smart value, and not just static text.

To access fields within smart value objects, you use dot notation. For example, to access the display name of the assignee of an issue, you would use dot notation as follows: `{{issue.assignee.displayName}}`.

> **Tip**
>
> When you reference a field or value that does not exist in a particular issue, the smart value will be empty. You can instead specify that a smart value has a default value by using the pipe (|) symbol. For example, the smart value `{{issue.description|No description was supplied}}` will return the text **No description was supplied** if the **Description** field is empty.

Smart values can be used in **Advanced compare condition**, **JQL condition**, and **User condition**, as well as in most rule actions.

Let's take a look at an example rule that uses smart values.

Creating a rule to add a comment when issues first become assigned

In this example rule, we are going to add a comment to the issue when the issue is first assigned, which will notify the reporter that we're working on their request:

1. In your Service Management project, navigate to **Project settings**, click the **Automation** tab, and then click on **Create rule**.

2. Select **Issue assigned** and then click **Save**.

3. Then select **New condition** followed by **Advanced compare condition**.

    We need to examine the changelog to ensure that the previous assignee was empty before continuing. The changelog contains all the fields that were changed in the issue during the update that caused the trigger to fire. For each changed field, the changelog will contain the **from** and **to** values, as well as the text representations of those values in the **fromString** and **toString** fields.

Set the condition fields as follows and click **Save**:

First value: `{{changelog.assignee.fromString}}`

Condition: `equals`

Second value: Leave blank

4. Now, select **New action** and then **Comment on issue**.

    Add the following text to the **Comment** field and click **Save**:

    `Hi {{issue.reporter.displayName}}`

    `We're now looking into your issue {{issue.summary}}.`

    `We'll get back to you soon with an update.`

    `{{issue.assignee.displayName}}.`

    The rule should look as follows:

Figure 3.2 - Using smart values in a rule

5. Finally, name the rule `Comment to reporter on issue assigned` and click **Turn it on** to save and enable the rule.

In this section, we learned how we can use smart values in our rules to make them more flexible and, in the next section, we will introduce you to smart value functions.

Smart value functions

In addition to the ability to access data fields with smart values, you can also manipulate these data values with the addition of functions.

Functions are generally appended to the end of smart values using dot notation. For example, to truncate the issue summary to the first 50 characters and add an ellipsis to the end of the truncated summary, we would use the following smart function: `{{issue.summary.abbreviate(50)}}`.

> **Important note**
> Smart value functions can only be applied to fields of the corresponding type. For example, date and time functions can only be applied to the *created*, *updated*, *duedate*, *resolutiondate*, and any custom fields with *Date Picker* or *Date Time Picker* types.

Smart functions can also be chained together, allowing us to perform multiple transformations in a single step. For example, the following smart function chain will convert the summary to lowercase, extract the fifth to tenth characters, and then append an exclamation to the end: `{{issue.summary.toLowerCase().substring(5,10).concat("!")}}`.

Let's look at an example of using smart value functions in a rule.

Creating a rule to add a comment asking for screenshots

In this example, we are going to create a manually triggered rule that a user can invoke to create a customized comment on the issue requesting the reporter to upload attachments to help further diagnose an issue:

1. In your Service Management project, navigate to **Project settings**, click the **Automation** tab, and then click on **Create rule**.

2. Select **Manual trigger** and click **Save**.

3. Next, select **New action** followed by **Comment on issue**.

    Add the following text to the **Comment** field and click on **Save**:

    ```
    Hi {{issue.reporter.displayName.split(" ").first}}
    ```

    ```
    We require a little more info in order to diagnose your
    issue further.
    ```

    ```
    Please take a screenshot and attach it to this issue by no
    later than {{now.plusBusinessDays(2).fullDate}}.
    ```

    ```
    Thank you :)
    ```

    ```
    {{issue.assignee.displayName}}
    ```

    The rule should look similar to the following screenshot:

Figure 3.3 - Using smart value functions

4. Finally, name the rule `Ask reporter to attach screenshot` and click **Turn it on** to save and enable the rule.

> **Important note**
> In Jira Cloud, it is possible to use the *Create variable* action to create a custom smart value based on other smart value functions and expressions that you can then make use of in later conditions and actions.

In this section, we learned what smart values are and how we can use them to access data in automation rules. We also learned how to find the correct smart value for triggers and how to find the associated smart value fields. We also looked at smart value functions and saw how we can chain them together to apply multiple transformations in a single step.

In the next section, we will look at how we can use smart values to manipulate and format dates in automation rules.

Using smart value date functions

As a project management and tracking tool, having the ability to manipulate dates in Jira is critical to the correct operation of the application, and smart values in automation rules give us a lot of flexibility in how we can use and manipulate dates and times in rules.

In this section, we will look at how we can use smart values to format dates and times for inclusion in other date and time fields, as well as how to format them for use in other fields such as text fields, the advanced field editor, or for use in notifications.

We will also explore all the available formats and functions applicable to dates and see how we can use these in automation rules.

> **Tip**
>
> You can access the current date and time using the smart value *{{now}}*. All formatting and date manipulation functions that can be used with date fields can also be used with the *{{now}}* smart value.

Let's take a look at how we can format dates using smart value functions.

Formatting dates

The ability to format dates and times gives us flexibility in how we can display these to users, in either comments, text fields, or notifications. It also allows us to be able to specify the exact format to use when communicating with external systems that require date and time inputs in specific formats and in reformatting dates and times received from external systems.

Finally, being able to control the format of dates and times allows us to manipulate them using smart value functions and ensure that we can set a date or time field with the resulting calculation correctly.

In the following table, we can see how the date, *Tuesday, December 31, 2019 10:25:30 PM CET* will be formatted using each of the available date and time formats available to automation rules:

Format	Output
Default	Tuesday, December 31, 2019 10:25:30 PM CET
*jiraDate / asJiraDate	2019-12-31
*jiraDateTime / asJiraDateTime	2019-12-31T22:25:30.0+0100
jqlDate / asJqlDate	2019-12-31
jqlDateTime / asJqlDateTime	2019-12-31 22:25:30
shortDate / asShortDate	12/31/19
shortTime / asShortTime	10:25 PM
shortDateTime / asShortDateTime	12/31/19 10:25 PM
mediumDate / asMediumDate	Dec 31, 2019
mediumTime / asMediumTime	10:25:30 PM
mediumDateTime / asMediumDateTime	Dec 31, 2019 10:25:30 PM
longDate / asLongDate	December 31, 2019
longTime / asLongTime	10:25:30 PM CET
longDateTime / asLongDateTime	December 31, 2019 10:25:30 PM CET
fullDate / asFullDate	Tuesday, December 31, 2019
fullTime / asFullTime	10:25:30 PM CET
fullDateTime / asFullDatetime	Tuesday, December 31, 2019 10:25:30 PM CET
format("pattern") e.g. format("dd/MM/yyyy") / as("pattern") e.g. format("dd/MM/yyyy")	31/12/2019

* Use these formats when you need to set a **Date Picker** or **Date Time Picker** field in Jira

Figure 3.4 - Available date formats

As you can see from the preceding list, dates and times can be formatted for display in a variety of ways, and it is also possible to use a custom pattern if none of the standard ones are suitable.

> **Tip**
>
> The pattern syntax used for the custom formatters `format("pattern")` and `as("pattern")` are defined by the underlying Java platform and the full syntax descriptions can be found at the following link, `https://docs.oracle.com/en/java/javase/11/docs/api/java.base/java/time/format/DateTimeFormatter.html`, under the heading *Patterns for Formatting and Parsing*.

Formatting dates with locales and time zones

In addition to the formats that we have just looked at, with smart values, it is also possible to format dates and times for specific locales and time zones, or even the locale or time zone of a specific user, such as the assignee or reporter of an issue.

The following formatting functions are provided to enable locale- and time zone-based formatting of dates and times:

- **locale(string locale)/withLocale(string locale)**: Formats the date field using the given locale. For example, you can use `{{issue.created.withLocale("fr_CA")}}` to format the issue created date using Canadian French, or `{{issue.created.withLocale(issue.reporter.locale)}}` to format the issue created date using the reporter's locale.

- **convertToTimeZone(string timezone)**: Converts the time in the **DateTime** field to the given time zone. For example, you can use `{{issue.created.convertToTimeZone("America/New_York")}}` to format the issue created date to display in the current time zone in New York, or `{{issue.created.convertToTimeZone(issue.reporter.timeZone)}}` to format the issue created date to the reporter's time zone.

- **setTimeZone(string timezone)**: Sets the time zone component of the **DateTime** field to the given time zone. This function will change the time zone without converting the time.

The full list of supported locales can be found at `https://www.oracle.com/java/technologies/javase/jdk11-suported-locales.html#modules`. The list of time zones is defined by the tz database and the full list can be found at `https://en.wikipedia.org/wiki/List_of_tz_database_time_zones`.

Let's see how we can use date formats in an example rule.

Creating a rule to create onboarding sub-tasks

In this rule, when a new employee onboarding request is created, we need to ensure that certain tasks, such as provisioning a laptop and desk phone, are completed before the new employee starts.

We want the sub-task summaries to include the start date so that it is immediately apparent to the user assigned to the request when the task is due:

1. In your Service Management project, navigate to **Project settings**, click on the **Automation** tab, and then click on **Create rule**.

2. Select the **Issue created** trigger and click **Save**.

3. Then select **New condition** followed by **Issue fields condition**.

   Complete the fields as follows, and then click **Save**:

   Field: Request Type

   Condition: equals

   Value: Onboard new employees

4. Next, select **New action**, followed by **the Create sub-tasks** action.

   Add two sub-tasks with the following summaries:

   Provision new laptop by {{issue.duedate.longDate}}

   Setup new desk phone by {{issue.duedate.longDate}}

   The rule should look similar to the following screenshot:

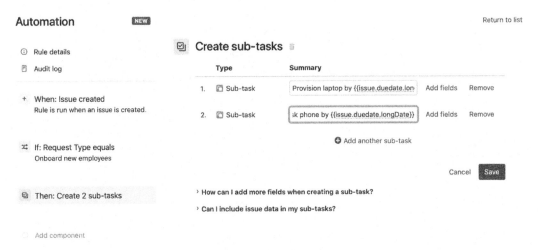

Figure 3.5 - Using the smart value date format

5. Finally, click **Save**, name the rule `Create onboarding sub-tasks`, and click **Turn it on** to save and enable the rule.

Now that we've seen how to format dates and time, let's take a look at how we can manipulate them using smart value functions.

Manipulating dates

In addition to providing the ability to format dates, a number of smart value functions are provided that enable us to perform operations on dates. These operations allow us to perform comparisons on dates and times, perform basic arithmetic on dates and times, and manipulate the various components of dates and times.

Let's take a look at the functions you can use to manipulate dates in your rules. The first set of functions relate to date comparisons and allow you to compare one date with another:

- **isBefore(date)**: Checks whether the date field used to call the function is before the date supplied as the `function` parameter. This function will return **true** if the date is earlier than the `date` parameter, and **false** otherwise.

- **isAfter(date)**: Checks whether the date field used to call the function is after the date supplied as the `function` parameter. This function will return **true** if the date is later than the `date` parameter, and **false** otherwise.

- **isEquals(date)**: Checks whether the date field used to call the function is equal to the date supplied as the `function` parameter. This function will return **true** if the date is exactly equal to the `date` parameter, and **false** otherwise.

- **compareTo(date)**: Checks whether the date field used to call the function is earlier than, equal to, or later than, the date supplied as the parameter. This function returns a negative integer (such as `-1`) when the date field used to call the function is earlier than the date in the parameter, `0` if they are equal, or a positive integer (such as `1`) if the date field is later than the date field in the parameter.

The next set of functions allows us to manipulate dates and times in various ways:

- **diff(date)**: This function calculates the difference between the date field used to call the function and the date supplied as the parameter. The result can be refined to display the difference, using any of the components of a date, including *millis*, *seconds*, *minutes*, *hours*, *days*, *weeks*, *months*, *years*, or *businessDays* by appending this to the end of the function. For example, `diffDate(date).seconds` will display the difference between the dates in seconds. The default output is *prettyPrint*, which displays the difference in words, for example, *2 days 3 hours*.

- **plusDays(int days)/minusDays(int days)**: Adds or subtracts the given number of days to or from the respective date component and returns a new date with the relevant calculation applied.

- **plusHours(int hours)/minusHours(int hours)**: Adds or subtracts the given number of hours to or from the respective date component and returns a new date with the relevant calculation applied.

- **plusWeeks(int weeks)/minusWeeks(int weeks)**: Adds or subtracts the given number of weeks to or from the respective date component and returns a new date with the relevant calculation applied.

- **plusMillis(int millis)/minusMillis(int millis)**: Adds or subtracts the given number of milliseconds to or from the respective date component and returns a new date with the relevant calculation applied.

- **plusMinutes(int minutes)/minusMinutes(int minutes)**: Adds or subtracts the given number of minutes to or from the respective date component and returns a new date with the relevant calculation applied.

- **plusMonths(int months)/minusMonths(int months)**: Adds or subtracts the given number of months to or from the respective date component and returns a new date with the relevant calculation applied.

- **plusSeconds(int seconds)/minusSeconds(int seconds)**: Adds or subtracts the given number of seconds to or from the respective date component and returns a new date with the relevant calculation applied.

- **plusYears(int years)/minusYears(int years)**: Adds or subtracts the given number of years to or from the respective date component and returns a new date with the relevant calculation applied.

- **plusBusinessDays(int days)/minusBusinessDays(int days)**: Adds or subtracts the given number of business days to or from the respective date component and returns a new date with the relevant calculation applied. A business day is defined as the hours of 9 a.m. to 6 p.m., Monday to Friday.

- **toBusinessDay/toBusinessDayBackwards**: Returns the first business day after or before the date used to call the function, respectively.

- **toStartOfDay/toDateTimeAtStartOfDay**: Sets the time components to zero (that is, midnight) for the given date using the server's default time zone. The first function is used for **DateTime** fields, while the second function will convert a **Date** field to a **DateTime** field and set the time component accordingly.

- **toCurrentTime/toDateTimeAtCurrentTime**: Sets the time components to the current time for the given date. The first function is used for **DateTime** fields, while the second function will convert a **Date** field to a **DateTime** field and set the time component accordingly.

- **withNextDayOfWeek(string dayOfWeek)**: Sets the date to the next matching day of the week. It accepts MON, TUE, WED, THU, FRI, SAT, or SUN as values for the dayOfWeek parameter.

- **withDayOfMonth(int dayOfMonth)**: Sets the day of month component of the **Date** or **DateTime** field to the supplied dayOfMonth. The allowable range for the dayOfMonth parameter is 1 to 31.

- **withHour(int hour)**: Sets the hour component of the **DateTime** field to the supplied hour. The allowable range for the hour parameter is 0 to 23.

- **withMillis(int millis)**: Sets the milliseconds component of the **DateTime** field to the supplied millisecond. The allowable range for the millis parameter is 0 to 999.

- **withMinute(int minute)**: Sets the minute component of the **Date** or **DateTime** field to the supplied minute. The allowable range for the minute parameter is 0 to 59.

- **withMonth(int month)**: Sets the month component of the **Date** or **DateTime** field to the supplied month. The allowable range for the month parameter is 1 to 12.

- **withSecond(int second)**: Sets the second component of the **DateTime** field to the supplied second. The allowable range for the second parameter is 0 to 59.

- **withYear(int year)**: Sets the year component of the **Date** or **DateTime** field to the supplied year. The allowable range for the year parameter is any valid year in the Gregorian calendar.

- **withDayOfYear(int dayOfYear)**: Sets the day of year component of the **Date** or **DateTime** field to the supplied dayOfYear. The allowable range for the dayOfYear parameter is 1 to 365.

- **startOfMonth/endOfMonth**: Sets the date component of the **Date** or **DateTime** field to the first or last calendar day of the month in the field's month component.

- **firstBusinessDayOfMonth/lastBusinessDayOfMonth**: Sets the day of month component of the **Date** or **DateTime** field to the first or last business day of the month in the field's month component.

- **firstOfTheMonth(int dayOfWeek)/lastOfTheMonth(int dayOfWeek)**: Sets the date component of the **Date** or **DateTime** field to the first or last weekday of the month based on the day of the week supplied in the parameter. The day of the week parameter is in the range 1 to 7, 1 being Monday and 7 being Sunday. For example, calling `{{datefield.firstOfTheMonth(3)}}` will set the date to the first Wednesday of the month.

- **ofTheMonth(int weekOfMonth, int dayOfWeek)**: Sets the date component of the **Date** or **DateTime** field to the supplied day of the week in the supplied week of the month. The range for the `weekOfMonth` parameter is from 1 to 5 and the range for the `dayOfWeek` parameter is 1 to 7, 1 being Monday and 7 being Sunday. For example, to set the date to the third Monday of the month, you would use `{{datefield.ofTheMonth(3, 1)}}`.

Now that we've taken a look at the various functions available to manipulate dates and times, let's take a look at a couple of examples of how to use them in rules.

Creating a rule to update the due date based on sub-tasks

For this example, we have a number of sub-tasks for each user story in the software project, and we would like to update the due date of the user story to 5 business days from the current date when the last sub-task transitions to **In Progress**:

1. In your Software project, navigate to **Project settings**, click the **Automation** tab (or **Project automation** tab if you're using Jira Server), and then click on **Create rule**.

2. Select the **Issue transitioned** trigger and set the **To status** field to **In Progress** and then click **Save**.

3. Then select **New condition** followed by **Issue fields condition**.

   Set the condition fields as follows and click **Save**:

   Field: `Issue Type`

   Condition: `equals`

   Value: `Sub-task`

4. Next, select **Branch rule / related issues**, set **Type of related issues** to **Parent**, and then click **Save**.

5. Now select **New condition**, followed by **Related issues condition**.

    Set the condition fields as follows and then click **Save**:

    Related issues: `Sub-tasks`

    Condition: `All match specified JQL`

    Matching JQL: `status = "In Progress"`

6. Select **New action** and then select **Edit issue action**. In the **Choose fields to set** dropdown, select **Due date** and enter `{{now.plusBusinessDays(5)}}` in the **Due date** field and click **Save**.

    Your rule should now look similar to the following screenshot:

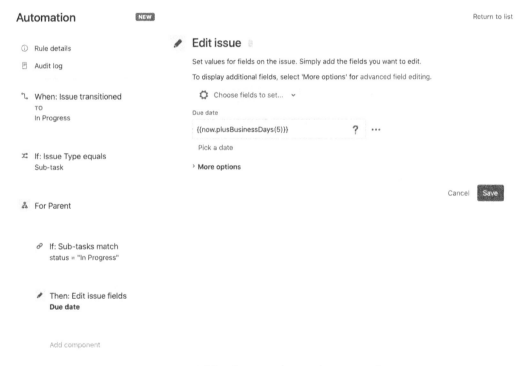

Figure 3.6 - Adding business days to the current date

7. Finally, name your rule `Set user story due date` and click **Turn it on** to save and enable the rule.

Let's now take a look at another example of using smart value functions to manipulate dates.

Creating a rule to set the due date

For this example, we want to set the due date of an issue to the 15th of the current month if the issue is created before the 15th of the month, and to the 15th of the following month if the issue is created after the 15th of the month:

1. In your Software project, navigate to **Project settings**, click the **Automation** tab (or the **Project automation** tab if you're using Jira Server), and then click on **Create rule**.

2. Select **Issue created** and then click **Save**.

3. Next, select **New condition**, followed by **If / else block**, and add an **Advanced compare condition** to the If block.

4. Set the fields for the **Condition** as follows and then click **Save**:

    First value: `{{issue.created}}`

    Condition: `greater than`

    Second value: `{{now.startOfMonth.plusDays(15)}}`

5. Now select **New action** and then **Edit issue**. Select **Due date** from the **Choose fields to set** dropdown and then set the **Due date** field to `{{now.endOfMonth.plusDays(15)}}` and click **Save**.

    Your rule should now look as per the following screenshot:

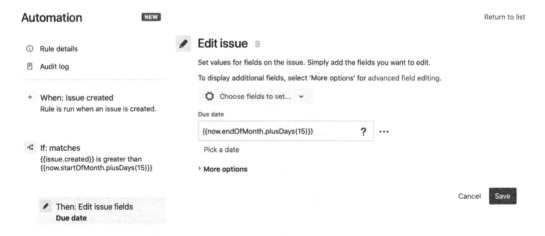

Figure 3.7 - Setting the date to the middle of next month

6. Now that we've dealt with due dates for next month, let's complete the rule for due dates this month. Click on **Add else** in the rule-chain view and then click **Save**.

7. Next, add a **New action** field, followed by **Edit issue**. Again, select **Due date** from the **Choose fields to set** dropdown and then set the **Due date** field to `{{now.withDayOfMonth(15)}}` and click **Save**.

Your rule should look similar to the following screenshot:

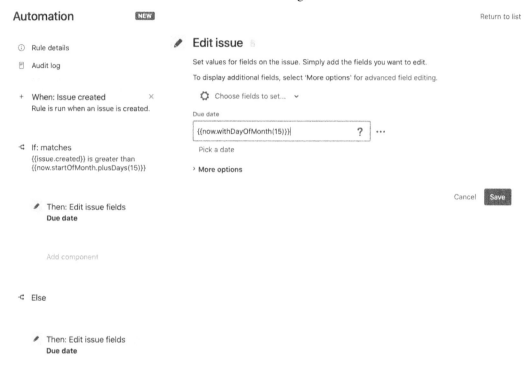

Figure 3.8 - Setting the date to the middle of the current month

8. Finally, name the rule `Set due date to middle of the month` and click **Turn it on** to save and enable the rule.

In this section, we have taken a look at the various smart value date and time functions available and learned how to use these to manipulate dates in automation rules. Next, we'll take a look at how we can use smart values to work with text.

Using smart value text functions

In a similar fashion to working with dates and times, smart value functions that deal with text strings allow us to manipulate any text field type, including the sub-attributes of fields where they are also text-type fields.

In this section, we will look at how smart value functions for text allow us to manipulate text, encode it for use in HTML, JSON, XML, or URLs, and how we can use functions to test for specific characteristics within blocks of text.

Let's take a look at the functions available to manipulate text in automation rules. The first set of functions we'll look at deal with text comparisons and return either **true** or **false** depending on whether the check passes or fails:

- **startsWith(string)/endsWith(string)**: Checks whether the text field starts or ends with the given string, respectively
- **equals(string)/equalsIgnoreCase(string)**: Checks whether the text field equals the given string exactly or ignoring capitalization, respectively
- **isAlpha**: Checks whether the text field contains only letters
- **isNumeric**: Checks whether the text field contains only numbers
- **isAlphaNumeric**: Checks whether the text field contains only letters and numbers
- **isEmpty**: Checks for the absence of data in the text field
- **isNotEmpty**: Checks for the presence of data in the text field

The next set of functions allows us to convert text into other types, such as numbers, dates, or lists:

- **asNumber**: Converts the text field to a number allowing you to perform numeric operations and calculations on the converted value.

> **Tip**
> Use the *isNumeric* test on the text field prior to conversion to ensure you don't get errors by trying to convert text that cannot be represented as numbers.

- **toDate/toDate(string pattern)**: Converts a text field to a date. Use the second form of the function to specify what the format of the date in its textual representation should be. Refer to the *Formatting dates* section for examples of how to define the pattern.
- **split(string separator)**: Splits a text field into a list of items around the separator. The resulting list of items can then be manipulated using the smart value list functions.
- **match(string regularExpression)**: Performs a regular expression search on the text field. Multiple matches of regularExpression are returned as a list of items that can be manipulated further using the smart value list functions.

> **Tip**
>
> A *regular expression* is a special text string for describing a search pattern. These patterns are usually used to perform find or find-and-replace operations on text strings or to validate input. In Jira automation, regular expressions are based on the underlying Java implementation, which can be found at `https://docs.oracle.com/javase/8/docs/api/java/util/regex/Pattern.html`.

The following set of functions allows us to change the way text is displayed, extract portions of text, or even replace blocks of text:

- **abbreviate(int maxLength)**: Abbreviates the text field to the maximum length specified and adds an ellipsis ("…") to the end of the text.

- **toLowerCase**: Converts the text field to all lowercase.

- **toUpperCase**: Converts the text field to all uppercase.

- **capitalize**: Converts the first character of the text field to uppercase.

- **reverse**: Reverses all the characters of the text field.

- **trim**: Removes all leading and trailing white spaces from the text field.

- **concat(string)**: Appends the given string to the end of the text field.

- **charAt(int index)**: Returns the character at the specified position in the text. The first character is at index 0.

- **indexOf(string) / lastIndexOf(string)**: Finds the first or last position of the given string within the text field.

- **length**: Returns the total number of characters of the text field.

- **quote**: Formats the text field into a literal expression that can then be used in a regular expression in the match function. For example, if the text field contains regular expression special characters, such as * or \, these will be treated as normal (or literal) characters rather than as regular expressions.

- **remove(string)**: Removes all occurrences of the given string from the text field.

- **replace(string target, string replacement)**: Replaces the target string in the text field with the replacement string value.

- **replaceAll(string regex, string replacement)**: Replaces all occurrences in the text field of the regular expression `regex` with the replacement string.

- **left(int length)/right(int length)**: Returns the specified number of characters from either the left or right of the text field, respectively.

- **leftPad(int length, string)/rightPad(int length, string)**: Adds the given string to either the left or right of the text field until the text reaches the total length specified.

- **substring(int start)**: Returns a portion of the text field beginning at the start index.

- **substring(int start, int end)**: Returns a portion of the text field beginning at the start index and ending at the end index.

- **substringAfter(string)/substringAfterLast(string)**: Returns a portion of the text field after the first or last occurrence of the supplied string, respectively.

- **substringBefore(string)/substringBeforeLast(string)**: Returns a portion of the text field before the first or last occurrence of the supplied string, respectively.

- **substringBetween(string open, string close)**: Returns a portion of the text field between the given start and end strings.

The final set of functions allows us to encode text to comply with specific standards. This is especially useful when integrating with external systems or when sending email notifications from rules:

- **htmlEncode**: Use this function to ensure the text field value is correctly encoded when including the field in HTML output.

- **jsonEncode)**: Use this function to ensure the text field value is correctly encoded when including the field in JSON output.

- **urlEncode**: Use this function to ensure the text field value is correctly encoded when using the field to create a URL link.

- **xmlEncode**: Use this function to ensure the text field value is correctly encoded when including the field in XML output.

Now that we've looked at the various functions available that we can use to manipulate text, let's take a look at how we can leverage these in automation rules.

Creating a rule to auto-close an issue

A common scenario faced by many teams is that after a ticket has been resolved, the reporter replies to say thank you. This will generally cause the ticket to re-open and someone will have to manually go and resolve the ticket again.

In this example, we'll use text smart value functions to examine the latest comment and auto-resolve the issue if we find the words "thank you":

1. In your Service Management project, navigate to **Project settings**, click the **Automation** tab, and then click on **Create rule**.

2. Select the **Issue transitioned** trigger, set the **From status** field to **Resolved**, the **To status** field to **In Progress**, and then click **Save**.

3. Now select **New condition** followed by **Advanced compare condition**.

   Complete the condition fields as follows and click **Save**:

   First value: `{{issue.comments.last.body.trim.toLowercase}}`

   Condition: `contains regular expression`

   Second value: `thank\s+you`

   The rule should now look as follows:

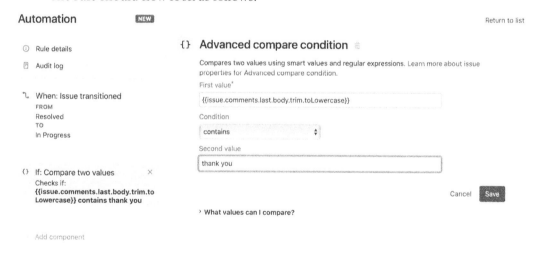

Figure 3.9 - Using text smart value functions in conditions

4. Next, select **New action** and then **Transition issue**. Set **Transition the issue by** to **Selecting the destination status**, and, in the **Destination status** field, select **Resolved** and then click **Save**.

5. Name the rule `Auto-resolve thank you comments` and click **Turn it on** to save and enable the rule.

In this section, we have seen how we can use smart value functions to compare and manipulate text values. In the next section, we'll take a look at how we can use smart values and functions to work with lists of items.

Using smart value list functions

There are a number of scenarios you'll come across when authoring automation rules, where you'll be presented with a list of items. This could be a list of versions or components attached to an issue, or a list of issues, such as all the sub-tasks of a particular issue.

Smart value functions for lists give us the ability to work with these lists of items by iterating over each item and being able to perform additional functions against attributes of the items. We also have access to functions that allow us to perform simple calculations against all the items in a list.

In this section, we'll take a look at the smart value functions available for accessing and formatting lists of items.

We'll cover examples of iterating over lists using smart values when we look at sending notifications via email and Slack in *Chapter 4, Sending Automated Notifications*.

Let's now take a look at the smart value functions available for working with lists:

- **isEmpty**: Checks whether a list contains any items. This function will return **true** if the list is empty and **false** if it contains items.
- **size**: Returns the number of items in the list.
- **join(string separator)**: Joins all the items in the list into a single text value, separated by the supplied separator.
- **get(int index)/getFromEnd(int index)**: Gets the item in the specified location from the front or end of the list, respectively. The position of items in the list are counted starting from 0 (zero) on either end of the list.
- **first**: Retrieves the first item of the list.
- **last**: Retrieves the last item of the list.
- **average**: Computes the average of all the items in a numerical list.
- **max**: Finds the item with the largest number in a numerical list or finds the latest date in a list of dates.

- **min**: Finds the item with the smallest number in a numerical list or finds the earliest date in a list of dates.

- **sum**: Computes the sum of all the items in a numerical list.

Let's take a look at how we can incorporate what we have learned about lists into a practical example that uses a smart value list function to calculate the sum of story points in sub-tasks.

Creating a rule to sum up sub-task story points in a parent story

In this example, we are tracking story points against sub-tasks and would like to ensure that the parent story always reflects the correct total of story points whenever the story points in one of its sub-tasks' changes. You will need to enable the configuration context for the **Story Points** custom field to include **sub-tasks** in addition to **Epics** and **Stories**:

1. In your Software Project, navigate to **Project settings**, click the **Automation** tab (or the **Project automation** tab if you're using Jira Server), and then click on **Create rule**.

2. Select **Field value changed**, set **Fields to monitor for changes** to **Story Points**, and then click **Save**.

3. Now select **New condition** followed by **Issue fields condition**.

    Set the condition fields as follows and click **Save**:

    Field: `Issue Type`

    Condition: `equals`

    Value: `Sub-task`

4. Then select **Branch rule / related issues** and set **Type of related issues** to `Parent` and click **Save**.

5. Next, select **New action** and then select **Edit issue**.

6. In the **Choose fields to set** dropdown, find and select **Story Points** in the **Story Points** field.

    Add the following smart value expression and click **Save**:

    ```
    {{issue.subtasks.Story Points.sum}}
    ```

Your rule should now look as per the following screenshot:

Automation   `NEW`   Return to list

ⓘ Rule details   ✏ **Edit issue** 🗑

🗒 Audit log   Set values for fields on the issue. Simply add the fields you want to edit.

                                    To display additional fields, select 'More options' for advanced field editing.

Ⅰ **When:** Value changes for   ⚙ Choose fields to set... ⌄
   Story Points
                                    Story Points

⤭ **If:** Issue Type equals   ┌──┐ •••
   Sub-task   │ {{issue.subtasks.Story Points.sum}}│   │
                                    └──┘

                                    › **More options**

⚘ **For** Current issue   Cancel   **Save**

   ✏ **Then:** Edit issue fields
      Story Points

      Add component

Figure 3.10 - Using a smart value list function to sum list item values

7. Finally, name the rule `Keep parent in sync with sub-task story points` and click **Turn it on** to save and enable the rule.

In this section, we have learned how we can use smart value list functions to iterate over items in a list and how to perform operations against values in a list.

Next we'll take a look at the mathematical operations available for use in automation rules.

Using smart value math expressions and functions

So far, we have seen how to use smart values for working with dates, text, and lists and how they are able to help you create powerful and flexible automation rules.

In this section, we are going to look at math expressions and functions. Math expressions and functions will allow you to perform calculations directly in numeric fields as well as allow you to reference numeric fields in calculations for display in text fields. In Jira, all numeric fields are based on floating-point numbers.

To use any of the math expressions, they need to be surrounded by the following smart value block in order to be recognized as shown in the following example:

```
{{#=}} <math expression> {{/}}
```

The {{#=}} operator signifies to the automation engine that you are about to perform a calculation and is a custom addition to the underlying Mustache library.

> **Important note**
> Jira Cloud offers additional capabilities for working with numbers, including the ability to format numbers using locales or with custom patterns.

Let's take a look at the math expressions in common between Jira Cloud and Jira Server first.

Math expressions support the usual operations you'd expect to see, as can be seen in the following table:

Operator	Description
+	Additive operator
-	Subtraction operator
*	Multiplication operator
/	Division operator
%	Remainder operator (modulo)
^	Power operator

Figure 3.11 - Basic math expression operators

In addition to the basic operations, math expressions support Boolean operators as well, and the supported operators can be seen in the following table:

Operator	Description
= OR ==	Equals
!= OR <>	Not equals
<	Less than
<=	Less than or equal to
>	Greater than
>=	Greater than or equal to
&&	Boolean AND
||	Boolean OR

Figure 3.12 - Boolean math expression operators

Math expressions also support a number of functions that can be used, and we can see a full list of supported functions in the following table:

Function	Description
NOT(expression)	Boolean negation, 1 (means true) if the expression is not zero
IF(condition,value_if_true,value_if_false)	Returns one value if the condition evaluates to true or the other if it evaluates to false
RANDOM()	Produces a random number between 0 and 1
MIN(e1,e2, ...)	Returns the smallest of the given expressions
MAX(e1,e2, ...)	Returns the biggest of the given expressions
ABS(expression)	Returns the absolute (non-negative) value of the expression
ROUND(expression,precision)	Rounds a value to a certain number of digits, uses the current rounding mode; helpful with formatting numbers
FLOOR(expression)	Rounds the value down to the nearest integer
CEILING(expression)	Rounds the value up to the nearest integer
LOG(expression)	Returns the natural logarithm (base e) of an expression
LOG10(expression)	Returns the common logarithm (base 10) of an expression
SQRT(expression)	Returns the square root of an expression
SIN(expression)	Returns the trigonometric sine of an angle (in degrees)
COS(expression)	Returns the trigonometric cosine of an angle (in degrees)
TAN(expression)	Returns the trigonometric tangents of an angle (in degrees)
ASIN(expression)	Returns the angle of asin (in degrees)
ACOS(expression)	Returns the angle of acos (in degrees)
ATAN(expression)	Returns the angle of atan (in degrees)
SINH(expression)	Returns the hyperbolic sine of a value
COSH(expression)	Returns the hyperbolic cosine of a value
TANH(expression)	Returns the hyperbolic tangents of a value
RAD(expression)	Converts an angle measured in degrees to an approximately equivalent angle measured in radians
DEG(expression)	Converts an angle measured in radians to an approximately equivalent angle measured in degrees

Figure 3.13 - Supported math functions

There are also a few constant values that are supported for use in math expressions, and these are listed here:

Constant	Description
e	The value of *e*
PI	The value of PI
TRUE	The value 1
FALSE	The value 0
NULL	The null value

Figure 3.14 - Support constant values

In addition to the preceding common functions and operations, Jira Cloud introduces some additional numerical operations. These operations do not need to be surrounded by the smart value block we learned about earlier, but rather can be applied directly to numerical smart values or fields.

Let's take a look at these additional numerical operations:

- **abs**: Returns the absolute value of a number
- **round**: Returns a number rounded to the nearest whole number
- **floor/ceil**: Returns the lower or upper value of a number, respectively
- **plus(value)/minus(value)**: Adds or subtracts the number or smart value in the parameter to or from the numerical value or field used to call the operation
- **multiply(value)/divide(value)**: Multiplies or divides the number or smart value in the parameter with or by the numerical value or field used to call the operation
- **gt(value)/gte(value)**: Checks whether the numerical smart value is greater than, or greater than or equal to, the value given in the parameter
- **eq(value)**: Checks whether the numerical smart value is equal to the value given in the parameter
- **lt(value)/lte(value)**: Checks whether the numerical smart value is less than, or less than or equal to, the value given in the parameter

Jira Cloud also adds the ability to format numerical values using smart value functions, and these functions are listed here:

- **format**: Formats the numerical field using the numerical format of the US locale.
- **formatWithLocale(locale)**: Formats the numerical field using the numerical format of the supplied locale, for example, `fr_CA`.
- **format(string pattern)**: Formats the numerical field using a custom pattern. The patterns you can use rely on the underlying Java implementation and can be found at the following link: `https://docs.oracle.com/javase/tutorial/ java/data/numberformat.html`.
- **asPercentage/asPercentage(string locale)**: Formats the numerical field as a percentage in the US locale or as a percentage in the locale specified.
- **asCurrency/asCurrency(string locale)**: Formats the numerical field as a currency in the US locale or as a currency in the locale specified.

As we've seen, there is a comprehensive number of smart value functions that we can make use of to perform advanced mathematical operations in automation rules. Let's now take a look at using math expressions in an example.

Creating a rule to keep an original estimate for an epic in sync with its child issues

In this example, we're going to update the original estimate of an epic any time tracking fields in the epic's underlying issues change:

1. In your Software project, navigate to **Project settings**, click the **Automation** tab (or the **Project automation** tab if you're using Jira Server), and then click on **Create rule**.

2. Select the **Field value changed** trigger and, in the **Fields to monitor for changes** list, select **Time tracking** and then click **Save**.

3. Next, select **New condition** and then **Related issues condition**.

   Set the fields of the condition as follows and click **Save**:

   Related issues: `Epic`

   Condition: `Exists`

4. Now select **Branch rule / related issues** and, in the **Type of related issues** field, select `Epic (parent)` and click **Save**.

5. Then, select **Edit issue**. In the **Choose fields to set** dropdown, find and select `Original Estimate (System)`.

Add the following math expression to the **Original Estimate (System)** field and click **Save**:

```
{{#=}}{{fieldChange.to}}/60 - {{fieldChange.from}}/60 +
{{issue.original estimate}}/60{{/}}
```

The rule should now look similar to the following screenshot:

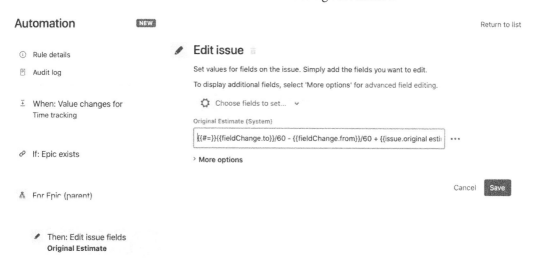

Figure 3.15 - Using math expressions in a rule

6. Finally, name the rule `Keep Epic estimates in sync` and click **Turn it on** to save and enable the rule.

In this section, we have seen the comprehensive list of smart value mathematical functions available for use in your automation rules and how we can use these to manipulate numerical values.

Summary

In this chapter, you have learned how to enhance the functionality of automation rules by using smart values and smart value functions.

We learned which smart values are set by the various triggers and how you can access their attributes or fields. In addition, you learned about smart value functions and how they can be used in isolation against a particular field or chained together to perform multiple operations on data in a single step.

Finally, we learned about the various smart value functions available for dates, text, lists, and numerical values and how these can be used to format and manipulate data to create extremely powerful and flexible rules.

Smart values and their associated functions can be used in nearly every field in automation rule conditions and actions, and we'll learn throughout the rest of this book how they will help us to create much more powerful and richer rules as a result of their use.

In the next chapter, we will be looking at how to send notifications to various channels from your automation rules.

4

Sending Automated Notifications

Sending the right notification at the right time, with relevant contextual information, is important. It ensures that the desired action is taken by the recipient of the notification.

Jira has always had the ability to send email notifications to users when changes to issues are made. However, these are, by necessity, very generalized. They do not contain relevant contextual information and are exceedingly difficult to customize.

Automation rules allow us to overcome some of this limitation by enabling us to send custom notifications based on any rule condition we require, and not only via email; we also have the ability to send notifications to mobile phones via SMS and to chat applications such as **Slack** and **Microsoft Teams**.

This chapter will introduce you to the notification capabilities in automation rules and show you how to send custom email notifications to users, groups, or indeed any valid email address. We'll also learn how to send messages to Slack channels and to Microsoft Teams channels. Finally, we'll learn how to use **Twilio** to send text messages via SMS to mobile devices.

In this chapter, we will cover the following topics:

- Sending email notifications using automation
- How to send notifications to Slack

- How to send notifications to Microsoft Teams
- Sending SMS notifications with Twilio

Technical requirements

The requirements for this chapter are as follows:

- **Jira Cloud environment**: If you don't already have access to Jira, you can create a free Jira Cloud account at `https://www.atlassian.com/software/jira/free` and ensure that you have both Jira Software and Jira Service Management selected; or
- **Jira Server environment**: If you are using Jira Server (available from `https://www.atlassian.com/software/jira/download`), ensure that you have licenses for both Jira Software and Jira Service Management. In addition, you will also need to ensure that you install the *Automation for Jira* app from the Atlassian Marketplace.

In both instances, you will need to have at least Project Administrator access to a Jira project.

You will also need access to any of the following tools:

- **Slack**: If you don't already have access to Slack, you can sign up for an account at `https://www.slack.com`.
- **Microsoft Teams**: You can sign up for a Teams account at `https://teams.microsoft.com` if you don't already have one.
- **Twilio**: Sign up at `https://www.twilio.com` if you need an account.

You can download the latest code samples for this chapter from this book's official GitHub repository at `https://github.com/PacktPublishing/Automate-Everyday-Tasks-in-Jira`.

The Code in Action videos for this chapter are available at: `https://bit.ly/2Y9p0cR`

Sending email notifications using automation

Jira has always had the ability to send notifications to users via email when certain events take place, for example, when an issue has been updated or a comment has been added. You can also send emails to various users containing the results of saved filters on a scheduled basis and with Jira Service Management, you can create custom templates for sending notifications to customers via email in place of the standard event notifications.

With the **Send email** action available to automation rules, we are able to extend this capability and send customized email notifications to any email address, user field, or group of users whenever the rule is activated.

In this section, we'll look at how to introduce custom email notifications in automation rules and how these notifications can provide more specific context to the user.

> **Tip**
> You should always take care when creating custom email notifications in an automation rule. Make sure that you do not end up spamming the user with multiple notifications for the same event.

Before we look at how to use email notifications in a rule, let's take a quick look at the **Send email** action itself.

The following screenshot shows the fields available in the **Send email** action:

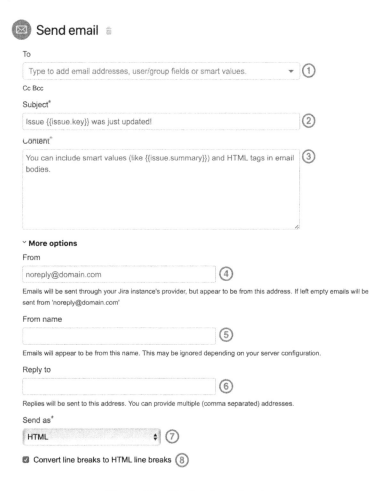

Figure 4.1 – The Send email action

Let's take a quick look at each of the fields available in the **Send email** action:

1. The **To** field is where we configure the email recipients. This can be in the form of one or more email addresses, or you can use the drop-down menu to select one or more Jira users or user groups. You can also use smart values and smart value functions to extract email addresses from issue fields.

    You can additionally set the email **CC** and **BCC** fields in the same manner by clicking on the corresponding links under the **To** field to reveal the relevant input field.

2. The **Subject** field is where we configure the email notification subject. You can use smart values and smart value functions in this field to reference data from any issue field.

3. The **Content** field is where you supply the email message itself. You can use HTML tags to format the message and you can also use smart values and smart value functions to reference and manipulate any data from the issue that triggered the automation rule.

4. Under the **More options** disclosure, you will find the **From** field. This field is only applicable to Jira Server and Data Center. It is not editable in Jira Cloud.

    If you are using Jira Server or Data Center, you should ensure that the email address you enter here uses a valid sender domain as many SMTP servers are configured to only accept outgoing mail from valid domains in order to prevent themselves from being used as spam relays.

5. The **From name** field is the human-readable sender name that will appear in the email notification. In Jira Cloud, this will default to *Jira automation*, and in Jira Server and Data Center, it will not be present.

6. Optionally, if you want users to be able to reply to the email and potentially capture the reply as a comment against the issue, you can use the **Reply to** field to enter the email address you have configured in the **Incoming Email** system configuration for Software and Core projects, or, for Service Management projects, in the project's **Email requests** setting.

    You should also ensure that the issue key is present in the **Subject** line if you make use of the **Reply to** feature.

7. The **Send as** field allows you to select whether this notification will be sent as plain text or HTML. If the email notification is being sent to another application, you will probably want to set this to plain text.

8. Leaving the **Convert line breaks to HTML line breaks** option selected will automatically insert HTML line break tags (`<br>`) in the message body for each new line when the **Send as** field is set to **HTML**. While convenient, it has the ability to play havoc with your HTML formatting if you forget to take this into consideration.

> **Important note**
> If you are using Jira Server or Jira Data Center, you (or a Jira administrator) need to have configured an outgoing SMTP mail server in the **Jira Administration | System | Outgoing Mail** settings. Without a configured outgoing mail server, rules with email notifications will still execute successfully, however, no emails will actually be sent.

Let's take a look at a rule that makes use of email notifications.

Creating a rule to notify customers when a new version is released

In this example, we want to be able to notify customers when a new software version is released and list the items that were fixed or added in the newly released version.

All the customers for this example belong to a user group called *Customers*. This will allow us to add any new customers to the group and not have to modify the automation rule for each new customer.

Due to the differences in the way automation rules handle multiple issues in Jira Cloud and Jira Server, we'll present this rule twice in order to highlight the differences between the two environments.

Using Jira Cloud to notify customers when a new version is released

In Jira Cloud, we need to make use of the **Lookup issues** action, which will allow us to iterate up to 100 issues in a single operation.

Let's see how to build this rule using Jira Cloud:

1. In your Jira Software project, navigate to **Project settings**, click on the **Automation** link in the project settings menu, and then click **Create rule**.

2. Select the **Version released** trigger and click **Save**.

3. Next, select **New action** and then select the **Lookup issues** action.

    Add the following query to the **JQL** field and click **Save**:

    ```
    fixVersion = {{version.name}}
    ```

    As you can see, we are using a smart value to reference the version name in this JQL query and so we cannot validate the query.

4. Then, select **New action** followed by the **Send email** action.

    Complete the action's fields as follows:

    To: Customers

    Subject: {{version.project.key}} version {{version.name}} is released!

    Content:

    ```
    We have just released Version <strong>{{version.name}}</strong> for {{version.project.key}}.
    <br/>
    This version includes the following fixes and features:
    <ul>
    {{#lookupIssues}}
        <li>
            <a href="{{url}}">{{issuetype.name}}: {{key}} - {{summary}}<a/>
        </li>
    {{/}}
    </ul>
    We hope you enjoy it!<br/><br/>
    Regards,<br/>
    The {{version.project.key}} development team
    ```

5. Next, expand the **More options** disclosure and uncheck the **Convert line breaks to HTML line breaks** option, as we have included explicit HTML line breaks in the content field, and then click **Save**.

Your rule should look similar to the following screenshot:

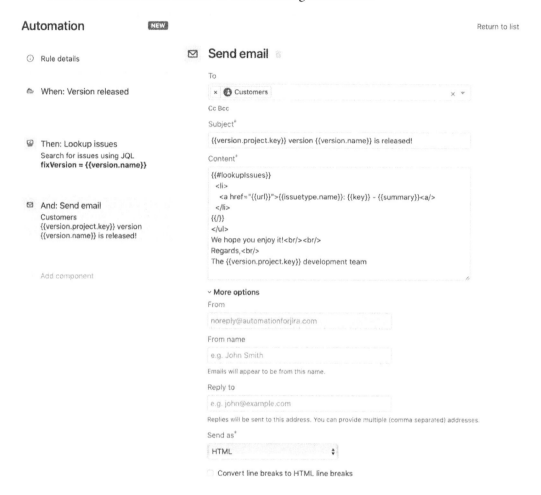

Figure 4.2 – Sending an email notification in Jira Cloud

6. Finally, name your rule `Version released customer notification` and click **Turn it on** to save and enable the rule.

Now that we've learned how to send an email notification in Jira Cloud using the **Lookup issues** action, let's see how we need to adjust this rule to work in Jira Server.

Using Jira Server to notify customers when a new version is released

Automation rules in Jira Server do not have the **Lookup issues** action. Instead, we can choose to process issues in certain triggers and branch rules in bulk.

Let's see how to replicate the version-released rule in Jira Server:

1. In your Jira Software project, navigate to **Project settings**, click on the **Project automation** link in the project settings menu, and then click **Create rule**.

2. Select the **Version released** trigger and click **Save**.

3. Next, select **Branch rule/related issues** and select **Issues fixed in version** in the **Type of related issues** field.

4. Expand the **More options** disclosure and ensure the **Process all issues produced by this trigger in bulk** option is checked and click **Save**.

5. Now, select **New action** followed by the **Send email** action.

    Complete the action's fields as follows:

    To: Customers

    Subject: {{version.project.key}} version {{version.name}} is released!

    Content:

```
We have just released Version <strong>{{version.name}}</
strong> for {{version.project.key}}.
<br/>
This version includes the following fixes and features:
<ul>
{{#lookupIssues}}
   <li>
     <a href="{{url}}">{{issuetype.name}}: {{key}} -
     {{summary}}<a/>
   </li>
{{/}}
</ul>
We hope you enjoy it!<br/><br/>
Regards,<br/>
The {{version.project.key}} development team
```

6. Next, expand the **More options** disclosure and uncheck the **Convert line breaks to HTML line breaks** option as we have included explicit HTML line breaks in the content field, and then click **Save**.

Your rule should look similar to the following screenshot:

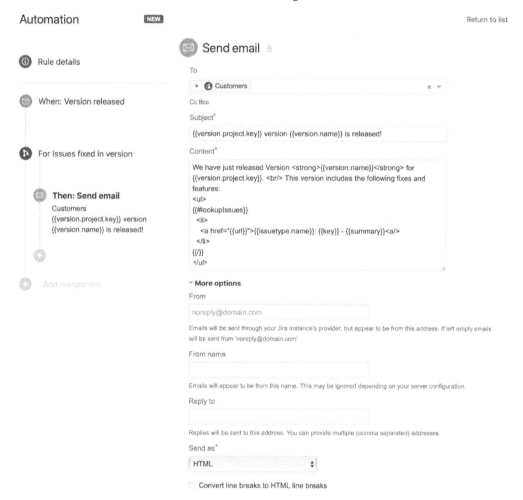

Figure 4.3 – Sending an email notification in Jira Server

7. Finally, name your rule Version released customer notification and click **Turn it on** to save and enable the rule.

In this section, we have learned how to use the **Send email** action to send custom notifications to users from automation rules.

In the next section, we'll look at how we can integrate Slack notifications within our automation rules.

How to send notifications to Slack

Slack is a popular workspace communications tool that allows users to chat in so-called channels or via direct messages with one another.

One of the actions we have available to our automation rules is the **Send Slack message** action, which gives us the ability to send messages to Slack channels or to an individual user.

In this section, we'll learn how we can integrate with Slack to send notifications from automation rules.

Integrating with Slack

Before we get to sending a Slack notification from an automation rule, we first need to set up an incoming webhook in Slack to be able to receive the messages from Jira.

There are two ways we can achieve this. The first is by creating a custom app in Slack and configuring it with an incoming webhook and then selecting the channel that will receive the notifications.

The second and simplest way to integrate Slack with automation rules is to create a legacy incoming webhook, which also allows the configured channel to be overridden.

> **Important note**
>
> If you use the custom app method of creating incoming webhooks in Slack, you will need to create a webhook for each channel you need to send a notification to as this method does not allow you to override the default channel that you selected when creating the webhook. It is better to use the *legacy webhook* method instead, which we'll cover in this section.

Let's take a look at how to establish an incoming webhook in Slack using the legacy incoming webhook option, which we'll then use in an automation rule to post a message to the **#general** channel in Slack:

1. Navigate to the following URL in your browser: `https://my.slack.com/services/new/incoming-webhook/`.

   You should be presented with a screen similar to the following screenshot, after being asked to log in if required:

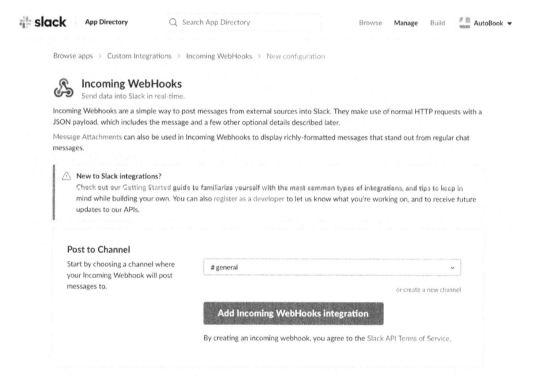

Figure 4.4 – Adding an incoming webhook to Slack

2. In the **Post to Channel** field, select the **#general** channel and click the **Add Incoming WebHooks integration** button.

3. In the following screen, you will be presented with your new **webhook URL**. You can also use this page to customize the icon, label, and username that will be used for this integration. For now, make a note of the **webhook URL** that was generated as we'll need it to complete the setup of the automation rule later.

Now that we've set up Slack to receive incoming messages via a webhook, let's set up an automation rule to make use of this integration.

Creating a rule to notify open issues in a sprint

In this example, we want to send a notification to the development team's **#sprint-update** channel in Slack on a daily basis, listing the issues still outstanding for the current sprint:

1. In your Jira Software project, navigate to **Project settings**, click on the **Automation** link in the project settings menu, and then click **Create rule**.

2. Select the **Scheduled** trigger and, in the **Fixed rate scheduled** tab, enter 1 Days in the **Run this rule every** field and click **Save**.

3. Next, select **New action** and then select the **Lookup issues** action.

    Enter the following query in the **JQL** field and click **Save**:

    ```
    Sprint in openSprints() AND status != Done
    ```

4. Then, select **New action** followed by the **Send Slack message** action.

    Complete the action fields as follows and then click **Save**:

    Webhook URL: Use the webhook URL you configured previously in Slack.

    Message:

    ```
    Hey Team, we still have the following issues left to
    complete this sprint:
    ```
    ```
    {{#lookupIssues}}
    ```
    ```
    <{{url}}|{{key}} - {{summary}}>
    ```
    ```
    {{/}}
    ```
    ```
    We can do this!
    ```

    Channel or user: #sprint-updates

The automation rule should look similar to the following screenshot:

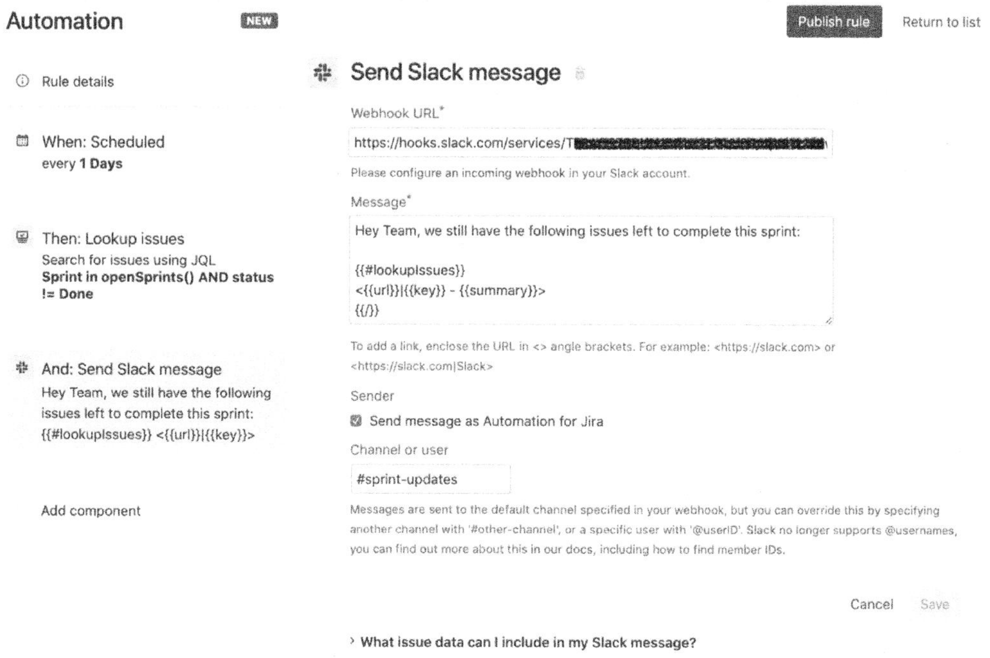

Figure 4.5 – Sending a Slack message

5. Finally, name the rule `Open issues in sprint notification` and click
    Turn it on to save and enable the rule.

6.   Now that you've set up the automation rule, every day around the time you created the rule, you should receive a notification in the Slack channel you configured that should look similar to the following screenshot:

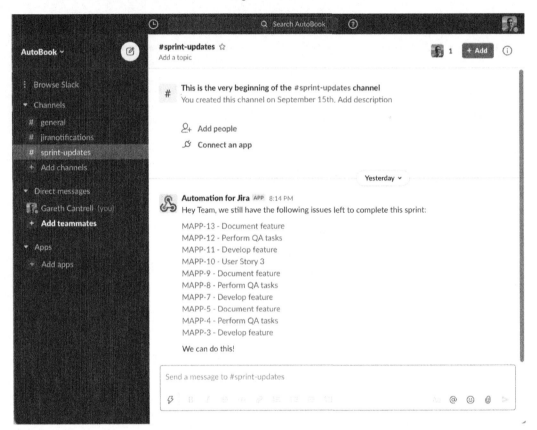

Figure 4.6 – Receiving a notification in a Slack channel

> **Tip**
> To create this rule in Jira Server, instead of the **Lookup issues** action, you will need to enter the JQL query in the trigger configuration, expand the **More options** disclosure, and ensure that the **Process all issues produced by this trigger in bulk** option is selected.

In this section, we have learned how to integrate Slack notifications in automation rules and how to send notifications to Slack channels. In the next section, we'll explore how to integrate with Microsoft Teams to send notifications to a Teams channel in a similar manner to Slack.

How to send notifications to Microsoft Teams

Microsoft Teams is a collaboration platform from Microsoft and part of the Microsoft 365 offering. As with Slack, it allows teams to collaborate in channels or via direct messages with other individuals.

As we saw in the previous section, automation provides a **Send Microsoft Teams message** action that allows us to send messages to a Microsoft Teams channel.

In this section, we will learn how to integrate with Microsoft Teams to send notifications to channels using automation rules.

Integrating with Microsoft Teams

The first thing we need to do before we can use Microsoft Teams in automation rules is to set up an incoming webhook so that our rule can send messages to a channel in Teams.

In Microsoft Teams, we need to add the Incoming Webhook connector to our team before we can send messages to a channel from an automation rule.

Let's look at how we can configure a team and channel in Microsoft Teams using the *Incoming Webhook connector*:

1. Open your Microsoft Teams app and open the Teams app store from the sidebar.

2. Select **Connectors** from the menu and then find the **Incoming Webhook** connector.

3. In the pop-up window, click on **Add to a team**, and then select the team and channel you want to add the connector to and click **Set up a connector**.

4. In the following screen, provide a name for your incoming webhook such as *Jira Notifications*, upload a new image if you like, and click on **Create**.

    The following screenshot shows the URL for your new Incoming Webhook connector that you will need to copy so that you can use it when configuring your automation rule:

Figure 4.7 – Setting up a Microsoft Teams Incoming Webhook connector

Now that we've set up our Incoming Webhook connector in Microsoft Teams, we are ready to use it in an automation rule to send notifications to our configured channel.

Creating a rule to notify a Microsoft Teams channel when a high-priority issue is raised

In this example, we'll use an automation rule to watch for issues raised with a high or highest priority alert and then send a notification to the team channel using *Microsoft Teams*:

1. In your Jira Service Management project, navigate to **Project settings**, click on the **Automation** link in the project settings menu, and then click **Create rule**.

2. Next, select the **Issue created** trigger and click **Save**.

3. Then, select **New condition** followed by the **Issue** fields condition.

4. Complete the fields as follows and click **Save**:

    Field: `Priority`

    Condition: `is one of`

    Value: `Highest, High`

5. Next, select **New action** followed by the **Send Microsoft Teams message** action.

6. Complete the action fields as follows and click **Save**:

    Webhook URL: Use the webhook URL you configured previously in Microsoft Teams.

    Message Title: `High Priority Ticket`.

    Message:

```
{{issue.key}} - {{summary}} has just been created with
*{{issue.priority.name}}* priority.
Your urgent attention is required.
```

> Tip
>
> If you leave the **Include issue summary in message** option checked, the notification in Microsoft Teams will include the issue status, issue type, and assignee in the message, as well as a **View in Jira** button that will open the Jira ticket in your web browser when clicked.

Your rule should look similar to the following screenshot:

Automation   NEW   Return to list

ⓘ Rule details

+ When: Issue created
   Rule is run when an issue is created.

↔ If: Priority is one of
   Highest, High

🗂 Then: Send Microsoft Teams
   message
   {{issue.key}} - {{summary}} has just
   been created with *
   {{issue.priority.name}}* priority. Your
   urgent attention is required.

   Add component

Send Microsoft Teams message

To connect to Microsoft Teams, you first need to add an Incoming Webhook connector in your
Team channel:

   1. Head on over to Teams and select the channel you wish to connect.
   2. From More Options (...), choose Connectors and setup a custom webhook.
   3. Give it a name, click create. Copy and paste the webhook URL into below.

See our documentation for more detailed instructions and an example!

Webhook URL *

https://outlook.office.com/webhook/c3▓▓▓▓▓▓▓▓▓▓▓▓▓▓▓▓▓▓▓▓▓▓▓▓▓▓▓▓▓

Message Title *

High Priority Ticket

Message *

{{issue.key}} - {{summary}} has just been created with *{{issue.priority.name}}* priority.

Your urgent attention is required.

☑ Include issue summary in message
∨ More options

Message image

https://d283vu6e5qi87p.cloudfront.net/automation/prod/automation-logo.svg

                                                                        Cancel   Save

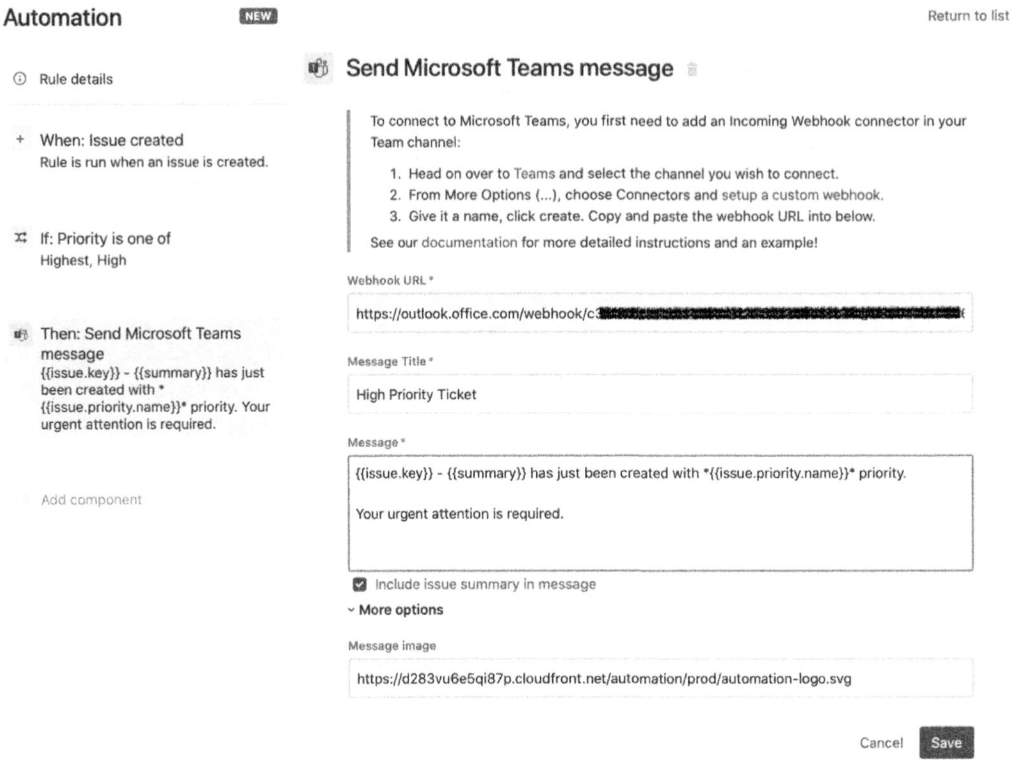

Figure 4.8 – Sending a message with Microsoft Teams

7. Finally, name the rule `High priority issue notification` and click **Turn it on** to save and enable the rule.

8. Creating a new high or highest priority issue in your Service Management project will cause a notification similar to the following screenshot to be sent to your configured Microsoft Teams channel:

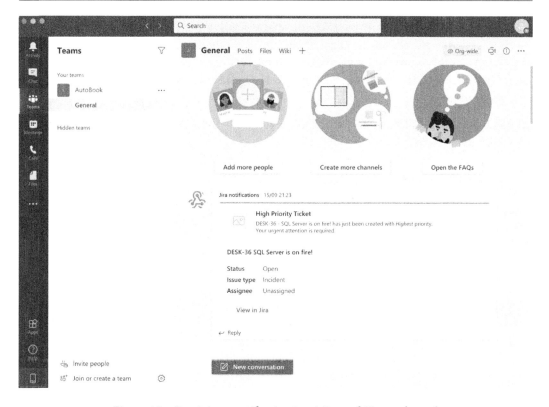

Figure 4.9 – Receiving a notification in a Microsoft Teams channel

In this section, we have learned how to set up an Incoming Webhook connector in Microsoft Teams and how to use it in an automation rule to send notifications to the team channel that was configured in the connector.

In the next section, we'll look at how to send SMS notifications to mobile phones using *Twilio*.

Sending SMS notifications with Twilio

Twilio is a communications platform offered as a cloud-based service that allows developers to integrate voice, video, and text communications into their applications using a **REST API**.

Using the **Send Twilio notification** action in our automation rules allows us to make use of the Twilio platform to send SMS messages to mobile phones.

In practice, you would usually have a dedicated on-call tool integrated with Jira that has the capability to contact the correct team member using a customizable schedule via various methods, including via mobile phone text message (SMS). However, the **Send Twilio notification** action will allow you to build a simple on-call schedule using *automation rules*.

In this section, we will learn how to integrate with Twilio to send notifications as SMS messages using automation rules.

Integrating with Twilio

Integrating with Twilio is a relatively straightforward process. You will need a Twilio account and a telephone number from which your SMS messages will be sent.

> **Important note**
>
> Twilio accounts are free to set up and you can get a trial number free of charge. However, you will be charged for every SMS message you send through the platform and you will need to pay for a phone number in your country of choice.

Let's take a look at how we can get set up with Twilio so that we can send SMS messages from our automation rules:

1. Navigate to `https://www.twilio.com` and sign up for an account or log in to your existing account.

2. If you don't already have a phone number, click on the **Get a Trial Number** button on your project dashboard.

    Once you have a phone number, your Twilio dashboard should look similar to the following screenshot:

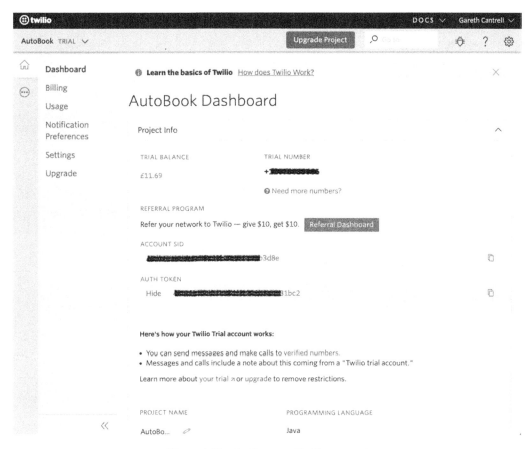

Figure 4.10 – Setting up a Twilio account

3. You will need to copy your **TRIAL NUMBER, ACCOUNT SID, and AUTH TOKEN** information from your Twilio dashboard when we come to configure the automation rule. To copy your **ACCOUNT SID** and **AUTH TOKEN** fields, you can click on the icon at the right of the respective field.

Now that we have a Twilio account and phone number, we can create an automation rule to send SMS messages to a mobile phone.

Creating a rule to send an after-hours notification via SMS message

In this example, for any incidents with a priority of highest or high and raised before 8 a.m. or after 6 p.m., we will send an SMS notification using *Twilio* to a mobile number.

To keep things simple, we will assume that there is a single mobile device that is in the possession of the team member who is on-call after hours.

Let's create the rule to send an SMS message:

1. In your Jira Service Management project, navigate to **Project settings**, click on the **Automation** link in the **Project Settings** menu, and then click **Create rule**.

2. Next, select the **Issue created** trigger and click **Save**.

3. Then, select **New condition** followed by **Issue fields condition** so we can narrow down our rule to only incidents.

   Complete the condition fields as follows:

   Field: `Issue Type`

   Condition: `equals`

   Value: `Incident`

4. Now click **Save** so we can add our next condition.

5. Select **New condition** and then select the **Issue fields** condition to narrow down the priorities we want to respond to.

   Complete the condition fields as follows:

   Field: `Priority`

   Condition: `is one of`

   Value: `Highest, High`

   Click **Save** so that we can move on to our final condition.

6. Now select **New Condition** followed by **JQL condition** and enter the following **JQL** query and click **Save**:

   ```
   NOT(created > startOfDay("+8h") AND created <
   endOfDay("-6h"))
   ```

7. Next, select **New action** and then the **Send Twilio notification** action.

    Complete the fields as follows and click **Save**:

    Account SID: Copy the account SID from your Twilio dashboard.

    Auth token: Copy the auth token from your Twilio dashboard.

    From: Copy the trial number or phone number from your Twilio dashboard.

    To: The mobile number to send the text message to in international format.

    Message body:

    ```
    A new incident, {{issue.key}} - {{issue.summary.
    abbreviate(100)}}, requires urgent attention!
    ```

    Your automation rule should look similar to the following screenshot:

Figure 4.11 – Sending an SMS message via Twilio

8. Finally, name the rule `High priority after-hours notification` and click **Turn it on** to save and enable the rule.

9. Creating an issue in the Service Management project with a high or highest priority should result in an SMS message being sent that looks similar to the following screenshot:

Figure 4.12 – Receiving an SMS message notification via Twilio

In this section, we have learned how to use the Twilio platform to send text messages via SMS to a mobile phone number from an automation rule. The ability to send an SMS message notification gives you another channel to ensure that your notifications are delivered in a timely manner and express the desired level of urgency.

Summary

In this chapter, you have learned how to use automation rules to send custom email notifications to users, groups of users, or indeed any valid email address.

You have also learned how to send notifications to two of the most widely used chat systems, Slack and Microsoft Teams.

Finally, we have learned how to integrate with Twilio to send text messages via SMS to mobile phones.

With these skills, you will now be able to leverage automation rules to send customized notifications at exactly the right time and with the relevant contextual information, and this will encourage your users to take the desired actions.

In the next chapter, we will explore how to use automation rules to integrate with external systems that can accept web requests and how to accept requests from external systems.

5
Working with External Systems

Applications rarely exist in isolation. They tend to specialize in doing one thing well, but to be truly useful, they need to co-exist with other applications within your organization.

This is especially true for Jira, and this can be seen in the Atlassian Marketplace where, among the large number of available apps, hundreds of them exist solely to integrate Jira with other applications and systems.

Even with the number of integrations with various applications available as plugins to Jira, there will often be occasions where the integration you need is not catered for, or where an existing integration does not quite meet your specific requirements.

In recent years, many applications and systems have embraced JSON-based REST APIs to enable third-party systems to integrate with them, and automation rules in Jira provide us with the components necessary to take advantage of this.

In this chapter, we will learn how we can send requests to external systems using automation rules and how to work with the data that is returned from these requests. In addition, we will explore how we can use automation rules to set up incoming webhooks that can listen for requests from external systems to trigger a rule.

We will cover the following topics in this chapter:

- How to send requests to external systems

- Working with data returned from requests

- How to receive requests using incoming webhooks

- Working with data in incoming webhooks

Technical requirements

The requirements for this chapter are as follows:

- **Jira Cloud environment**: If you don't already have access to Jira, you can create a free Jira Cloud account at `https://www.atlassian.com/software/jira/free` and ensure that you have both Jira Software and Jira Service Management selected.

- **Jira Server environment**: If you are using Jira Server (available from `https://www.atlassian.com/software/jira/download`), ensure you have licenses for both Jira Software and Jira Service Management. In addition, you will also need to ensure that you install the *Automation for Jira* app available from the Atlassian Marketplace.

- **Confluence Cloud environment**: If you don't already have access to Confluence, you can use the application switcher menu in your Jira Cloud instance to set up a Confluence site in your cloud account. If you don't have a Jira Cloud account, you can set up a free Confluence Cloud account at `https://www.atlassian.com/software/confluence/free`.

- **Confluence Server environment**: If you are using Jira Server, you can either download and install Confluence Server from `https://www.atlassian.com/software/confluence/download` or you can create and use a Confluence Cloud account.

In both instances, you will need to have at least **Project Administrator** access to a Service Management project and a Scrum Software project to be able to follow the examples in this chapter. For the examples in this chapter, we have used the *IT Service Management project template* to create the Service Management project and the *Scrum Software project template* to create the Software project.

You can download the latest code samples for this chapter from this book's official GitHub repository at `https://github.com/PacktPublishing/Automate-Everyday-Tasks-in-Jira`. The Code in Action videos for this chapter are available at `https://bit.ly/2LJAJvN`.

How to send requests to external systems

The ability to send requests to external systems from your automation rules opens up a whole new realm of extremely powerful possibilities. This functionality can be used to send notifications, or issue data or any custom data to any application or system that accepts web requests over HTTP or HTTPS. For example, you could use this functionality to kick off a build process in a build tool such as Bamboo or Jenkins, or to initiate a password change in a centralized user directory system if it supports this.

In this section, we will look at the **Send web request** component and how to use it in automation rules to send requests to external systems. We'll begin by taking a look at the various configuration options available in the action.

In the following screenshot, we can see the configuration options for the **Send web request** action:

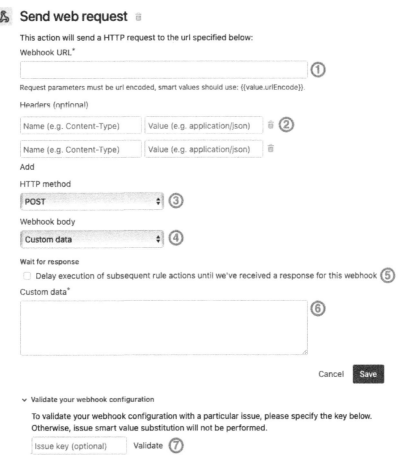

Figure 5.1 – Configuring the Send web request action

Let's take a look at each field in the configuration screen and how we can make use of it:

1. **Webhook URL** is where you enter the web address of the external system you want to call. You can send requests to both secure (HTTPS) and non-secure (HTTP) web addresses; however, security experts recommend using secure connections wherever possible.

   You can use smart values to populate the field or portions of the field; however, you must always remember to use the smart value function `urlEncode` to ensure the smart value is properly encoded. For example, you should insert the issue key in the field as `{{issue.key.urlEncode}}`.

2. The **Headers** field is where you add any HTTP request headers required by the external system you're going to connect to, such as an **Authorization** header, which allows you to submit credentials or authorization tokens to the remote system, or the **Content-Type** header, which informs the remote system of the nature of the data you will be sending. We'll be making use of both of these headers in our example when we publish release notes to Confluence.

   > **Tip**
   > Header names are generally case-insensitive. However, you should always ensure that you use the case defined in the official specifications to avoid any unexpected results. Wikipedia maintains a handy list of the standard request headers, complete with examples of accepted input for each header, at `https://en.wikipedia.org/wiki/List_of_HTTP_header_fields`.

   You can add as many HTTP request headers as you need by clicking on the **Add** link below the **Name** field. If you need to remove a header, you can do so by using the trash can icon to the right of the **Value** field.

3. The **HTTP method** field allows you to select the correct method required by the external resource to perform the selected operation. The **Send web request** action supports the following standard HTTP methods:

   GET: Generally used to retrieve a resource from the external system.

   POST: Generally used to create a resource in the external system using the data located in the request body.

   PUT: Generally used to replace a resource or create it if it does not exist, with the resource data located in the request body.

   PATCH: Generally used to update a resource, with the updated data located in the request body.

   DELETE: Generally used to delete a resource from the external system.

4. **Webhook body** allows you to choose whether or not your request will contain data in the HTTP request body. The following options are available in this field:

    Empty: Select this option when you do not need to send data to the external system in the request body. Usually used with **GET** and **DELETE** requests.

    Issue data: Select this option to send the issue data as a JSON-formatted text string to the external system. The format for issue data is documented in the REST API call `Get issue` at the following link: `https://developer.atlassian.com/cloud/jira/platform/rest/v3/api-group-issues/#api-rest-api-3-issue-issueidorkey-get`.

    Custom data: Selecting this option will cause the **Custom data** field (6) to be shown. This option is usually needed when using the **POST**, **PUT**, or **PATCH** methods and the external system is not expecting data in the Jira issue format.

5. The **Wait for response** option will cause the rule to wait for a response after contacting the external system and then populate the response in the `{{webhookResponse}}` smart value field. We will explore this in more detail in the next section, *Working with data returned from requests*.

6. **Custom data** is where you construct the request body that the external system is expecting. This data can be any JSON, XML, or even web form URL-encoded data, depending on what the external system is expecting.

    You can also use smart values and smart value functions to inject data from the issue into this field. You should also always use the relevant encoding smart value function, which we covered in *Chapter 3*, *Enhancing Rules with Smart Values*, as the final function to ensure the value is properly encoded for the type of content you're sending.

    For example, if you're sending an abbreviated issue description in a JSON-formatted object, you should express this as `{{issue.description.abbreviate(255).jsonEncode}}` to ensure that the content of the description field is properly encoded.

> **Tip**
> Always make sure when sending custom data that you use the **Headers** field to specify the correct content type of your data to the external system with the *Content-Type* header name. For example, if you're sending JSON data, set *Content-Type* to *application/json*, or to *application/xml* for XML data.

7. Once you've configured your web request with the correct URL, headers, method, and optional data, you should always test that the request generated, and response received, are what you're expecting.

    You can do this by expanding the **Validate your webhook configuration** disclosure and clicking the **Validate** link. Supplying an optional issue key will ensure that any smart values are substituted during the validation process.

    When you click the **Validate** link, a request with your configured options and data will be generated and sent to the external system and the response received will be captured and presented back to you, similar to the following screenshot:

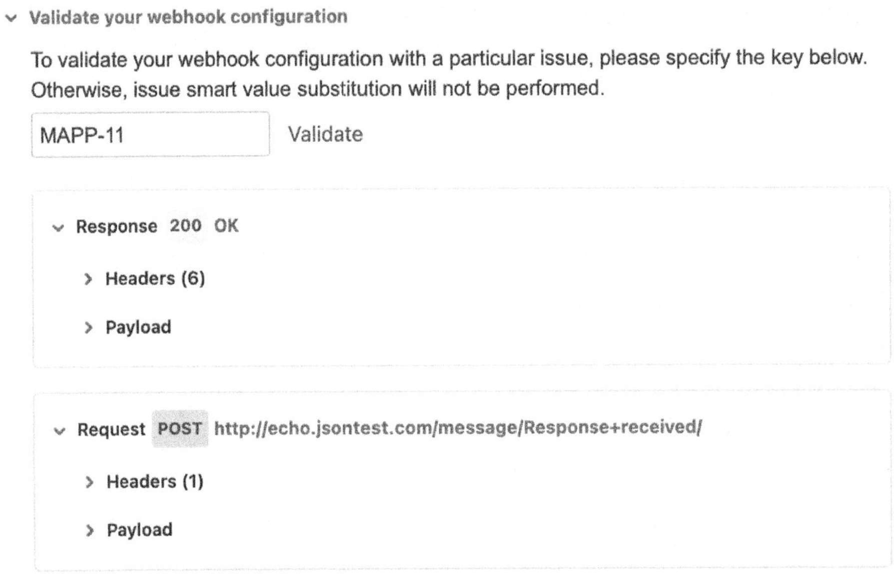

    ˅ **Validate your webhook configuration**

    To validate your webhook configuration with a particular issue, please specify the key below. Otherwise, issue smart value substitution will not be performed.

    | MAPP-11 | Validate

    ˅ **Response 200 OK**

    > **Headers (6)**

    > **Payload**

    ˅ **Request POST** http://echo.jsontest.com/message/Response+received/

    > **Headers (1)**

    > **Payload**

Figure 5.2 – Validating a web request configuration

As you can see, validating the request will return the response received from the external system, as well as the request that was generated and sent to the external system. Expanding the **Payload** disclosures will reveal the actual data received and sent by the web request, allowing you to ensure that the data in both directions is what you expected to see.

Now that we've learned about the various configuration options for sending a web request, let's look at using these in an automation rule.

Creating a rule to publish release notes to Confluence

In *Chapter 4*, *Sending Automated Notifications*, we showed you how to create a rule to send an email notification to various stakeholders when a software version is released in Jira.

We are going to revisit that rule in this example. However, instead of sending an email notification when a version is released, we will instead publish a page to Confluence using the **Send web request** action.

For this example, we have created a new Confluence space and a Releases page. Individual release notes pages will be created as children of the Releases page.

To make things easier, we'll create a **Release Notes Template** page in Confluence, complete with all the relevant smart values populated. Once we have our template, we need to copy the page using its storage format so we can include it in the **Send web request** body in our automation rule.

In the following screenshot, we can see the completed template and the option to view the storage format of the page:

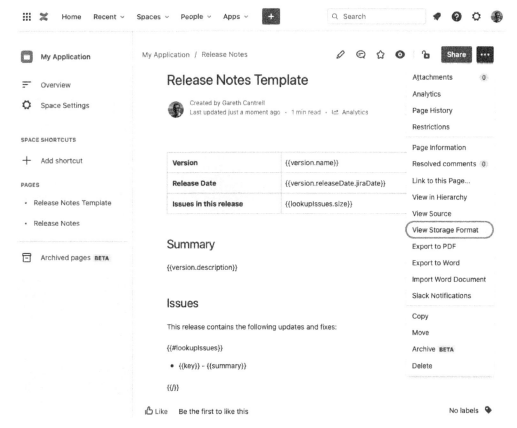

Figure 5.3 – Getting the Release Notes Template page source

Copy all the code in the storage format view into a text editor, and then we'll modify the `{{#lookupIssues}}` section as follows to ensure that the smart value substitutions work as expected:

```
<ul>
{{#lookupIssues}}
<li><p>{{key}} - {{summary}} </p></li>
{{/}}
</ul>
```

Next, we will escape all the double quote characters in the code by prepending a backslash to them and then remove all the new lines so that the entire code is on a single line.

> **Tip**
> We use the storage format when working with Confluence as this gives us access to the underlying HTML formatting of the page, including the XML used to define the various Confluence macros in the page, and allows us greater flexibility in making adjustments to the final content that will be displayed when the page is published.

Finally, we need to ensure that you have a valid API token, which will be needed to authorize the web request later in the rule:

1. Navigate to `https://id.atlassian.com/manage-profile/security/api-tokens` and click on **Create API token**.

> **Important note**
> You cannot use two-step authentication for the account that you use in an automation rule. Two-step verification is designed for human users who have access to a secondary device and is impossible to implement for an automated system.

2. Give your token a label, for example, `Automation Rules`, and click **Create**.

3. Copy the token somewhere safe, as you will not be able to retrieve it once you close the pop-up window.

4. We now need to encode our credentials for use in our automation rule. You can use an online tool such as the one at `https://www.base64encode.org` to perform the encoding.

Enter your email address, followed immediately by a colon (:) and then your API token, click the **Encode** button, and then copy the resulting encoded value somewhere safe.

> **Tip**
>
> If you're using Confluence Server, you need only the username and password of a user who can create pages in the Confluence space. To encode the credentials, replace the email address in the preceding *step 4* with the username, and the API token with the user's password.

Now, let's move on to building the automation rule:

1. In your Jira Software project, navigate to **Project settings**, click on the **Automation** link in the **Project Settings** menu, and then click **Create rule**.

2. Select the **Version released** trigger and click **Save**.

3. Next, select **New action** followed by the **Lookup issues** action.

    Add the following query to the **JQL** field and click **Save**:

    ```
    fixVersion = "{{version.name}}"
    ```

4. Then, select **New action** followed by the **Send web request** action. Ensure you have two **Headers** fields and then complete the fields as follows:

    Webhook URL: `https://<your_site>.atlassian.net/wiki/rest/api/content`

    First **Headers** field:

    Name: `Content-Type`

    Value: `application/json`

    Second **Headers** field:

    Name: `Authorization`

    Value: `Basic <your base64-encoded credentials>`

    HTTP method: `POST`

    Webhook body: `Custom data`

5. We need to retrieve the page ID of the Release Notes page as this will be the parent of our release pages. To do so, navigate to the Release Notes page in Confluence, and then click the **Page Information** item in the ellipsis menu. Copy the URL and extract the **pageId** value for use in the ancestors item in the JSON.

You also need to ensure you use the correct Confluence space key. In our example, this is **MA**.

Tip

The JSON structure necessary to create a page in Confluence Cloud using the REST API is documented at https://developer.atlassian.com/cloud/confluence/rest/api-group-content/#api-api-content-post. This page also documents all the other API calls and data structures available for Confluence. The Confluence Server API definitions are nearly identical to Confluence Cloud and can be found at https://docs.atlassian.com/ConfluenceServer/rest/latest/#api/content-createContent.

The completed JSON structure should look similar to the following:

```
{
    "type": "page",
    "title": "Version {{version.name.jsonEncode}}",
    "space": {
        "key": "MA"
    },
    "ancestors": [
        {
            "id": "33051"
        }
    ],
    "body": {
        "storage": {
            "value": "<table data-layo
ut=\"default\"><colgroup><col style=\"width:
212.0px;\" /><col style=\"width: 416.0px;\" /></
colgroup><tbody><tr><th><p><strong>Version</strong></
p></th><td><p>{{version.name.jsonEncode}}</p></td></
tr><tr><th><p><strong>Release Date</strong></p></
th><td><p>{{version.releaseDate.jiraDate}}</p></
td></tr><tr><th><p><strong>Issues in this release</
```

```
strong></p></th><td><p>{{lookupIssues.size}}</p></
td></tr></tbody></table><h1>Summary</h1><p>{{version.
description.jsonEncode}}</p><h1>Issues</h1><p>This
release contains the following updates and fixes:</
p><ul>{{#lookupIssues}}<li><p>{{key}} - {{summary.
jsonEncode}}</p></li>{{/}}</ul>",
                "representation": "storage"
        }
    }
}
```

If the JSON structure looks like the preceding code, copy the JSON into the **Custom data** field, after which your rule should look similar to the following screenshot:

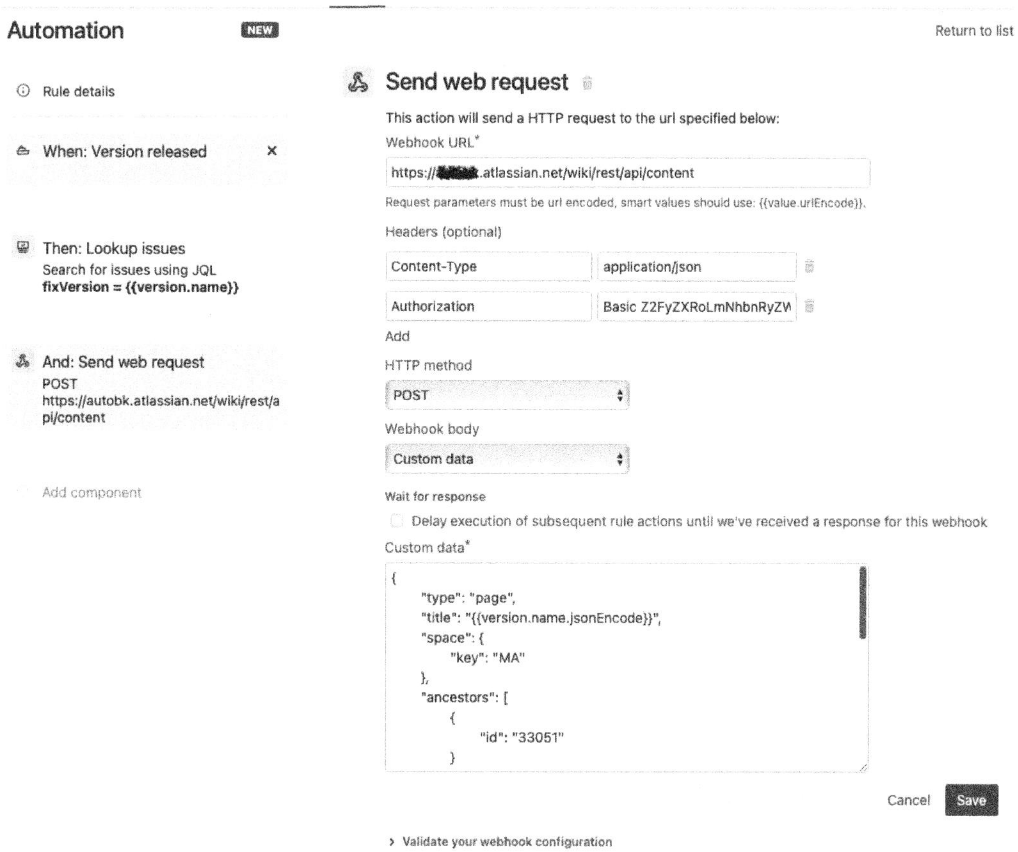

Figure 5.4 – Configuring the Send web request

6. Finally, click **Save**, name the rule `Publish release notes to Confluence`, and click **Turn it on** to save and enable the rule.

    When you release a version in your Jira Software project now, you should have a published page in Confluence under **Release Notes** that looks similar to the following screenshot:

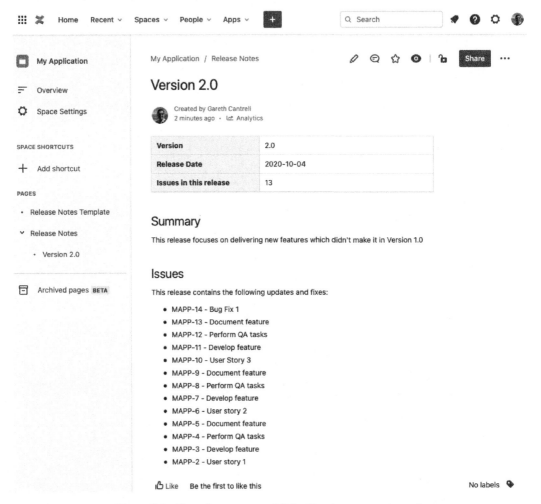

Figure 5.5 – The release notes published by the automation rule

We have now learned how to send a web request to an external system using automation rules. In the next section, we'll expand on this and see how we can incorporate the data returned from the external system in subsequent rule components.

Working with data returned from requests

Many systems you will integrate with not only accept data you send, but also respond with additional data depending on the request. With automation rules, we are able to retrieve the response from a request and utilize this data in subsequent conditions and actions in our rules. This ability gives our rules even greater flexibility and power as we can now make decisions and perform actions based on the specific content returned from the external system.

When configuring the **Send web request** action, checking the **Wait for response** checkbox will cause the action to wait for a response after sending the initial data to the external system, after which it will populate the smart value, `{{webhookResponse}}`, with the response from the external system.

The `{{webhookResponse}}` smart value contains a number of fields that you can access in your subsequent rule components, and these are as follows:

- **{{webhookResponse.status}}**: The status field holds the HTTP response code received from the external system. This will usually be `200` or `201` for successful requests, or in the range `300` to `599` for redirection and errors. You can find more about HTTP response codes at `https://en.wikipedia.org/wiki/List_of_HTTP_status_codes`.

- **{{webhookResponse.headers}}**: The headers field is a list of the response headers returned from the external system. You can reference individual headers by name, for example, `{{webhookResponse.headers.Content-Type}}` will retrieve the **Content-Type** header returned by the external system.

- **{{webhookResponse.body}}**: The body field will contain the body of the response from the external system. If the external system response is a JSON object, you can access any of the fields using **dot notation**.

- **{{webhookResponses}}**: If you have multiple **Send web request** actions in your rule, each response, if present, will be added to this list and you can use the smart value list functions that we covered in *Chapter 3, Enhancing Rules with Smart Values*, to work with the list items.

Let's now take a look at how we can incorporate the response from a web request into an automation rule.

Creating a rule to add incident managers as watchers

In this example, we are going to add the members of the VIP group that we created in *Chapter 1*, *Key Concepts of Automation*, as watchers to issues whose priority is set to **Highest** when the issue is either created or updated.

As Jira itself has a powerful REST API, we can treat it as an external system in our automation rules and retrieve data for use in our rules that we wouldn't ordinarily have access to.

Let's take a look at the rule:

1. In your Jira Service Management project, navigate to **Project settings**, click on the **Automation** link in the **Project Settings** menu, and then click **Create rule**.

2. Select the **Multiple issue events** trigger and, in the **Issue events** field, select Issue Created and Issue Updated. Then click **Save**.

3. Now select **New condition**, followed by **Issue fields condition**, and complete the fields as follows and then click **Save**:

   Field: Issue Type

   Condition: equals

   Value: Incident

4. Then select **New condition**, followed by **Issue fields condition**, and complete the fields as follows and then click **Save**:

   Field: Priority

   Condition: equals

   Value: Highest

5. Next, select **New action** and then **Send web request**. Complete the fields as follows and then click **Save**:

   Webhook URL: https://<your_site.domain.com>/rest/api/3/group/member?groupname=VIP

   Headers, Name: Authorization

   Headers, Value: Basic <your base64-encoded credentials>

   HTTP method: GET

   Webhook body: Empty

   Wait for response: Select the checkbox

The response from this API call returns a list of users in the **values** array that belong to the **groupname** we specified in the query parameter, similar to the following:

```
{
    "values": [
        {
            "self": "https://<your-site>.atlassian.net/rest/
            api/3/user?accountId=5b10a2844c20165700ede21g",
            "name": "Joe Soap",
            "key": "jsoap",
            "accountId": "5b10a2844c20165700ede21g",
            "emailAddress": "joe.soap@company.com",
            "avatarUrls": {},
            "displayName": "Joe Soap",
            "active": true,
            "timeZone": "Europe/London",
            "accountType": "atlassian"
        }
    ]
}
```

You can find more information about this API call at `https://developer.atlassian.com/cloud/jira/platform/rest/v3/api-group-groups/#api-rest-api-3-group-member-get`.

6. To complete the rule, select **New action** and then select **Manage watchers**.

    In the **Add these watchers** field, we will need to reference all the **accountId** items from the **values** array. We can do this using smart value list functions by using the following smart value in the field:

    `{{webhookResponse.body.values.accountId}}`

Your rule should look similar to the following screenshot:

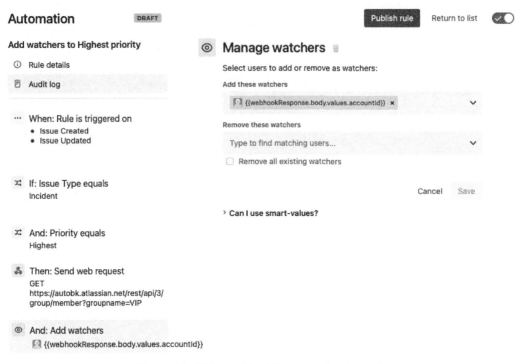

Figure 5.6 – Using webhookResponse data in a rule

7. Finally, click **Save**, name the rule `Add watchers to Highest priority incidents`, and then click **Turn it on** to save and enable the rule.

In this section, we have learned how to expose the response returned from an external system request and how we can use this data to create much more powerful automation rules.

In the next section, we will learn how we can listen for web requests from external systems and how these can be used to trigger our automation rules.

How to receive requests using incoming webhooks

In the previous two sections, we learned how to use automation rules to send notifications and data to external systems and how to work with the response data received from an external system.

In addition to this, automation rules also allow us to receive notifications and data from external systems using the **Incoming webhook** trigger. This component will create a unique URL for each trigger that can then be called by an external system and will trigger the automation rule to run. These incoming webhooks can receive a list of issues on which to act as well as custom data in the form of JSON objects, which can be used in later rule components to make decisions using conditions or to create or update issues using the custom data provided.

The following screenshot shows the configuration options for the **Incoming webhook** trigger:

⌘ Incoming webhook ✎

Incoming webhooks are a simple way to trigger an automation rule from external sources without requiring any extra authentication. Learn more.

This rule will run when a HTTP POST is sent to the following url:

Webhook URL*

https://automation.atlassian.com/pro/hooks/▮▮▮▮▮▮▮▮▮▮▮▮▮▮▮▮▮▮▮   ①

Copy URL • Regenerate

Execute this automation rule with: ②

○ Issues provided in the webhook HTTP POST body

◉ Issues provided by running the following JQL search

○ No issues from the webhook

JQL*

priority > Medium   ③

🔵 Insert account id   ⚙ Resolve users   🔍 Validate query

If smart-values are used JQL can not be validated.

> Please ensure that the request you send explicitly includes the Content-Type header set to application/json. For example if you're using curl:

```
curl -X POST -H 'Content-type: application/json' \
https://automation.atlassian.com/pro/hooks/▮▮▮▮▮▮▮▮▮▮▮▮▮▮▮▮
```

Cancel   **Save**

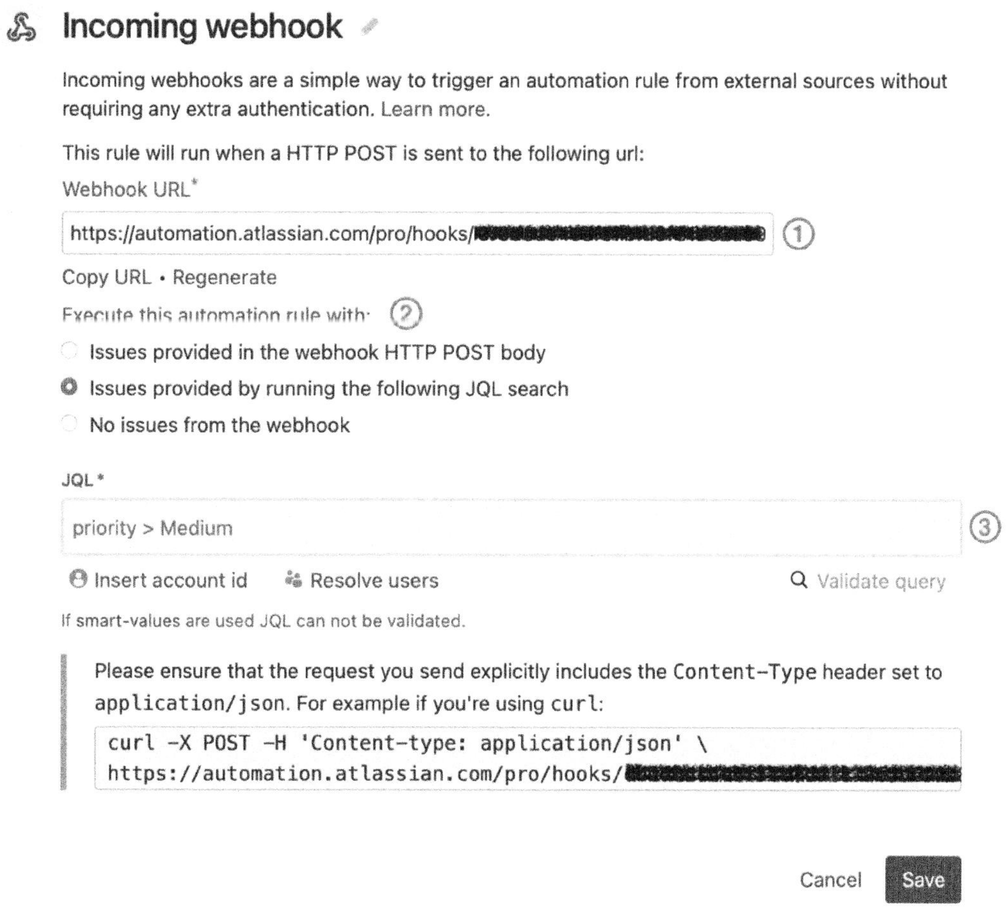

Figure 5.7 – Configuring the Incoming webhook trigger

Let's now take a look at how each of the configuration options works:

1. The **Webhook URL** is the unique URL that will cause the rule to run when an external system sends an HTTP **POST** request to it.

    This URL is generated automatically and requires no authentication to use. If the URL is compromised, you can use the **Regenerate** link to generate a new URL for the webhook and update any external systems that use it.

    > **Important note**
    >
    > Incoming webhooks only support the HTTP **POST** method. They will not respond to HTTP **GET** or any other method. In addition, you need to ensure that the external system that sends a request to the webhook sets the *Content-Type* request header to *application/json*.

2. The **Execute this automation rule** options allow you to define how the incoming webhook will process issues, if at all, using the following options:

    Issues provided in the webhook HTTP POST body allows you to specify which issues will be in scope for the actions you specify later in the rule.

    You can specify a single issue by including the issue key in the URL by appending the query parameter `issue`, for example, `https://automation.atlassian.com/pro/hooks/<unique-webhook-token>?issue=MAPP-1`. To specify multiple issues, you should include either the issue key or the issue ID in an `"issues"` list in the JSON-formatted request body as follows:

    ```
    {
        "issues": [
            "MAPP-1",
            "MAPP-2",
            "10123"
        ]
    }
    ```

    Issues provided by running the following JQL search will display the **JQL** field (3), which allows you to input a JQL query to search for the relevant issues.

    No issues from the webhook means the webhook is not expecting to operate on any existing issue. You could use this option if you needed to create issues as a result of the webhook being called, for example.

3. As mentioned in *step 2* above, the **JQL** field is displayed when you use the **Issues provided by running the following JQL search** option and allows you to define a JQL query to return the issues that will be updated as a result of calling the webhook. You can use smart values and functions in the query. However, doing so means you cannot validate the query using the **Validate query** link.

Let's now look at how we can use an incoming webhook to trigger an automation rule that we've seen in order to configure incoming webhooks.

Creating a rule to resolve open issues using an automation webhook

Many software projects have some form of automated build and deploy tool that automates the building, testing, and deployment of code.

In this example, we are going to assume that the developers will move their issues to the *Waiting for deploy* status once they have completed development. When our automated deployment starts, we want to automatically resolve all issues in the currently open sprint that are awaiting deployment by having our build and deploy tool an automation rule in Jira.

In our example Jira Software project, we are using the *Software Simplified* workflow, so we will edit the workflow from the **Project Settings** screen and add a new *Waiting for deploy* status and allow all statuses to transition to it. In addition, add the *Resolve issue* screen to the *Done* transition to allow comments to be added when resolving issues.

Now that we've adjusted our workflow to take this new status into account, let's create the automation rule:

1. In your Jira Software project, navigate to **Project settings**, click on the **Automation** link in the project settings menu, and then click **Create rule**.

2. Select the **Incoming webhook** trigger, configure it as follows, and then click **Save**:

    Execute this automation rule with: `Issues provided by running the following JQL search`

    JQL: `sprint in openSprints() AND status = "Waiting for deploy"`

3. Now, select **New action**, followed by the **Transition issue** action, and then select `Done` in the **Destination status** field.

4. In addition, we want to add a comment to these issues to the effect that the issue was automatically resolved by the build system.

    To do this, expand the **More options** disclosure, add the following JSON in the **Additional fields** editor, and then click **Save**:

```
{
    "update": {
        "comment": [
            {
                "add": {
                    "body": "Issue automatically resolved
                        by build system"
                }
            }
        ]
    }
}
```

Your rule should now look similar to the following screenshot:

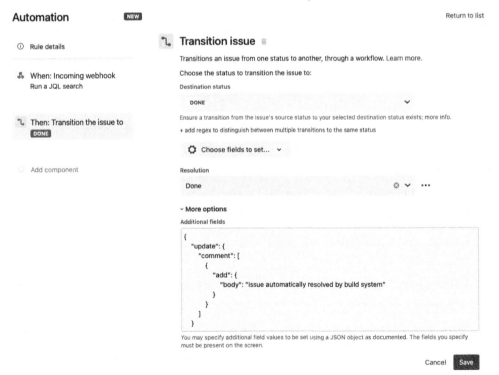

Figure 5.8 – Configuring a rule with an incoming webhook

5.   Finally, name your rule `Release issues waiting for deploy` and click **Turn it on** to save and enable the rule.

In this section, we have learned how to create and use incoming webhooks to trigger automation rules. In the next section, we'll learn how we can also make use of data supplied by the external system to further enhance our automation rules.

Working with data in incoming webhooks

Having the ability to trigger actions in Jira from external systems enables you to create really powerful integrations with automation rules.

As we saw in the previous section, you can act on specific issues by including them in the incoming request body. However, with the **Incoming webhook** trigger, you can also consume any valid JSON object sent in the request body, and this data is made available to your subsequent rule components in the `{{webhookData}}` smart value, where you can access any of the JSON object fields using dot notation.

This powerful functionality will enable you to integrate with any external system that can send web requests and allow you to extract valuable data for use in your issues. For example, you could potentially set up your monitoring tools to send notifications to an automation rule when an incident occurs and use the data it provides to create a new incident and set affected components based on which asset caused the incident.

Let's now take a look at how we can configure an automation rule that makes use of custom data from an incoming web request.

Creating a rule to raise new issues using an automation webhook

Being able to collect information about your deployed software when something goes wrong is invaluable for many developers and many software applications allow users to submit feedback when an error occurs.

In this example, we are going to create an automation rule using an incoming webhook to receive a bug report and automatically create a bug in our Jira project to track it.

We are going to expect a JSON object with the following structure to process this incoming information:

```json
{
    "summary": "some summary text",
    "bugDescription": "some descriptive text",
    "softwareVersion": "version string"
}
```

If you were including this in a product, you could probably add more relevant data, such as stack traces to the JSON structure to make the bug report more contextual.

Let's now take a look at how to build this automation rule:

1. In your Jira Software project, navigate to **Project settings**, click on the **Automation** link in the **Project Settings** menu, and then click **Create rule**.

2. Select **Incoming webhook** and then, in the **Execute this automation rule with** field, select No issues from the webhook as we're going to be using this rule to create an issue. Then click **Save**.

3. Next, select **New action**, followed by the **Create issue** action, and complete the action's fields as follows.

   Project: Same project

   Issue type: Bug

   Summary: {{webhookData.summary}}

   Description: {{webhookData.bugDescription}}

4. We also want to capture the software version that was deployed when this bug was submitted, and we'd like to add some labels to the issue to make it easier to find bugs raised from the in-product feedback collector.

   To do this, expand the **More options** disclosure and then add the following JSON to the **Additional fields** editor:

```json
{
    "fields": {
        "versions": [
            { "name": "{{webhookData.softwareVersion}}" }
        ],
        "labels": [
```

```
                    "bugfix",
                    "feedback"
         ]
       }
     }
```

Your rule should now look similar to the following screenshot:

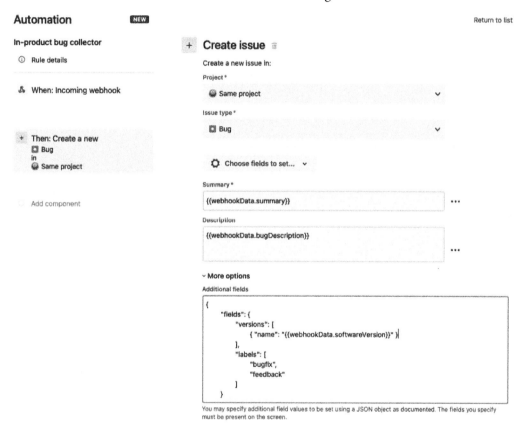

Figure 5.9 – Consuming incoming webhook data

5. Click on **Save**, name your rule `In-product bug collector`, and then click
    Turn it on to save and enable the rule.

You have now learned how to consume request data from an external system in an
incoming webhook.

The ability to consume incoming data from external systems and use it to make decisions
and effect changes to issues using automation rules gives you some extremely powerful
options in terms of automating your projects in Jira.

Summary

In this chapter, you have learned how you can integrate to external systems using automation rules by sending web requests and how you can include custom data in these requests using smart values and smart value functions.

We have also learned how to ensure we can receive a response from a request to an external system and how we can extract the data for use in subsequent rule components.

Next, we learned to set up an incoming webhook using automation rules to listen for requests coming from external systems and how to optionally process data sent in the request body and use this in subsequent rule components.

As we have seen in this chapter, the ability to integrate with external systems using automation rules opens a world of possibilities to your Jira projects. For example, you could start a software build or deployment from your build tool when you release a version or complete a sprint in Jira Software. In Service Management, you could integrate with your user directory service to automatically provision new accounts based on service requests or reset passwords automatically, if supported.

In the next chapter, we will look at how we can use the skills learned in this and previous chapters to help build automations in your Service Management instances.

Section 3: Advanced Use Cases with Automation

In this section, we will focus on advanced use cases targeted specifically at Jira Service Desk and Software, before taking a look at best practices and some troubleshooting tips. Finally, we will take an introductory look at advanced automation using scripting across both the Jira cloud and Jira server.

This section comprises the following chapters:

- *Chapter 6, Automating Jira Service Management*
- *Chapter 7, Automating Jira Software Projects*
- *Chapter 8, Integrating with DevOps Tools*
- *Chapter 9, Best Practices*
- *Chapter 10, Troubleshooting Tips and Techniques*
- *Chapter 11, Beyond Automation; an Introduction to Scripting*

6
Automating Jira Service Management

Today, Jira Service Management is used by many organizations to provide customer support portals, **human resources (HR)** services, and **information technology (IT)** service desks, among others.

The most common use case for Jira Service Management, however, is as an **IT Service Management (ITSM)** solution to enable the efficient provision of IT services within an organization.

One of the best ways to improve efficiency and drive down the cost per ticket in an IT service desk request is to automate mundane tasks and processes wherever possible.

Some of the most common tasks wherein automation provides immediate benefits are the categorization and routing of tickets, keeping customers updated as to the status of their requests, maintaining **service-level agreement (SLA)** compliance, freeing up support staff from repetitive tasks, and closing out older requests to ensure they are not clogging up your request queues.

In this chapter, we will cover the following topics:

- Processing incoming requests
- Monitoring SLA compliance
- Automating common and repetitive tasks

By the end of this chapter, you will have a better understanding of how you can use automation rules in Jira Service Management to improve the efficiency of your service desks. In addition, reducing the amount of human intervention necessary to complete common tasks will also reduce the cost per ticket of service desk requests.

Technical requirements

The requirements for this chapter are as follows:

- **Jira Cloud environment**: If you don't already have access to Jira, you can create a free Jira Cloud account at `https://www.atlassian.com/software/jira/free` and ensure that you have both **Jira Software** and **Jira Service Management** selected.

- **Jira Server environment**: If you are using Jira Server (available from `https://www.atlassian.com/software/jira/download`), ensure you have licenses for both Jira Software and Jira Service Management. In addition, you will also need to ensure that you install the *Automation for Jira* app available from the Atlassian Marketplace.

- **Microsoft Azure Active Directory (Azure AD)**: Azure AD is Microsoft's cloud-based identity service. You can sign up for a free Azure account at `https://azure.microsoft.com/free`.

In both instances, you will need to have at least **Project Administrator** access to a Service Management project and a Scrum Software project to be able to follow the examples in this chapter. For the examples in this chapter, we have used the *IT Service project template* to create the Service Management project and the *Scrum Software project template* to create the software project.

You can download the latest code samples for this chapter from this book's official GitHub repository at `https://github.com/PacktPublishing/Automate-Everyday-Tasks-in-Jira`. Please visit the following link to check the CiA videos: `https://bit.ly/2NhMFp9`

Processing incoming requests

One of the more time-consuming tasks in a service desk is the categorization and routing of incoming requests to the correct teams.

Having a mature service request catalog and using this as a basis to create relevant request types in the Jira Service Management portal solves the initial categorization issue when customers create requests; however, in many organizations requests are still received via email, and these generally require human intervention to categorize and route to the relevant team.

In this section, we will look at automation rules to automatically triage incoming requests and then route them to the correct teams for processing.

In our first example, we will look at how we can use automation rules to triage requests originating from incoming emails.

Creating a rule to triage email requests

One of the benefits of having a well-structured customer portal is that you can make use of your organization's service request catalog to drive the correct selection of service requests using request types, and at the same time using pre-selected components in each service request to narrow down the categorization of the request.

> **Tip**
> To pre-define a value for any field in a request type, add that field to the request form as a hidden field. Doing this will force you to supply the field with a default value that you can then rely on in later automations.

This approach ensures that tickets reaching your service desk queues have already been categorized with the correct components, which we can use to drive the automations.

However, email requests are still widely used to create service desk requests, and these typically end up in a service queue that requires human intervention to triage and correctly categorize.

In this example, we'll use an automation rule to triage and categorize incoming emails with the correct components based on the presence of specific keywords in the email. To keep things simple, we'll only examine the issue summary, which is set from the email subject.

Let's take a look at the rule, as follows:

1. In your Jira Service Management project, navigate to **Project settings**, click on the **Automation** link in the **Project Settings** menu, and then click **Create rule**.

2. Select the **Issue created** trigger and click **Save**.

3. Then, select **New condition** followed by **Issue fields condition**. Complete the fields as follows, and then click **Save**:

   Field: Request Type

   Condition: equals

   Value: Emailed request

4. Next, select **New condition** and then select **If / else block**. Click **Add conditions** and select **Issue fields condition**, and complete the fields as follows before clicking **Save**:

   Field: Summary

   Condition: contains

   Value: vpn

5. Select **New action** and then **Edit issue**. Choose the Components field from the **Choose fields to set** list, and then select the VPN Server component and click **Save**.

6. Click on **Add else** in the rule-chain view on the left and then click **Add conditions**. Select **Issue fields condition** and complete the fields as follows, then click **Save**:

   Field: Summary

   Condition: contains

   Value: password

7. Now, select **New action** and **Edit issue**. As before, choose the Components field from the **Choose fields to set** list, and then select the Active Directory component and click **Save**.

8. The rule should now look similar to the one shown in the following screenshot:

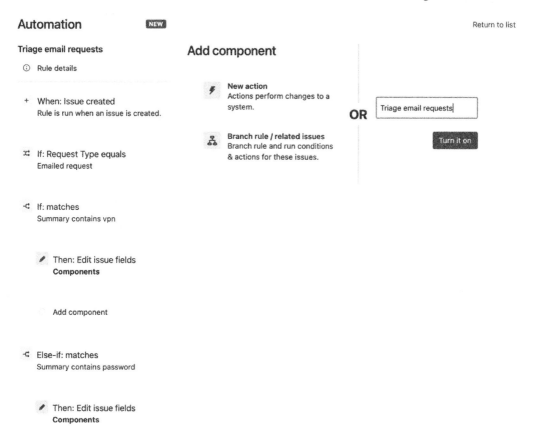

Figure 6.1 – Triaging incoming email requests

9. You could continue to add else-if blocks for as many components as you need; however, for this example, we'll stop here and name the rule `Triage email requests`, and then click **Turn it on** to save and enable the rule.

Now that we've learned how to categorize incoming requests that we've received via email, let's see how we can extend this to route and assign requests to the correct teams.

Creating a rule to automatically route requests

Using automation rules to automatically categorize incoming requests will help shorten the response time for ticket handling. However, we can take this one step further and automatically route and assign the request to the correct team, further shortening the response and resolution times.

In this example, we are going to make use of the ability to pre-define components for each request type and use these to assign incoming requests to the correct team. In addition, we will ensure that the automatic categorization rule we created previously can feed into this rule.

We will be referring to the *Network Team* and *System Administrator Team* user groups, so you will need to create these user groups in your instance for this rule to work correctly.

Let's get started with the rule, as follows:

1. In your Jira Service Management project, navigate to **Project settings**, click on the **Automation** link in the **Project Settings** menu, and then click **Create rule**.

2. Select the **Multiple issue events** trigger, and in the **Issue events** field select both `Issue Created` and `Issue Updated`, then click **Save**.

3. Next, select **New condition** and then **If / else block**. Click **Add conditions** and then select **Issue fields condition**. Complete the fields as follows, and then click **Save**:

    Field: `Components`

    Condition: `contains any of`

    Value: `VPN Server`

4. Then, select **New action** followed by **Assign issue**. Complete the fields as follows, and then click **Save**:

    Assign the issue to: `User in a group`

    Method to choose assignee: `Balanced workload`

    JQL to restrict issues: Leave empty

    Group: `Network Team`

5. Click on **Add else** in the rule-chain view on the left, then click on **Add conditions** and select **Issue fields condition**. Complete the fields as follows and then click **Save**:

    Field: Components

    Condition: contains any of

    Value: Active Directory

6. Click on **Add conditions** and select **Issue fields condition**. Complete the fields as follows, and then click **Save**:

    Field: Summary

    Condition: does not contain

    Value: password

7. Now, select **New action** and then **Assign issue**. Complete the fields as follows, and click **Save**:

    Assign the issue to: User in a group

    Method to choose assignee: Balanced workload

    JQL to restrict issues: Leave empty

    Group: System Administrator Team

8. You can continue to add further Else-If blocks to route more requests; however, for this example, we'll only create these two conditions.

9. Before we save this rule, we need to ensure that it can be triggered by the rule that categorizes incoming emails.

10. Click on **Rule details** in the rule-chain view on the left, and complete the following two fields:

    Name: Route incoming requests

    Allow rule trigger: Ensure the checkbox is selected

Your rule should now look similar to the one shown in the following screenshot:

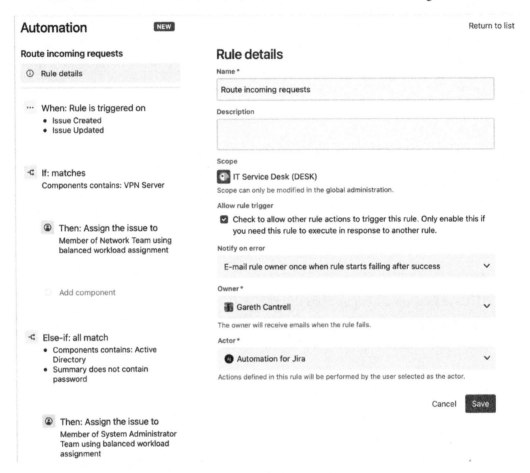

Figure 6.2 – Routing incoming requests

11. Finally, click **Save** and then click **Turn it on** to save and enable the rule.

In this section, we have learned how to use automation rules to process incoming requests to Jira Service Management by firstly categorizing them where appropriate, and then routing them to the correct teams for resolution.

In the next section, we will look at how to use automation rules to monitor SLA compliance.

Monitoring SLA compliance

SLAs are important metrics that are set to ensure that IT services are delivered within an agreed time period with respect to their priority and nature.

To maintain the agreed SLA compliance ratio of requests, we need to ensure that where possible, their priority is automatically increased when they are about to breach their SLA so that they gain a higher chance of their SLAs being met.

Additionally, this should be accompanied by appropriate notifications to the assigned agent, the service desk team, and the service desk manager, allowing for the appropriate response should the agent not be able to deliver a resolution with the SLA.

In this section, we will look at how to use automation rules to keep abreast of SLAs and how to manage requests when these are breached.

Let's look at an example by creating a rule to monitor the *Time to first response* SLA and notify the appropriate persons as applicable.

Creating a rule to monitor SLA breaches

To maintain the SLA success rate, we want to avoid requests breaching their SLAs in the first instance.

In this example, we are going to monitor the *Time to first response* SLA for high-priority requests and either notify a Slack channel if the request is unassigned or send a message to the assigned agent if the request has been automatically assigned. In addition, we will also send a notification to the service desk manager to alert them of the fact that the SLA is about to be breached so that they can take the appropriate action.

Let's get started with the rule, as follows:

1. In your Jira Service Management project, navigate to **Project settings**, click on the **Automation** link in the **Project Settings** menu, and then click **Create rule**.

2. Select the **SLA threshold breached** trigger and complete the fields as follows, and then click **Save**:

    SLA: `Time to first response`

    Trigger when SLA has: `will breach in the next 30 minutes`

3. Next, select **New condition** and then **Issue fields condition**. Complete the fields as follows, and click **Save**:

    Field: Priority

    Condition: is one of

    Value: Highest, High

4. The service desk manager needs to be notified irrespective of whether we send a general Slack notification or notify the request's assignee, so we'll send this notification first.

    Select **New action** followed by **Send email**. Complete the fields as follows, and then click **Save**:

    To: Manager

    Subject: {{issue.key}} is about to breach its SLA

    Content:

    An unassigned high-priority issue, {{issue.key}} - {{issue.summary}} is about to breach its "Time to first response" SLA in 30 minutes.

    A notification has also been sent to the #service-desk Slack channel.

    Regards,

    Your friendly SLA bot.

5. Then, select **New condition** and then **If / else block** as we want to have different outcomes depending on the assignment of the request. Click **Add conditions**, select the **Issue fields condition** and complete the fields as follows, and then click **Save**:

    Field: Assignee

    Condition: is empty

6. Now, select **New action** and then the **Send Slack message** action. Using the *Incoming Slack* webhook you configured in the *Integrating with Slack* section of *Chapter 4*, *Sending Automated Notifications*, complete the fields as follows, and then click **Save**:

Webhook URL: Use the webhook from *Chapter 4*, *Sending Automated Notifications*

Message:

```
:fire: <{{issue.toUrl}}|{{issue.key}} - {{issue.
summary}}> is currently unassigned and will breach its
'Time to first response' SLA in 30 minutes.
```

Channel or user: #service-desk

7. Then, click **Add else** in the rule-chain view on the left, and then click **Save**.

8. Select **New action** and then **Send email**. Complete the fields as follows, and then click **Save**:

To: Assignee

Subject: {{issue.key}} is about to breach its Time to first response SLA

Content:

```
Hi {{issue.assignee.displayName.split(" ").first}},

You have been assigned {{issue.key}} - {{issue.
summary}} which is about to breach its Time to first
response SLA in 30 minutes.

Please take appropriate action to ensure we meet our
SLA targets.

Thanks,
Your friendly SLA bot.
```

Now that you have configured the **Send email** action, your rule should look similar to the one shown in the following screenshot:

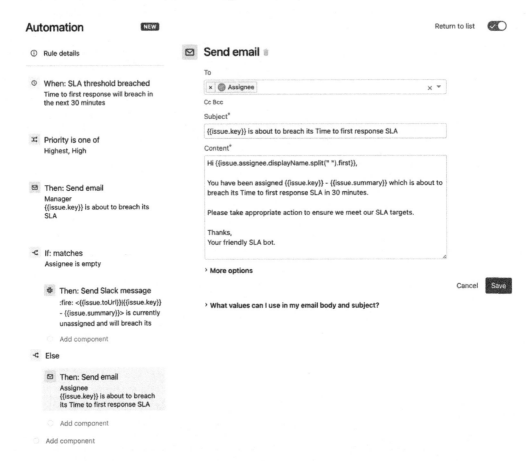

Figure 6.3 – Monitoring SLA breaches

9. Finally, name your rule `Time to first response monitor` and click **Turn it on** to save and enable the rule.

In this section, we learned how to monitor requests whose SLAs are about breach or that have already breached, and how to automatically prioritize and escalate these requests.

Next, we will look at how to improve service desk efficiency by automating common and repetitive tasks using automation rules.

Automating common and repetitive tasks

There are a number of requests received daily by IT service desks that are repetitive and mundane, and that are prime candidates for automation.

By automating tasks, not only are you reducing the need for human intervention and potential errors during the completion of these tasks, but you are also enabling increased productivity for the end user by reducing the time taken to fulfill their request.

In this section, we will take a look at using automation to handle password resets, which is quite possibly one of the most common requests handled by service desks.

Let's look at an automation rule that will automatically reset a user password when the user raises a password reset request in the service desk.

Creating a rule to automatically reset passwords

Probably one of the more frequent and time-consuming tasks faced by IT service desks is the request to reset a user's password, making it a prime candidate for automation.

To demonstrate how we could achieve this with automation rules in Jira Service Management, we are going to make use of **Microsoft's Azure AD** service, which has a well-defined **REpresentational State Transfer application programming interface (REST API)**.

> **Important note**
> We are going to assume that the only common information between users in Jira Cloud (or Jira Server) and Azure AD are the users' email addresses, as Jira Cloud does not allow access to user account names.

To begin, we first need to ensure that Jira is registered as an app with Azure AD and has the appropriate permissions assigned.

Let's start by completing the configuration we require in Azure AD, as follows:

1. Navigate to the **Azure Active Directory** component in your Azure portal and select **App registrations**, and then click on **New registration**.

2. Name your new app `Service Desk Autobot` and click **Register**.

You should now be presented with a screen similar to the one shown in the following screenshot. You will need to copy the **Application (client) ID (1)** and **Directory (tenant) ID (2)** IDs to use later in our rule:

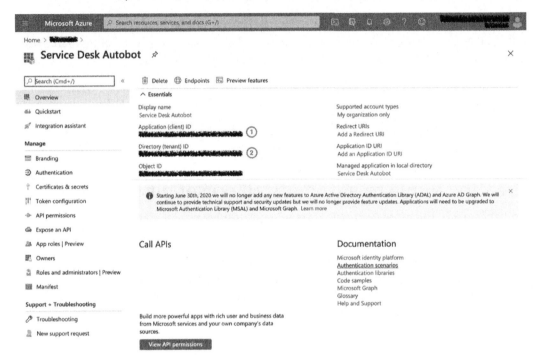

Figure 6.4 – Registering Jira as an app with Azure AD

3. The next step is to create a client secret that we can use to authenticate with from our automation rule. To do this, navigate to **Certificates & secrets** in the menu and click on **New client secret** in the **Client secrets** section.

    Add an optional description and select the length of time you want this secret to be valid for, and click **Add**.

Your screen should now look similar to the one shown in the following screenshot. Copy the newly added **client secret (1)** ID to a safe place for use later in our automation rule:

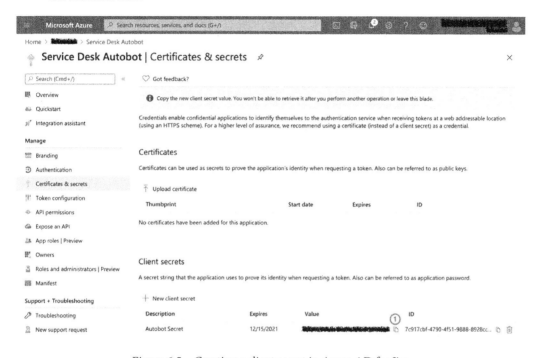

Figure 6.5 – Creating a client secret in Azure AD for Jira

4. We now need to give our new app the correct permissions in order to be able to reset passwords in Azure AD.

5. Navigate to the **API permissions** menu item and then click **Add a permission**. Then, select **Microsoft Graph**.

6. Next, select **Application permissions** and then narrow down the permissions to `Directory`, and check the **Directory.ReadWrite.All** permission. Finally, click **Add permissions**, as shown in the following screenshot:

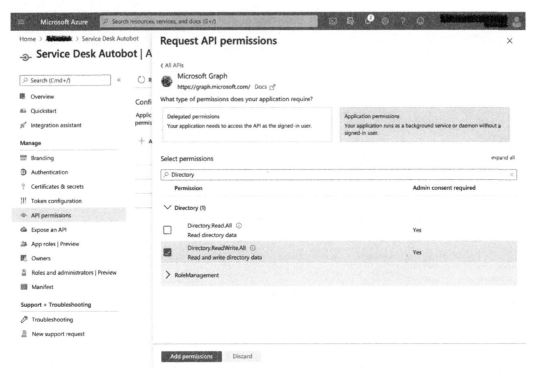

Figure 6.6 – Adding the correct Azure AD permissions for Jira

7. To simplify the interaction with our automation rule, we want to pre-authorize the permissions we just granted, so click on **Grant admin consent for** `<tenant>`.

The status for both **Microsoft Graph** API permissions should now have a green check next to them indicating they have been granted **Admin** consent, as can be seen in the following screenshot:

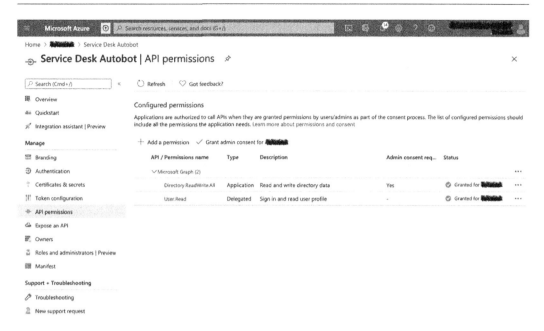

Figure 6.7 – Granting Admin consent to the API permissions

8. The final step in the Azure portal is to grant the **Company Administrator** role to your app. To do this, click on the Cloud Shell icon immediately to the right of the search bar and copy the following commands to the PowerShell terminal:

```
Connect-AzureAD

$displayName = "Service Desk Autobot"; $objectId =
(Get-AzureADServicePrincipal -SearchString $displayName).
ObjectId

$roleName = "Company Administrator"; $role =
Get-AzureADDirectoryRole | Where-Object {$_.DisplayName
-eq $roleName}

Add-AzureADDirectoryRoleMember -ObjectId $role.ObjectId
-RefObjectId $objectId
```

Your screen should now look similar to the one shown in the following screenshot:

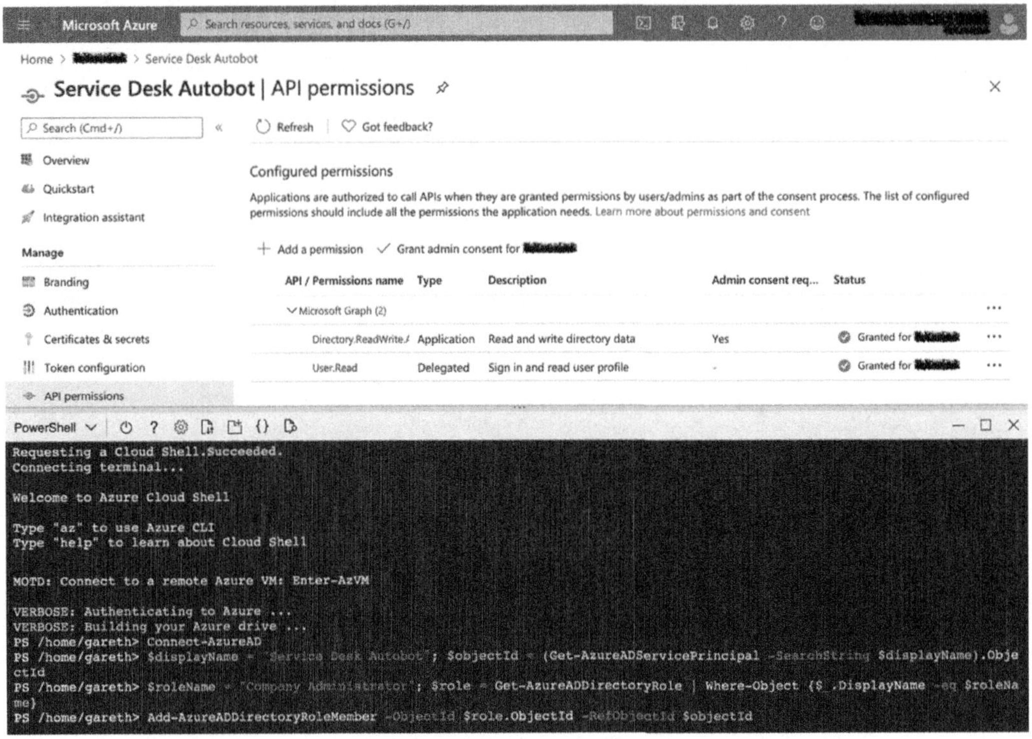

Figure 6.8 – Granting the Company Administrator role to Jira

Now that we have configured our app in Azure AD and you have a couple of users configured with email addresses that match their Jira email addresses, we can create our automation rule to automatically reset user passwords when a request is received in Jira Service Management. To do this, follow these steps:

1. In your Jira Service Management project, navigate to **Project settings**, click on the **Automation** link in the **Project Settings** menu, and then click **Create rule**.

2. Select the **Multiple issue events** trigger, and in the **Issue events** field select both `Issue Created` and `Issue Updated`, then click **Save**.

3. Then, select **New condition** and then **Issue fields condition**. Complete the fields as follows, and click **Save**:

    Field: `Components`

    Condition: `contains any of`

    Value: `Active Directory`

4. Select **New condition** followed by **Issue fields condition**, and complete the fields as follows before clicking **Save**:

   Field: Summary

   Condition: contains

   Value: password

5. Next, we'll use the https://www.passwordrandom.com external web service to generate a random, temporary password for the user, so we'll select **New action** followed by **Send web request** and complete the fields as follows:

   Webhook URL: https://www.passwordrandom.com/query?command=password&format=json

   HTTP method: GET

   Webhook body: Empty

   Wait for response: Ensure this is selected

6. If you validate your webhook configuration, you should receive a response, similar to the following:

```
{
    "char": [
        "LoyKI6;09jd"
    ]
}
```

   Click **Save** to move on.

7. In the next step, we need to log in to Microsoft Azure and retrieve an authentication token. To complete this step, we will need the **Application (client) ID** , **Directory (tenant) ID**, and the **Client secret** that we configured earlier in Azure AD.

   To do this, we need to send the following fields in **Uniform Resource Locator (URL)**-encoded format: resource, client_id, client_secret, and grant_type.

   To URL-encode the data, the field and the value are separated by = and each field-value pair is then separated using &; and finally, the entire text string needs to be URL-encoded, which you can do by pasting the complete string into a service such as https://www.urlencoder.org.

8. Select **New action** and then select **Send web request**. Complete the fields as follows, and then click **Save**:

Webhook URL: `https://login.windows.net/<Directory (tenant) ID>/oauth2/token`

Header Name: `Content-Type`

Header Value: `application/x-www-form-urlencoded`

HTTP method: `POST`

Webhook body: `Custom data`

Wait for response: Ensure the checkbox is selected

Custom data:

```
resource=https%3A%2F%2Fgraph.microsoft.com&client_
id=<Application (client) ID>&client_secret=<Client
secret>&grant_type=client_credentials
```

The preceding custom data corresponds to the following fields:

resource=`https://graph.microsoft.com`

client_id=`<Application (client) ID>`

client_secret=`<Client secret>`

grant_type=`client_credentials`

At this point, your rule should look similar to the one shown in the following screenshot:

Figure 6.9 – Configuring the login web request to Azure AD

9. A successful login request to Microsoft Azure will return the `token_type` and `access_token` you will need to complete the password reset request in the following **JavaScript Object Notation (JSON)** format, which we can access using the `{{webhookResponse.body.token_type}}` and `{{webhookResponse.body.access_token}}` smart values respectively, as follows:

```
{
    "token_type": "Bearer",
    "expires_in": "3599",
    "ext_expires_in": "3599",
    "expires_on": "1602958671",
    "not_before": "1602954771",
    "resource": "https://graph.microsoft.com",
    "access_token": "xxxxxx"
}
```

10. Now that we have successfully logged in to Microsoft Azure, we can use the authentication response and the reporter's email address to look up the ID of the user in the Azure AD. To do this, we need to select **New action** followed by another **Send web request** action, with the fields completed as follows:

Webhook URL: `https://graph.microsoft.com/v1.0/users?$filter=startsWith(mail,'{{reporter.emailAddress.urlEncode}}')`

Headers field: Make sure to use a space between the two smart values in the **Value** field

Name: `Authorization`

Value: `{{webhookResponses.get(1).body.token_type}}` `{{webhookResponses.get(1).body.access_token}}`

HTTP method: `GET`

Webhook body: `Empty`

Wait for response: Ensure the checkbox is selected

This request will return the user information from Azure AD in the following format, which we can access using the `{{webhookResponse.body.value.id}}` smart value, as follows:

```
{
    "@odata.context": "https://graph.microsoft.com/
v1.0/$metadata#users",
    "value": [
        {
            "businessPhones": [],
            "displayName": "Joe Bloggs",
            "givenName": "Joe",
            "jobTitle": null,
            "mail": "joe.bloggs@company.com",
            "mobilePhone": null,
            "officeLocation": null,
            "preferredLanguage": "en",
            "surname": "Bloggs",
            "userPrincipalName": "jblogs@tenant.onmicrosoft.
              com",
            "id": "2aa3af1f-c91f-4feb-89dc-de4d200da185"
        }
    ]
}
```

> **Tip**
> When receiving responses multiple web requests in an automation rule, each response is added to the `{{webhookResponses}}` smart value list in the order it was called in the rule, starting at position zero (0). We can therefore use the smart value list functions to retrieve the individual webhook responses when we need to reference them later in the rule. For example, `{{webhookResponses.get(1).body}}` will retrieve the JSON response from the *second* web request, while `{{webhookResponses.first.body}}` will retrieve the response from the first request.

11. Now that we have our authentication data, the ID of the user in Azure AD, and a temporary password from our first web request, we can combine these to actually perform the password reset.

Select **New action** followed by **Send web request**. Complete the fields as follows, and then click **Save**:

Webhook URL: `https://graph.microsoft.com/v1.0/users/` `{{webhookResponse.body.value.id}}`

First **Headers** field:

Name: `Authorization`

Value: `{{webhookResponses.get(1).body.token_type}}` `{{webhookResponses.get(1).body.access_token}}`

Second **Headers** field:

Name: `Content-Type`

Value: `application/json`

HTTP method: `POST`

Webhook body: `Custom data`

Custom data:

```
{
    "passwordProfile": {
        "forceChangePasswordNextSignIn": "true",
        "password": "{{webhookResponses.first.body.
        char}}"
    }
}
```

Wait for response: Ensure this option is selected so that we only continue with the rule if the response is successful.

The custom data in this example makes use of the Azure AD password profile structure of the user REST API defined in Microsoft's Graph API, available at `https://docs.microsoft.com/en-us/graph/api/resources/` `passwordprofile?view=graph-rest-1.0`.

Your rule should look similar to the one shown in the following screenshot:

Figure 6.10 – Configuring the reset password request

12. To complete the rule, we need to inform the user that their password has been reset, as well as what the new temporary password is for them to be able sign in again and change the password to one of their choice.

    Select **New action** and then **Send email**. Complete the fields as follows, before clicking **Save**:

    To: `Reporter`

    Subject: `Your request to reset your password has been completed.`

    Content:

    `Dear {{issue.reporter.displayName.split(" ").first}},`

    `Your request to reset your password has been completed.`

    `The new temporary password which has been generated for you is:`

    `{{webhookResponses.first.body.char}}`

    `You will be prompted to change this when you next log in.`

    `Thank you,`

    `The Service Desk Team.`

13. Finally, select **Rule details** from the rule-chain view on the left, name your rule `Password reset bot`, and ensure the **Allow rule trigger** checkbox is selected. Click **Save** and then click **Turn it on** to enable the rule.

In this section, we have learned how we can use automation rules to automate common and repetitive tasks faced by service desk teams by looking at one of the most common repetitive tasks—namely, resetting passwords.

As we have seen, using automation rules to automate these types of repetitive and time-consuming tasks will lead to improved overall efficiency of your service desk, reducing the cost per ticket and also improving end-user satisfaction.

Summary

In this chapter, you learned how adding automations to Jira Service Management can improve the efficiency of your IT service desks, reducing the cost per ticket and improving overall user satisfaction.

We learned how categorizing and processing incoming requests early in the request life cycle can increase the response and resolution times of requests as human intervention is no longer required for triage, and we now understand how monitoring SLA compliance with appropriate escalations can help to stay on top of important issues.

Finally, we learned how using automation bots to perform common and repetitive tasks such as resetting a user's password can drastically improve both the time to resolve a request and the end user's productivity, as they no longer have to wait for a service agent to manually perform the tasks.

By using the skills learned in this chapter and applying them to more processes within your service desk, you will not only enable your service agents to focus on more meaningful and urgent tasks but will also improve overall user satisfaction with IT services throughout the organization.

In the next chapter, we will explore how we can use automations to effectively manage Jira Software projects.

7
Automating Jira Software Projects

Tracking software development tasks and bugs is arguably what Jira is most well-known for; however, it has always come with administrative overhead in keeping issues aligned and ensuring that work across projects is synchronized.

Keeping on top of the administrative tasks in Jira can be frustrating at times and usually means that less time can be devoted to actual development work. Introducing automation can help cut down on many of the manual tasks, which leads to happier and more productive team members.

In this chapter, we will learn how to harness automation rules to provide simple yet effective productivity increases in Jira Software projects, such as how to keep versions synchronized across projects.

We'll also see how aligning the statuses of an issue hierarchy using automation can reduce a number of otherwise manual interactions and increase the efficiency of working with issues in a software project.

We will cover the following topics in this chapter:

- Managing versions across projects
- Ensuring epics and stories stay aligned
- Managing the scope of a sprint

Technical requirements

The requirements for this chapter are as follows:

- **Jira cloud environment**: If you don't already have access to Jira, you can create a free Jira cloud account at `https://www.atlassian.com/software/jira/free` and ensure that you have both **Jira Software** and **Jira Service Desk** selected.

- **Jira server environment**: If you are using Jira Server (available from `https://www.atlassian.com/software/jira/download`), ensure you have licenses for both Jira Software and Jira Service Desk. In addition, you will also need to ensure that you install the *Automation for Jira* app, available from the Atlassian Marketplace.

In both instances, you will need to have at least **Project Administrator** access to a Service Desk project and a Scrum software project to be able to follow the examples in this chapter. For the examples in this chapter, we have used the *IT service management project template* to create the Service Desk project and the *Scrum software project template* to create the Software project.

You can download the latest code samples for this chapter from this book's official GitHub repository at `https://github.com/PacktPublishing/Automate-Everyday-Tasks-in-Jira`. Please visit the following link to check the CiA videos: `https://bit.ly/3quqjil`

Managing versions across projects

A common use case with Jira Software projects is to have a public-facing project where your customers can log defects and feature requests against released software, and an internal project that is used by the development team to track their work.

Having this setup allows teams to triage incoming requests and select relevant issues to work on without clogging up their actual project with thousands of issues.

However, realizing the benefits from this setup requires that the software versions in both projects are synchronized, allowing customers to report issues against the correct versions of the released software.

In this section, we will explore how to use automation rules to manage the version synchronization between projects.

To do this, we will need to ensure that when we release a version in the internal project, we create a corresponding version in the public-facing project that customers can then use when reporting bugs or creating feature requests.

Let's take a look at a rule that enables us to keep versions in sync across projects.

Creating a rule to keep versions in sync across projects

In this example, we'll create a rule that will trigger for version releases in our internal project and create and release a corresponding version in the public-facing project that customers can then use when reporting issues.

> **Important note**
>
> Creating automation rules that span multiple projects requires the user to create the rule to have Jira administrator permissions. Project administrators are not permitted to create multi-project rules.

In this example, we are going to use two software projects in our rule. For the first software project, we will create a project using the Scrum software template named *My Application* with the project key *MAPP*. For the public-facing support project, we will create a project using the bug tracking software template named *My Application Support* with the project key *MAPS*.

Let's take a look at how to build this rule:

1. As we are working with more than a project, this rule needs to be set up by a user with Jira administrator permissions.

2. Navigate to **Settings** (the cog icon in the top menu), select **System**, click on the **Automation rules** tab in the left menu, and then click on **Create rule**.

3. Select the **Version released** trigger and click **Save**.

4. As both projects configured in this rule can cause this rule to fire, we need to ensure that it only continues executing when the MAPP project causes it to fire. To do this, select **New condition** followed by the **Advanced compare** condition. Complete the fields as follows and click **Save**:

   First value: `{{version.project.key}}`

   Condition: `equals`

   Second value: `MAPP`

5. Next, select **New action** and then **Create version**. In the **Version name** field, we need to use the `{{version.name}}` smart value to select the name of the version that caused the rule to fire.

   Expand the **More options** disclosure and select your application support project in the **Project** field. In the case of this example, it is **My Application Support (MAPS)**.

6. Click **Save**, and then select **New action** followed by **Release version** as we want to not only create the version in the support project but also release it to keep it in sync with the internal project.

   Expand the **More options** disclosure and select your application support project in the **Project** field. In this example, we'll be using the project named **My Application Support (MAPS)**.

   Your rule should look similar to the following screenshot:

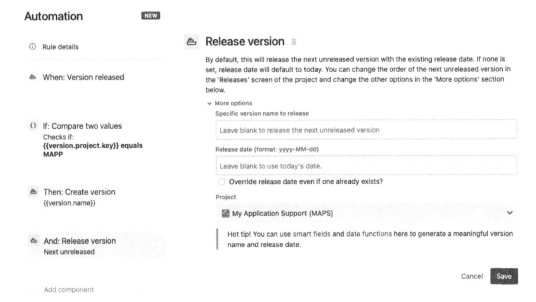

We've left **Specific version name to release** empty in this rule as the latest version in the support project will always be the version we've just created in the rule. If for some reason your support project could have later versions already defined, use the `{{version.name}}` smart value to ensure the correct version is released.

7. Next, click **Save**, and then select **Rule details** in the rule-chain view on the left. In the **Name** field, enter `Keep support project versions in sync`.

    Set the **Scope** field to `Multiple projects`, and in the **Restrict to projects** field, select your internal and support projects. In this case, we'll select `My Application` and `My Application Support`.

8. Finally, click **Save**, and then click **Turn it on** to publish and enable the rule.

In this section, we have learned how to use automation rules to keep versions synchronized across multiple projects, enabling customers to raise bugs and features outside of the development project.

In the following section, we will look at how to ensure that the status of epics in a software project stays aligned to the underlying stories in the project.

Ensuring epics and stories are aligned

Working in software projects using the **Scrum Agile framework** generally involves having a hierarchy of issue types.

In a typical Scrum-based agile hierarchy, you will have epics that define larger pieces of work, or business requirements, which may span multiple sprints.

These are broken down into stories (or user stories), which are high-level definitions of the requirements that can be delivered in a time-boxed period or sprint.

Stories can then be decomposed into tasks, modeled as sub-tasks of the story, which are specific, measurable items of work required to get the story done.

In this section, we'll look at how we can use automation rules to keep the statuses of the issues in this hierarchy in sync so that when work is started on a sub-task, the linked issues above the sub-task move to the correct status without needing manual intervention.

Creating a rule to keep epics and stories synchronized

In this example, we'll create a rule that triggers when a sub-task is transitioned to a new status, and depending on the status of the sub-task, the rule will automatically transition its parent story to the correct status if required.

In addition, we'll use the same rule to transition the epic linked to the story to the correct status when the story transitions to a new status, so we'll need to allow the rule to be triggered by other rules.

> **Important note**
>
> Allowing rules to be triggered by other rules can inadvertently lead to execution loops where a rule could be triggered indefinitely. The automation rule engine includes loop detection to prevent infinite loops; however, an incorrectly configured rule could still cause an execution loop up to a depth of 10 levels before the rule execution is terminated.

Let's take a look at this rule now:

1. In your Jira Software project, navigate to **Project settings**, click on the **Automation** link in the project settings menu, and then click **Create rule**.

2. Select the **Issue transitioned** trigger and click **Save**. Leave both the **From status** and **To status** fields blank as we want the rule to fire for every transition.

3. The first thing we want to check is whether progress has started on a sub-task and move its parent story to **In Progress**. We are going to use the **statusCategory** field in our condition to ensure that we catch any status of the sub-task that is deemed to be in progress.

    Select **New condition**, and then select the **If/else** block. Click **Add conditions**, and then select the JQL condition and enter the following query into the **JQL** field, then click **Save**:

    ```
    issueType = Sub-task AND statusCategory = "In Progress"
    ```

4. Now, select **Branch rule / related issues**, and in the **Type of related issues** field, select **Parent** and click **Save**.

5. Then, select **New action** followed by **Transition issue**. For this example, ensure that the **Destination status** field is set to **Copy from trigger issue**, and then click **Save**.

6. The next stage of the rule is to ensure the user story transitions to a completed status when all of its sub-tasks are done. To do this, click on **Add else** in the rule-chain view on the left, then click **Add conditions** and select the JQL condition.

    Enter the following query into the **JQL** field and click **Save**:

    ```
    issueType = Sub-task AND statusCategory = Done
    ```

7. Next, select **Branch rule / related issues**, and again, in the **Type of related issues** field, select **Parent**, and then click **Save**.

8. At this point, we need to check that all the sub-tasks for the parent issue selected in the **Branch rule** component are completed before continuing in this branch, so we select **New condition** and then select **Related issues condition**. Complete the fields as follows, and then click **Save**:

   Related issues: `Sub-tasks`

   Condition: `All match specified JQL`

   Matching JQL: `statusCategory = Done`

9. If the condition mentioned in *step 8* matches and all sub-tasks of the story have a status whose category is done, then we need to transition the story itself to a done status. To do this, select **New action** followed by **Transition issue** and ensure the **Destination** field is set to **Copy from trigger issue**, and then click **Save**.

   > **Important note**
   > When you use **Copy from trigger issue** for statuses, you need to ensure that both issue types use the same workflow or that the workflows share the same statuses. If this is not the case, you will need to select the actual status you wish to transition to.

10. Now that we've handled keeping the story in sync with its sub-tasks, we need to handle keeping epics in sync with their underlying stories.

    First, we'll handle moving epics to **In Progress** when progress starts on any underlying story by clicking on **Add else** in the rule-chain view on the left, then clicking **Add condition** followed by adding a JQL condition. Set the query in the **JQL** field as follows, and then click **Save**:

    `issueType = Story AND status = "In Progress"`

11. Then, select **Branch rule / related issues**, and in the **Type of related issues** field, select **Epic (parent)** and click **Save**.

12. Next, select **New action**, and then select **Transition issue**. Make sure the **Destination** field is set to **Copy from trigger issue** for this example, and then click **Save**.

13. The final conditional branch in this rule will ensure that an epic is automatically transitioned to a completed status when all of its underlying stories are complete.

   Do this by clicking **Add else** in the rule-chain view on the left. Next, select **Add condition**, and then select **JQL condition**.

   Set the query in the **JQL** field as follows, and then click **Save**:

   ```
   issueType = Story AND statusCategory = Done
   ```

14. Now, select **Branch rule / related issues**, and in the **Type of related issues** field, again select `Epic (parent)` and click **Save**.

15. Like we did for sub-tasks, we need to ensure that all the stories in the epic are completed before we can automatically transition the epic to a completed status.

   We do this by selecting **New condition**, followed by **Related issues condition**.

   Complete the condition fields as follows, and then click **Save**:

   Related issues: `Stories (or other issues in this Epic)`

   Condition: `All match specified JQL`

   Matching JQL: `statusCategory = Done`

16. To actually transition the epic, we need to add an action, so select **New action** followed by **Transition issue**.

   Ensure that the **Destination** field is set to **Copy from trigger issue** for this example, and then click **Save**.

17. One of the requirements for this rule is that it is able to fire itself to ensure that all issues in the hierarchy are updated to the correct status.

   In order to achieve this, we need to set the rule option that allows rules to be triggered by other rules.

   Select **Rule details** in the rule-chain view on the left. In the **Name** field, set the name of the rule to **Keep issue hierarchy statuses in sync** and ensure that the **Allow rule trigger** checkbox is selected.

Your rule should look similar to the following two screenshots:

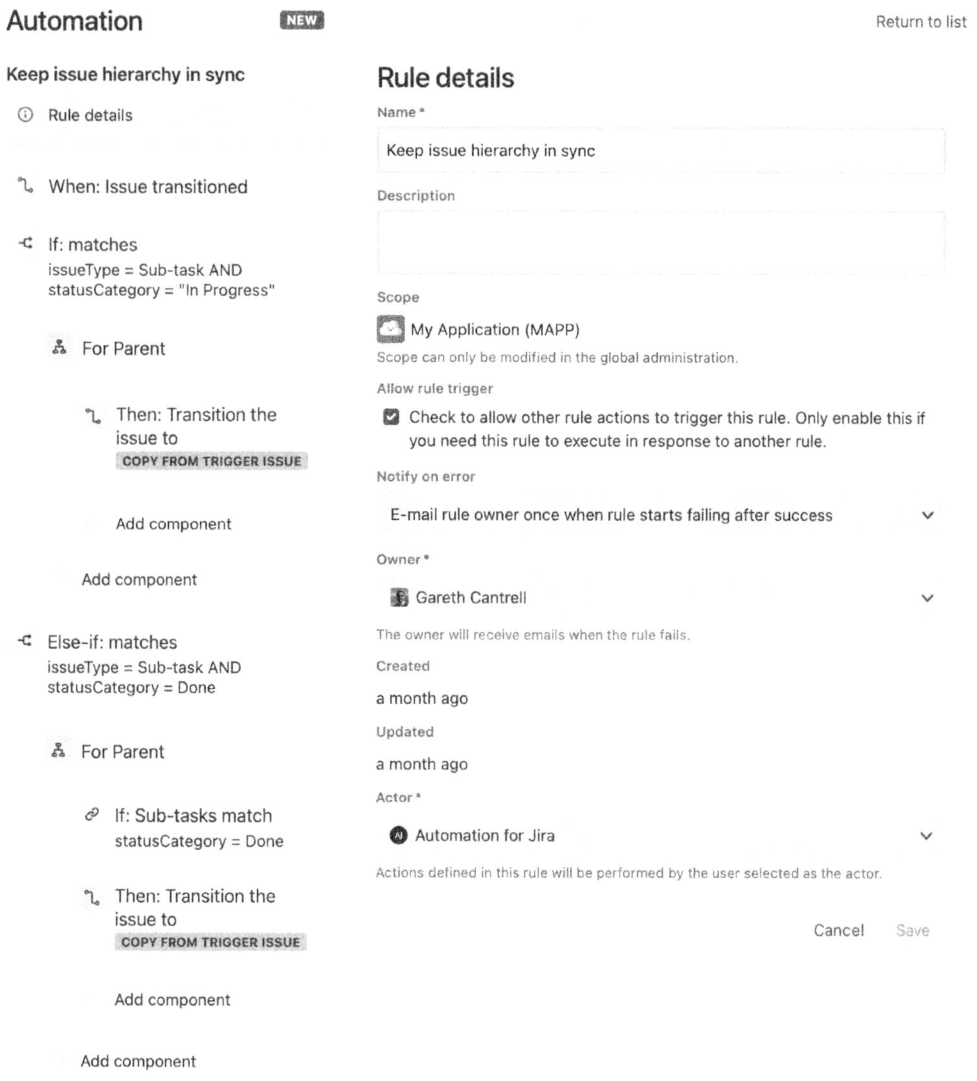
Automation
NEW
Return to list
Keep issue hierarchy in sync
Rule details
When: Issue transitioned
If: matches
issueType = Sub-task AND
statusCategory = "In Progress"
For Parent
Then: Transition the issue to
COPY FROM TRIGGER ISSUE
Add component
Add component
Else-if: matches
issueType = Sub-task AND
statusCategory = Done
For Parent
If: Sub-tasks match
statusCategory = Done
Then: Transition the issue to
COPY FROM TRIGGER ISSUE
Add component
Add component
Rule details
Name *
Keep issue hierarchy in sync
Description
Scope
My Application (MAPP)
Scope can only be modified in the global administration.
Allow rule trigger
Check to allow other rule actions to trigger this rule. Only enable this if you need this rule to execute in response to another rule.
Notify on error
E-mail rule owner once when rule starts failing after success
Owner *
Gareth Cantrell
The owner will receive emails when the rule fails.
Created
a month ago
Updated
a month ago
Actor *
Automation for Jira
Actions defined in this rule will be performed by the user selected as the actor.
Cancel
Save

Figure 7.2 – Rule to keep epics and stories in sync (part 1)

In the preceding screenshot, we can see the rule details and the first part of the rule chain dealing with keeping stories in sync with sub-tasks.

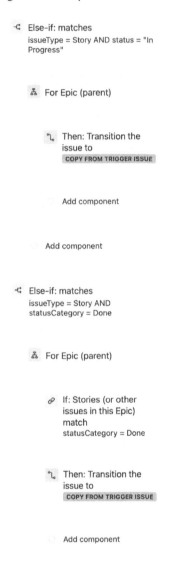

Figure 7.3 – Keeping epics and stories in sync (part 2)

In this screenshot, we can see the second part of the rule chain, which deals with keeping epics in sync with their underlying user stories.

18. Finally, click **Save**, and then click **Turn it on** to save and publish the rule.

In this section, we have learned how to use automation rules to keep a hierarchy of issues in sync with each other and how we can allow a rule to trigger itself in order to achieve this.

In the next section, we'll take a look at how we can automatically adjust the scope of a sprint by adding linked issues into the current sprint as well as notify the team when the scope of a sprint is changed.

Managing the scope of a sprint

During any development life cycle, it is inevitable that at some point there will be a change to the scope of the sprint, either due to last-minute changes to the requirements or by the need to include an urgent bug fix.

In this section, we'll firstly look at how we can change the scope of a sprint by including a newly linked issue to the sprint.

We'll also look at how we can use automation rules to monitor the sprint and notify the team when the scope changes.

Creating a rule to add a linked issue to the sprint

In this example, we are going to make use of the fact that we have both a private internal software development project (*My Application* with key *MAPP*) and a public support project (*My Application Support* with key *MAPS*) where customers can raise requests and report bugs.

We are also going to assume that we have a team that monitors the public support project and triages incoming requests.

Part of this triage involves examining high-priority bugs submitted by the organization's top customers and if verified, will create a linked bug in the private development project and add it to the current sprint.

Let's take a look at how we can achieve this with an automation rule:

1. As we are working with more than a project, this rule needs to be set up by a user with Jira administrator permissions.

2. Navigate to **Settings** (the cog icon in the top menu), select **System**, and then click on the **Automation rules** tab in the left menu and click **Create rule**.

3. Select the **Issue transitioned** trigger, set the fields as follows, and click **Save**:

    From status: `To Do`

    To status: `In Progress`

4. Next, we need to add in some conditions to ensure we only select the highest priority bugs in the support project.

    We will use multiple issue field conditions in this example as they have a performance advantage over using a JQL condition.

5. Check for the correct project by selecting **New condition** followed by **Issue fields condition**. Set the condition fields as follows and click **Save**:

    Field: `Project`

    Condition: `equals`

    Value: `My Application Support (MAPS)`

6. Next, we'll ensure that this rule only executes for bug issue types.

    Select **New condition**, and then select **Issue fields condition**. Set the condition fields as follows, and then click **Save**:

    Field: `Issue Type`

    Condition: `equals`

    Value: `Bug`

7. The last condition is to check that the bug has the highest priority.

    Select **New condition** followed by **Issue fields condition**, set the condition fields as follows, and click **Save**:

    Field: `Priority`

    Condition: `is one of`

    Value: `Highest`

8. The final step in this rule is to create the linked issue in our development project and add it to the current sprint.

    Select **New action**, and then select **Create issue**. From the **Choose fields to set** field, select **Description**, **Affects versions**, **Linked Issues**, **Priority**, and **Sprint**.

    Click the ellipsis button next to each of the fields, **Summary**, **Description**, **Affects versions**, and **Priority**, and select the **Copy from…** option.

Complete the remainder of the fields as follows and click **Save**:

Project: My Application (MAPP)

Issue type: Same issue type

Linked Issues: relates to

Issue: Trigger issue

Sprint: Active Sprint (My Application Scrum Board)

Your rule should now look similar to the following screenshot:

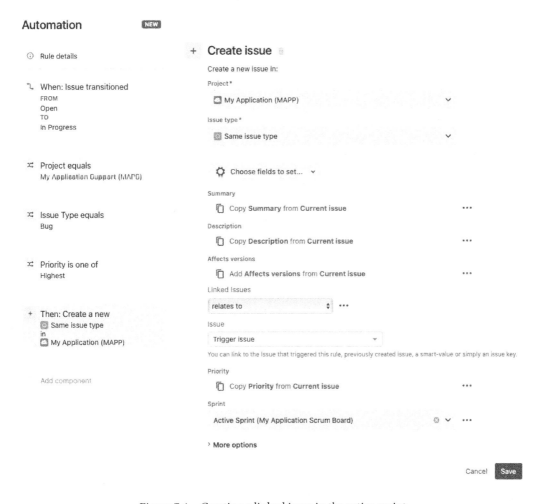

Figure 7.4 – Creating a linked issue in the active sprint

9. Finally, select **Rule details** in the rule-chain view on the left. In the **Name** field, enter `Add critical bug to active sprint`.

    Set the **Scope** field to **Multiple projects** and in the **Restrict to projects** field, select your internal and support projects. In this case, we'll select **My Application** and **My Application Support**.

10. Finally, click **Save**, and then click **Turn it on** to publish and enable the rule.

In this example, we have learned how to use automation rules to create a linked issue in a project and add it to the current sprint.

In the next example, we'll see how we can watch for scope changes to the current sprint and notify the development team when this occurs.

Creating a rule to notify the team when the scope changes

When the scope of an active sprint changes, we want to keep the team informed so that everyone on the team is kept abreast of what is happening.

To do this, we'll create a rule that listens for a change in the **Sprint** field of an issue and if that sprint is currently the active sprint, we'll send a notification to our team's Slack channel.

For this example, we'll send notifications to the **#sprint-updates** Slack channel using the Slack integration that we set up in *Chapter 4, Sending Automated Notifications*.

Let's take a look at how this rule works:

1. In your Jira Software project, navigate to **Project settings**, click on the **Automation** link in the **Project Settings** menu, and then click **Create rule**.

2. As there is no direct way to monitor changes to the active sprint, we'll instead set our rule to trigger when the **Sprint** field in an issue is changed.

    To do this, we'll select the **Field value changed** trigger. In the **Fields to monitor for changes** dropdown, select **Sprint**.

    Leave the **For** field blank that corresponds to **All issue operations**, and click **Save**.

3. We need to ensure that the sprint that the issue was added to corresponds with the currently active sprint.

We can achieve this by selecting **New condition** and then adding a JQL condition. Enter the following query in the **JQL** field and click **Save**:

```
sprint in openSprints()
```

4. Next, we'll select **New action** followed by **Send Slack message** and complete the fields as shown next, and then click **Save**:

Webhook URL: Use the incoming webhook URL that you configured in Slack in the *Integrating with Slack* section in *Chapter 4, Sending Automated Notifications*.

Message:

```
:mega: A new issue has just been added to the current
sprint <{{issue.url}}|{{issue.key}}: {{issue.summary}}> !
```

Channel or user: #sprint-updates.

Your rule should look similar to the following screenshot:

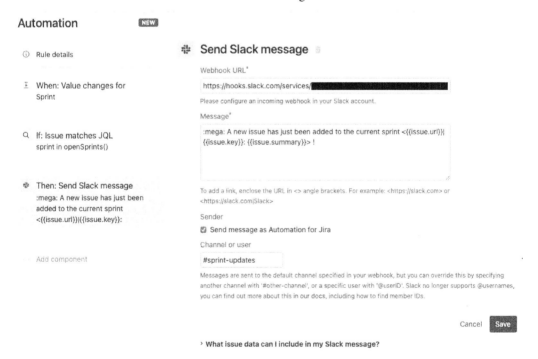

Figure 7.5 – Monitoring scope changes to a sprint

5. We also need to ensure that this rule can be triggered by other automation rules; otherwise, scope changes created by other rules will not cause notifications to be sent.

    Select **Rule details** in the rule-chain view on the left. In the **Name** field, set the name of the rule to **Send notification to Slack when Sprint scope changes** and ensure that the **Allow rule trigger** checkbox is selected.

6. Finally, click **Save**, and then click **Turn it on** to publish and enable the rule.

We have learned in this example how we can use the sprint field in an issue to monitor scope changes of a sprint and keep the team informed of these changes.

By cutting down on manual effort using automation to keep issues synchronized and teams updated, you will enable your teams to be more efficient as they no longer need to manage the project tool and can instead focus on their actual tasks.

Summary

In this chapter, we learned how we can use automation rules to minimize the administrative overhead usually involved in managing and working with Jira Software projects, and indeed these can be applied to most project types within Jira.

In particular, we learned how to keep versions synchronized across projects, which is especially useful when you have a software project spanning multiple Jira projects, whether they be internal team projects or, as in our example, public projects for customers to log and track requests.

Keeping hierarchies of issues in sync is a very common task faced in Jira projects and in this chapter, we learned how to use a looping rule to achieve this using the most common hierarchy encountered in Jira Software projects. Lastly, we learned how to maintain visibility of any scope changes to a sprint and how we can also use automation to adjust the scope of a sprint.

With the exception of the sprint-specific examples we have looked at, the topics we have covered in this chapter apply equally to any other style of software development, including Kanban and waterfall, with some minor adjustments.

Applying what we have learned in this chapter to your projects using automation will help reduce the amount of manual and repetitive administrative work and in doing so will enable your users to be both more efficient and productive.

In the next chapter, we'll look at how to leverage automation rules to integrate with tools such as GitHub and Bitbucket to support DevOps processes.

8
Integrating with DevOps Tools

One of the core tenets of DevOps, beyond cultivating the associated culture within your organization, is the practice of automating and optimizing processes through the use of technology. Using automation rules in Jira, we can optimize the process of software development by connecting DevOps tools such as Bitbucket and GitHub to issues in Jira, thereby allowing us to synchronize the status of issues automatically.

Beyond keeping issue statuses automatically synchronized to code commits, we can also make use of automation to keep track of and synchronize pull requests, create tasks to track these, and send notifications to the team to ensure maximum visibility of the process. All of this enables developers to spend more time focused on writing and delivering software and less time managing administrative tasks.

While integration with certain DevOps processes has been (and still is) possible in Jira using workflow triggers, in this chapter we will look at how automation rules can be used to create more flexible integrations than what has previously been possible. This will keep your workflow configuration clean and prevent lengthy workflow updates, especially when the workflow affects a large number of issues.

In this chapter, we will cover the following topics:

- Synchronizing issues and Git commits
- Keeping track of pull requests
- Automatically releasing versions using GitHub
- Synchronizing deployments with sprint completion

Technical requirements

The requirements for this chapter are as follows:

- **Jira Cloud environment**: If you don't already have access to Jira, you can create a free Jira Cloud account at `https://www.atlassian.com/software/jira/free` and ensure that you have both Jira Software and Jira Service Management selected.

- **Jira Server environment**: If you are using Jira Server (available from `https://www.atlassian.com/software/jira/download`), ensure that you have licenses for both Jira Software and Jira Service Management. In addition, you will also need to ensure that you install the *Automation for Jira* app, available from the Atlassian Marketplace.

For Jira, you will need to have at least **Project Administrator** access to a Scrum Software project and be able to follow the examples in this chapter. For the examples in this chapter, we have used the *Scrum project template* to create the software project.

You will also need access to the following tools:

- **Bitbucket Cloud**: Bitbucket Cloud is a hosted Git-based version control service from Atlassian. You can sign up for a Bitbucket account at `https://bitbucket.org` or by using the application switcher from your Jira Cloud account.

- **GitHub**: GitHub is a hosted software development and Git-based version control service from Microsoft. You can sign up for a GitHub account at `https://github.com`.

- **Jenkins**: Jenkins is a popular free, open source automation server that is used to facilitate **Continuous Integration (CI)** and **Continuous Delivery (CD)** by automating the building, testing, and deploying of software projects. You can download Jenkins from `https://www.jenkins.io`.

You can download the latest code samples for this chapter from this book's official GitHub repository at `https://github.com/PacktPublishing/Automate-Everyday-Tasks-in-Jira`. Please visit the following link to check the CiA videos: `https://bit.ly/2XWeuW7`

Synchronizing issues and Git commits

In the normal course of writing software, developers will normally move a story or task to an **In Progress** state, do the actual work of writing the code, commit the changes to a source repository such as Bitbucket or GitHub, and then switch back to Jira to move the story or task to the next status in the workflow.

All of this manual work requires unnecessary context switching, and because the process requires the developer to remember to switch between the various tools, it is very likely that sometimes issues are not updated, which makes it harder to track actual progress on the project.

Jira has, for some time, had the ability to integrate with tools such as Bitbucket and GitHub by allowing administrators to configure the underlying Jira workflows with triggers on various transitions.

While this approach does allow for automation of the process and frees up the developer from having to manually update their task statuses, it is limited to the transition on which the trigger is configured. Additionally, making adjustments to workflows is not always a straightforward task.

By using automation rules instead, we gain a lot more flexibility in how we synchronize code commits with their corresponding Jira issues.

Let's take a look at how we can leverage automation rules to achieve this.

Creating a rule to transition issues on code commits

For this example, we will create a rule that listens for a commit created using Bitbucket Cloud and transitions the corresponding issue to **In Progress** if it is not already in that status.

In addition, we will send a message for every commit to the *#sprint-updates* Slack channel, which we set up in *Chapter 4, Sending Automated Notifications*. In reality though, you would probably not want to spam the developers with commit notifications and rather wait for a more significant event, such as the creation of a pull request.

> **Tip**
>
> For automation rules to recognize the issue that needs to be updated, the commit message needs to include the issue key as part of the message. If your developers create a branch for each issue they work on, the issue key needs to be a part of the branch name.
>
> In both instances, the issue key must follow the standard Jira format of the project key, followed by a dash and then the issue number. For example, if the project key is PROJ and the issue number is 123, the issue key will be *PROJ-123*.

Let's firstly take a look at the rule in *Jira Cloud* using the DevOps triggers available to automation rules:

1. In your Jira Software project, navigate to **Project settings**, click on the **Automation** link in the **Project Settings** menu, and then click **Create rule**.

2. Select the **Commit created** trigger and then click **Save**.

> **Tip**
>
> If you do not already have a Git provider configured for your project, the commit created trigger will prompt you to create a connection, which you can do by clicking on the **Connect now** link.

3. Next, we'll send a Slack message to the **#sprint-updates** channel to notify the team that a commit has been created.

    Select **New action**, then select **Send Slack message** and complete the fields as follows, and then click **Save**:

    Webhook URL: Use the webhook URL you configured in *Chapter 4, Sending Automated Notifications*, in the *Integrating with Slack* section.

    Message:

    ```
    :pizza: A commit for <{{issue.url}}|{{issue.key}}> has
    been added with message {{commit.message}}>
    ```

    Channel or user: #sprint-updates

4. In this step, we'll add a condition to check that the current status of the issue is not **In Progress** before we transition it.

    Select **New condition**, followed by **Issue fields condition**, complete the following fields, and then click **Save**:

    Field: Status

    Condition: does not equal

    Value: In Progress

5. Next, if the condition from *step 4* is satisfied, we'll transition the issue to **In Progress**.

    Click on **New action** and then select **Transition issue**. Set the **Destination** field to **In Progress** and then click **Save**.

    Your rule should now look similar to the following screenshot:

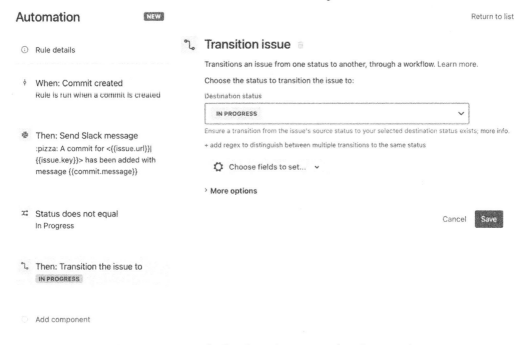

Figure 8.1 – Using the DevOps trigger to synchronize commits

6. Finally, name the rule Transition to In Progress on commit and click **Turn it on** to save and publish the rule.

Automation rules for Jira Server and Data Center do not currently include DevOps triggers, and so we need to make use of the incoming webhook trigger to achieve a similar result.

In this example, we'll first set up the incoming webhook automation rule in Jira, after which we'll copy the generated webhook URL, which we'll need to set up the outgoing webhook in the Bitbucket Cloud repository.

Let's now take a look at how we build this rule in *Jira Server* or *Jira Data Center*:

1. In your Jira Software project, navigate to **Project settings**, click on the **Project automation** link in the **Project Settings** menu, and then click **Create rule**.

2. Bitbucket Cloud sends a *push* webhook when a commit is created and sends a webhook payload, which you can read more about at `https://support.atlassian.com/bitbucket-cloud/docs/event-payloads/#EventPayloads-entity_repository`.

    In this example, we are assuming that the issue key is present in the commit message rather than the branch name. We will need to extract the issue key from the commit message in order to look up the correct Jira issue. Based on the Bitbucket payload structure detailed in the preceding link, we can find the commit message and extract the issue key using the following smart value:

    ```
    {{webhookData.push.changes.first().new.target.message.
    match("([A-Z][A-Z0-9]+-\d+)")}}
    ```

    > **Tip**
    >
    > If you are using branches per issue and the issue key is encoded in the branch name, you can extract the issue key from the branch name with the following smart value instead: `{{webhookData.push.changes.first().new.target.name.match("([A-Z][A-Z0-9]+-\d+)")}}`.

    Select the **Incoming webhook** trigger, complete the fields as follows, and then click **Save**:

    Webhook URL: Copy the autogenerated URL for use later in Bitbucket Cloud.

Execute this automation rule with: `Issues provided by running the following JQL search`

JQL: `key = {{webhookData.push.changes.first().new.target.message.match("([A-Z][A-Z0-9]+-\d+)")}}`

3. Next, we'll send a Slack message to the **#sprint-updates** channel to notify the team that a commit has been created.

    Select **New action**, followed by **Send Slack message**, complete the fields as follows, and then click **Save**:

    Webhook URL: Use the webhook URL you configured in *Chapter 4*, *Sending Automated Notifications*, in the *Integrating with Slack* section.

    Message:

    ```
    :pizza: A commit for <{{issue.url}}|{{issue.key}}> has
    been added with message {{commit.message}}
    ```

    Channel or user: `#sprint-updates`

4. In this step, we'll add a condition to check that the current status of the issue is not **In Progress** before we transition it.

    Select **New condition**, followed by **Issue fields condition**, complete the fields as follows, and then click **Save**:

    Field: `Status`

    Condition: `does not equal`

    Value: `In Progress`

5. Next, if the condition from *step 4* is satisfied, we'll transition the issue to **In Progress**.

    Click on **New action** and then select **Transition issue**. Set the **Destination** field to **In Progress** and then click **Save**.

Your rule should now look similar to the following screenshot:

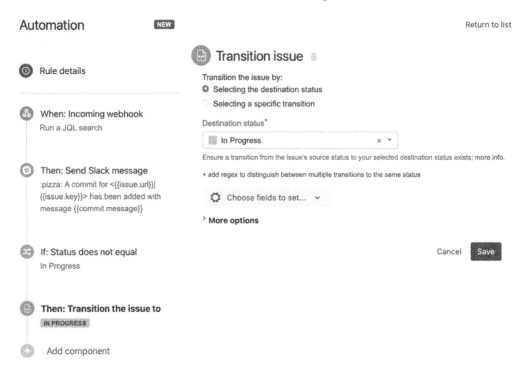

Figure 8.2 – Using an incoming webhook trigger to synchronize commits

6. Name the rule `Transition to In Progress on commit` and click **Turn it on** to save and publish the rule.

7. Next, we need to configure the outgoing webhook in Bitbucket Cloud.

    Navigate to your repository in Bitbucket Cloud and click on **Repository settings**, select the **Webhooks** link, and then click **Add webhook**.

    Name the webhook `Transition Jira issue on commit` and paste the Incoming webhook URL, which was generated in step 2, into the **URL** field.

    Leave the rest of the fields set to their default values and click **Save**.

Your Bitbucket Cloud webhook should look similar to the following screenshot:

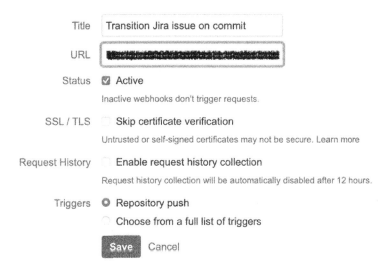

Figure 8.3 – Configuring the push webhook in Bitbucket Cloud

Now that we have completed the webhook setup in Bitbucket Cloud, any commits pushed to the Bitbucket repository will send a request to the **Webhook URL** that was autogenerated in *step 2*, causing our automation rule to fire and transition the issue related to the commit.

In this section, we have learned how to use the DevOps triggers available in Jira Cloud to automatically keep issues in Jira in sync with commits to a Git repository hosted in Bitbucket Cloud.

> **Important note**
>
> The DevOps triggers such as Commit created in Jira Cloud work with most major Git repositories, including Bitbucket Cloud, GitHub, and Gitlab, and the example we have looked at using Jira Cloud will work unchanged for any of these tools.

We also looked at how we can achieve a similar result for Jira Server and Jira Data Center using an incoming webhook for Bitbucket Cloud using issue keys in commit messages specifically.

In the next section, we'll look at how to use automation rules to keep track of pull requests created in Git-based repositories.

Keeping track of pull requests

A common feature of DevOps practices is the use of the so-called trunk-based development method, which is a key enabler for the application of **Continuous Integration** and **Continuous Delivery** or **Development (CI/CD)** to the software development process.

One of the ways to achieve this is by making use of short-lived branches taken from the master (or trunk) branch to perform development tasks. Jira facilitates this by allowing developers to automatically create branches for each development task when a source control repository such as Bitbucket or GitHub is configured for the software project.

These short-lived branches are usually merged back into the master/trunk branch by way of pull requests, which allow developers to review the changes introduced into the software before merging them into the master branch.

In this section, we will see how using automation rules allows us to keep track of these pull requests, which typically happen directly inside the source control repository, and to automatically synchronize and transition the affected issues in Jira.

We'll also see how to create automated tasks to track pull requests. These tracking tasks will allow product owners and the team to quickly see which issues have been merged without pull requests, or which issues have outstanding pull requests without leaving Jira.

Let's take a look at the first rule, which will synchronize the development issue and create the tracking task.

Creating a rule to track new pull requests

In this example, the first thing we want to achieve when managing pull requests is to transition the corresponding development issue into a **Waiting for review** status and then create a tracking task in Jira that is linked to the development issue under review.

> **Tip**
> The **Waiting for review** status will need to be added to your workflow for this example to work correctly. If you have used the default workflow from the *Scrum software project template*, you can do this by adding a new column to your scrum board through the board configuration. If you have a custom workflow, you will need to edit the workflow to add this status.

Additionally, we'll send a Slack message to the team to notify them that a new pull request task has been created. This will allow any member of the development team to pick up and review the pull request.

Let's take a look at how we build this rule:

1. In your Jira Software project, navigate to **Project settings**, click on the **Automation** link in the project settings menu, and then click **Create rule**.

2. Select the **Pull request created** trigger and then click **Save**.

3. Next, we want to transition the development issue to the **Waiting for review** status.

   Select **New action**, followed by **Transition issue** and then, in the **Destination status** field, select the **Waiting for review** option and then click **Save**.

4. Then we need to create the Jira task to track this pull request.

   Select **New action** and then select **Create issue**. In the **Choose fields to set** dropdown, ensure that **Description** and **Linked Issues** are selected, complete the fields as follows, and then click **Save**:

   Project: `Same project`

   Issue type: `Task`

   Summary: `Review PR: {{pullRequest.title}}`

   Description:

   `Review is required for PR: {{pullRequest.title}}`

   `Source branch: {{pullRequest.sourceBranch}}`

   `Destination branch: {{pullRequest.destinationBranch}}`

   `Access the PR here: {{pullRequest.url}}`

   Linked Issues: `blocks`

   Issue: `Trigger issue`

5.   To send a notification to the team via Slack, we'll select **New action** followed by
     Send Slack message.

     Complete the fields as follows and then click **Save**:

     Webhook URL: Use the webhook URL you configured in *Chapter 4, Sending
     Automated Notifications*, in the *Integrating with Slack* section.

     Message:

     ```
     :bellhop_bell: A new pull request has been created and is
     ready for review <{{createdIssue.url}}|{{createdIssue.
     key}}>
     ```

     Channel or user: #slack-updates.

     Your rule should look similar to the following screenshot:

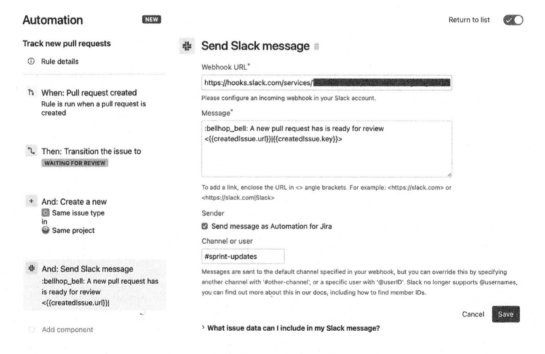

Figure 8.4 – Rule to track new pull requests

6.   Finally, name the rule `Track new pull requests` and click **Turn it on** to save
     and enable the rule.

In this example, we have learned how to use the built in DevOps triggers available in Jira Cloud to trigger rules when new pull requests are created in connected Git tools such as Bitbucket and GitHub, provided these tools are configured in Jira and connected to the software project.

The second rule we'll look at in this section will complete the loop of managing pull requests by handling the case when a pull request has been approved and merged.

Creating a rule to manage merged pull requests

In this example, we'll create an automation rule that will trigger when a pull request is merged. At this point, we want to transition the development issue from **Waiting for review** to **Waiting for deploy**.

> Tip
>
> The **Waiting for deploy** status will need to be added to your workflow in order for this example to work correctly. If you have used the default workflow from the *Scrum software project template*, you can do this by adding a new column to your scrum board through the board configuration. If you have a custom workflow, you will need to edit the workflow to add this status.

Additionally, we also want to automatically transition the tracking task that we created in the **Track new pull requests** rule to **Done**.

Let's now take a look at how we can build a rule to achieve this.

1. In your Jira Software project, navigate to **Project settings**, click on the **Automation** link in the **Project Settings** menu, and then click **Create rule**.

2. Select the **Pull request merged** trigger and then click **Save**.

3. As we only want to transition the issue if it is in *Waiting for review* status, we need to have a condition to check for this.

   Select **New condition** followed by **Issue fields condition**. Complete the condition fields as follows and then click **Save**:

   Field: Status

   Condition: equals

   Value: Waiting for review

4.   Next, select **New action** followed by **Transition issue** and then, in the **Destination status** field, select **Waiting for deploy** and then click **Save**.

5.   Now we want to automatically transition the tracking task that we created in the *Creating a rule to track new pull requests* section to **Done**. The tracking task was linked to the development task using a *blocks* link type, so in this rule, we'll need to use the inverse of the link type relationship to find the tracking task, which, in this case, is *is blocked by*.

    To achieve this, we will need to select the **Branch rule / related issues** component, complete the fields as follows, and then click **Save**:

    Type of related issues: `Linked issues`

    Link types: `is blocked by`

6.   As there might be other tasks linked to this issue using the same link type, we want to ensure that we only automatically transition the tracking task, so we'll need another condition.

    Select **New condition**, followed by **Issue fields condition**, complete the fields as follows, and then click **Save**:

    Field: `Summary`

    Condition: `starts with`

    Value: `Review PR:`

7.   Now select **New action** followed by **Transition issue**. In the **Destination status** field, select **Done** and then click **Save**.

The rule should now look similar to the following screenshot:

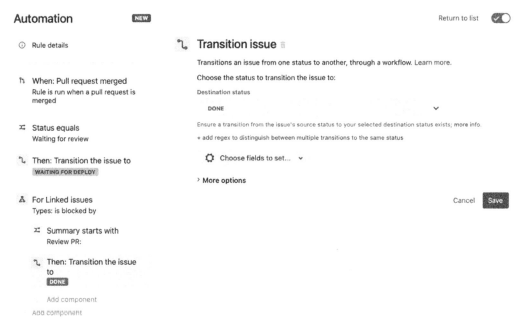

Figure 8.5 – Rule to manage pull request merges

8. Finally, name the rule `Manage pull request merges` and click **Turn it on** to save and enable the rule.

We now know how to integrate pull requests with Jira using automation rules. Firstly, to ensure that the development issues are synchronized with the actual work being done by the development team, and secondly, to keep track of which issues have been or still need to be merged into the master branch. In the next section, we'll see how to specifically use automation rules to integrate with the release functionality available in GitHub.

Automatically releasing versions using GitHub

Version control tools allow developers to tag specific revisions of their source code, which, in effect, creates a snapshot of the repository at a point in time. The most common use for tags is to identify the source components and files that make up a particular version or release of the software and tools such as GitHub and GitLab take this a step further by allowing developers to create a release based on a particular tag. These typically consist of the list of changes applicable to this particular release in the form of release notes. They can also include links to the list of assets that make up the release, which are typically downloadable binary packages.

Releases can be created using the tool's user interface, but most commonly are created automatically by build tools such as Bitbucket Pipelines or Jenkins upon the successful completion of a deployment build. These tools can, in turn, fire webhook events to notify other tools when a release has been created.

With automation rules in Jira, we can use incoming webhooks to receive these notifications and automatically release the corresponding version in Jira and simultaneously transition all the affected issues linked to that version to *Done*. Let's now take a look at a rule that will allow us to achieve that.

Creating a rule to synchronize version releases to GitHub releases

In this rule, we'll create an incoming webhook that can be called by GitHub when a release is created. The GitHub release webhook contains a JSON payload from which we'll be able to extract the name of the tag that identifies the release. In turn, this tag name should correspond to the versions in your Jira Software project.

The structure of the GitHub release payload is similar to the following, and we'll be using the `action` and `tag_name` fields in our rule:

```
{
    "action": "published",
    "release": {
        ...
        "tag_name": "1.0",
        ...
    }
}
```

You can read more about the event payload at the following URL: https://docs.github.com/en/free-pro-team@latest/developers/webhooks-and-events/webhook-events-and-payloads#release.

You can also learn more about GitHub webhooks and events in general at the following URL: https://docs.github.com/en/free-pro-team@latest/developers/webhooks-and-events/about-webhooks.

Let's take a look at the steps required to build an automation rule to synchronize the release of a Jira version when a version is released from GitHub:

1. In your Jira Software project, navigate to **Project settings**, click on the **Automation** link in the **Project settings** menu, and then click **Create rule**.

2. Select the **Incoming webhook** trigger and, in the **Execute this automation rule with** field, select the **No issues from the webhook** option and then click **Save**.

    Make sure to copy the webhook URL that was automatically generated as we'll need this later to configure the GitHub webhook.

3. GitHub will send a webhook event for different states of the release; however, for this rule, we are only interested in acting on the event when the release is published, which we can check by looking at the **action** field from the webhook payload.

    Select **New condition** followed by **Advanced compare condition**. Complete the fields as follows and then click **Save**:

    First value: `{{webhookData.action}}`

    Condition: `equals`

    Second value: `published`

4. The first thing we want to do if the condition in *step 3* matches is to automatically transition all the issues that belong to the release and are currently waiting to be deployed to **Done**.

    Select **Branch rule / related issue**, complete the fields as follows, and then click **Save**:

    Type of related issues: `JQL`

    JQL: `fixVersion = {{webhookData.release.tag_name}} AND status = "Waiting for deploy"`

5. Then we select **New action**, followed by **Transition issue**, and set the **Destination status** field to **Done** before clicking **Save**.

6. Next, we want to release the Jira version that corresponds to the tag name of the GitHub release.

    We need to do this outside the **Branch rule / related issues** block, so click on the last **Add component** link in the rule view on the left and then select **New action**, followed by **Release version**. Expand the **More options** disclosure, set the **Specific version name to release** field to the value `{{webhookData.release.tag_name}}` and then click **Save**.

The rule should now look similar to the following screenshot:

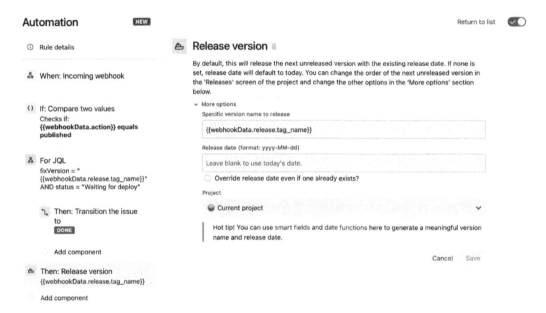

Figure 8.6 – Automatically releasing a Jira version from GitHub

7. Finally, name the rule `Synchronize versions with GitHub releases` and click **Turn it on** to save and enable the rule.

Now that we have the automation rule in Jira, we will need to complete the configuration in GitHub using the webhook URL generated previously in *step 2*.

Let's now configure our GitHub repository to send release notifications to our automation rule in Jira:

1. Navigate to your repository in GitHub, click on **Settings**, select the **Webhooks** tab from the menu on the left, and then click on the **Add webhook** button.

2. Complete the webhook fields as follows:

    Payload URL: Paste the webhook URL generated in *step 2* from the automation rule.

    Content type: `application/json`

    SSL verification: `Enable SSL verification`

3.   To ensure that we receive the correct event in the automation rule, select the **Let me select individual events** option in the **Which events would you like to trigger this webhook** field.

Make sure to deselect the **Pushes** option, select the **Releases** option, and then click **Add webhook**.

Your GitHub configuration should look similar to the following screenshot:

Figure 8.7 – Configuring the releases webhook in GitHub

We have now learned how to integrate Jira with GitHub releases and how we can use automation rules to release the corresponding version in Jira after transitioning all the affected development tasks to **Done**. In the next section, we'll look at how to automatically kick off deployment builds using Jenkins when a sprint is completed.

Synchronizing deployments with sprint completion

In Agile scrum, one of the artifacts created during a sprint is the **Product increment**, which is the deliverable produced by completion of the product backlog tasks during a sprint. In this section, we'll learn how to integrate with Jenkins using automation rules to automatically initiate the final deployment build when the sprint in Jira is closed.

During a sprint, in a trunk-based development model, developers will commit code to the branch in the source repository associated with the development task, which will generally initiate automated tests to verify that the new code does not negatively affect the build process. When pull requests are created and merged, further automated tests can be initiated followed by automated deployments to QA or staging servers. By the time the sprint is completed, all these processes result in the final task of deploying the resultant product increment to production, or by using a tool such as GitHub to create a release.

Let's take a look at how this is achievable using automation rules.

Creating a rule to start a deployment build

In this example, we'll create a rule that will initiate a production build of a software project each time a sprint is completed. To achieve this, we first need to configure the job in Jenkins to allow builds to be triggered remotely by scripts.

> **Tip**
> If you do not already have a Jenkins instance, you can sign up for an AWS account at `https://aws.amazon.com` and launch a new EC2 instance based on the *Jenkins Certified by Bitnami* AMI. This AMI contains full instructions on how to get up and running with Jenkins in AWS.

We'll start by navigating to the project in Jenkins. In the project's **Configuration** screen, select the **Build Triggers** tab and then select the **Trigger builds remotely** option. Jenkins requires an authentication token to be provided to ensure that only remote systems that know this token can kick off the build job.

This token can be any text string of your choosing. In our example, we're going to use `MY_SECURE_AUTH_TOKEN` as the **Authentication Token**. Once you have configured Jenkins, the **Build Triggers** section should look similar to the following screenshot:

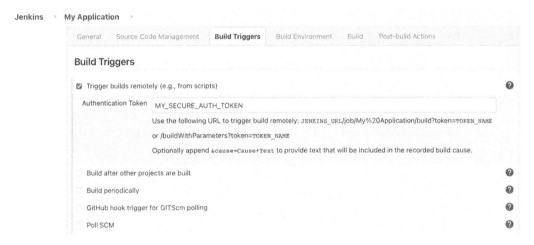

Figure 8.8 – Configuring Jenkins to allow the triggering of builds remotely

Now that we have Jenkins configured, let's build the automation rule to initiate deployment when our sprint is completed:

1. In your Jira Software project, navigate to **Project settings**, click on the **Automation** link in the **Project settings** menu, and then click **Create rule**.

2. Select the **Sprint completed** trigger and, in the **Boards** field, select the Scrum board for your project and then click **Save**. In this example, we'll select **My Application Scrum Board**.

3. Sending API requests to Jenkins requires us to acquire an API crumb from the Jenkins crumb issuer service. This service returns a crumb that we later need to use to interact with the API in the following format:

```
{
    "_class": "hudson.security.csrf.DefaultCrumbIssuer",
    "crumb": "18b1846…",
    "crumbRequestField": "Jenkins-Crumb"
}
```

To do this, select **New action** and then select **Send web request**. Complete the web request fields as follows and then click **Save**:

WebhookURL: `https://<your_jenkins_host>/crumbIssuer/api/json`

Headers name: `Authorization`

Headers value: `Basic <your base64-encoded credentials>`

HTTP method: `GET`

Webhook body: `Empty`

Wait for response: Ensure that this option is checked so that we can retrieve the crumb in the `{{webhookResponse}}` smart value.

4.   Next, we need to make the call to the Jenkins API to kick off the deployment build that we configured in Jenkins.

We will also need to send the Jenkins crumb that we retrieved in *step 3* in the *Jenkins-Crumb* header.

Again, select **New action** followed by **Send web request**. Complete the fields as follows and then click **Save**:

Webhook URL: `https://<your_jenkins_host>/job/<your_job_name>/build?token=<YOUR_AUTHORIZATION_TOKEN>`

Fill the following in the first **Headers** field:

Name: `Authorization`

Value: `Basic <your base64-encoded credentials>`

Fill in the following second **Headers** field:

Name: `Jenkins-Crumb`

Value: `{{webhookResponse.body.crumb}}`

HTTP method: `POST`

Webhook body: `Empty`

Wait for response: Ensure that this option is checked so that we can retrieve the status of the request from the `{{webhookResponse}}` smart value.

5. If the build is successfully kicked off in Jenkins, we want to transition all the issues in the sprint that were waiting for deployment to **Done**.

    Typically, Jenkins will respond with an HTTP 201 status; however, we'll check for any success status code that is in the range 200 to 299.

    > **Tip**
    >
    > The `{{webhookResponse}}` smart value will always contain the response from the latest **Send web request** action in your rule. If you want to refer to the response from a previous web request, you can use the `{{webhookResponses}}` list, which will contain the responses in order of the web request actions, starting from position zero (0). Also note that responses will only be added to this list if you have checked the **Wait for response** option in the corresponding **Send web request** action.

    Select **New condition** followed by **Advanced compare condition**. Complete the fields as follows and then click **Save**:

    First value: `{{webhookResponse.status}}`

    Condition: `exactly matches regular expression`

    Regular expression: `2\d\d`

6. Next, select **Branch rule / related issues** followed by **Issues in the sprint** in the **Type of related issues** field and then click **Save**.

7. Then, select **New condition** followed by **Issue fields condition**. Complete the condition fields as follows and then click **Save**:

    Field: `Status`

    Condition: `equals`

    Value: `Waiting for deploy`

8. Now we need to transition the issues if they match the condition in *step 7*.

    Select **New action** followed by **Transition issue**. In the **Destination status** field, select **Done** and then click **Save**.

Your rule should look similar to the following screenshot:

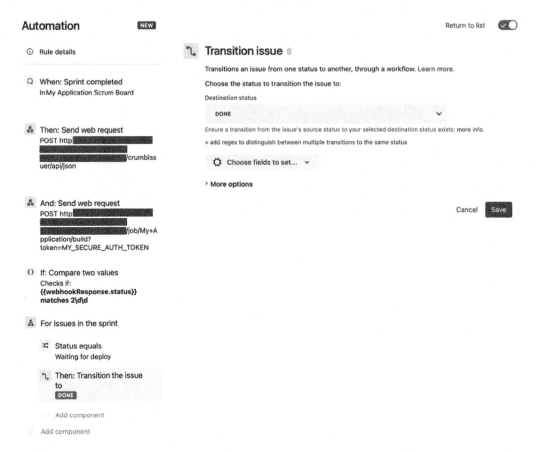

Figure 8.9 – Rule to start Jenkins deployment upon sprint closure

9. Finally, name the rule `Start deployment on sprint closure` and click **Turn it on** to save and enable the rule.

This concludes the final section of this chapter, in which we have learned how to use automation rules to integrate with Jenkins to automatically kick off deployment builds when a sprint is completed and to transition all the affected development tasks to **Done**.

Summary

In this chapter, we have learned how using automation rules can help us with DevOps practices by optimizing our development and operations processes.

We have covered how to use the built-in DevOps automation triggers available in Jira Cloud to integrate with our source repositories, such as Bitbucket or GitHub. This allows us to keep development issues in Jira in sync with the code as it is committed to the source repository.

In addition, we have also learned how we can achieve similar integrations when using Jira Server or Data Center by using incoming webhooks in our rules in place of the DevOps triggers available to Jira Cloud.

Next, we learned how we could use the DevOps pull request triggers available in Jira Cloud to automatically synchronize the development tasks in Jira. We also learned how to create and manage tracking tasks, which provide greater visibility into the overall development process within Jira.

We then learned how, when using GitHub to manage software releases, we can also use automation rules to release transition the affected issues in Jira to **Done** and how to automatically keep the version in Jira in sync when creating a GitHub release. Finally, we learned how to automatically initiate a deployment build of a software project in Jenkins whenever a sprint in Jira is completed.

By introducing automation rules into our Jira processes, we can streamline our DevOps processes and drastically reduce the amount of time developers need to perform tasks in multiple tools.

In the next chapter, we will be exploring some best practices to follow when creating automation rules in Jira.

9
Best Practices

The ability to automate tasks and processes in Jira opens up a whole new world of possibilities for streamlining your projects and improving productivity.

This, in turn, brings about its own complexities, and if approached in a haphazard manner, you could very well end up with a bunch of rules that instead of increasing productivity end up causing more pain than before you started.

Having a set of guidelines to help you get the most out of your automation journey is what this chapter is all about.

We will learn where to begin by planning your rules, before diving into implementing them and how to approach writing your rules to ensure you maximize performance. Finally, we will be looking at some best practices to organize your rules to make it easier to manage and maintain them.

In this chapter, we'll cover the following topics:

- Planning your rules
- Thinking about performance
- Organizing your rules

Technical requirements

The requirements for this chapter are as follows:

- **Jira cloud environment**: If you don't already have access to Jira, you can create a free Jira cloud account at `https://www.atlassian.com/software/jira/free` and ensure that you have both **Jira Software** and **Jira Service Management** selected.

- **Jira server environment**: If you are using Jira Server (available from `https://www.atlassian.com/software/jira/download`), ensure you have licenses for both Jira Software and Jira Service Management. In addition, you will also need to ensure that you install the *Automation for Jira* app, available from the Atlassian Marketplace.

You will need to be a global Jira administrator in order to follow the examples in this chapter. In addition, we have used the *Scrum software project template* to create the two software projects that these examples run against.

You can download the latest code samples for this chapter from this book's official GitHub repository at `https://github.com/PacktPublishing/Automate-Everyday-Tasks-in-Jira`. Please visit the following link to check the CiA videos: `https://bit.ly/3oVOYw1`

Planning your rules

Before you jump in and start creating automation rules, you should have a clear purpose about what you want to automate and how to approach your desired outcome, and these are things that you should think about in the planning stages.

Having an automation strategy in place first will ensure that your automation rules are fit for purpose, are efficient, and meet the objectives of the organization.

In this section, we will look at some of the best practices for planning your rules.

Planning your automation strategy

It is worth keeping in mind that the primary purpose of automation is to streamline your business and to ensure that your processes work more efficiently.

When planning what to automate, one of the first things you should do is engage with your users. This will uncover valuable insight into which tasks they spend the most time doing and how you could leverage automation rules to increase their productivity.

You should also take into account the usage patterns of existing requests in your system to identify whether there are any automation opportunities you could apply to improve overall efficiency.

By planning your rules ahead of time and ensuring they align with your overall business and process objectives, you will have a clear idea of what you should automate to ensure the overall success of your automation efforts.

Next, we'll look at why using the appropriate scope for your rules should be taken into account during rule planning.

Scoping your rules

As we saw in *Chapter 1, Key Concepts of Automation*, rules in Jira can be applied in one of four scopes:

- **Single or project-specific rules**: This scope is applied automatically to a rule when it is created within a project. An example rule in this scope would be the scheduled creation of a project-specific task.

- **Multi-project rules**: This scope is enabled by naming specific projects to which a rule applies and can only be applied by a Jira administrator. An example of a rule in this scope would be keeping software versions in sync between two projects.

- **Global rules**: This scope is applied automatically when a rule is created from the global administration view by Jira administrators. Rules in this scope apply to every project in the instance. An example rule in this scope would be to close an issue when it is marked as a duplicate.

- **Project type-specific rules in the Jira cloud**: This scope is applicable to the Jira cloud only and allows a rule to be applied to all projects of a specific type. For example, a rule to close a customer request that has not been updated for 5 business days could be applied to all *service projects*.

This is an important aspect to consider as part of the planning for your automation rules.

One of the main purposes of using automation is to improve the efficiency of processes and this is true when deciding how to scope the automation rules themselves.

It is common for multiple projects in a Jira instance to share workflows and other common configurations. In the case where a rule is also common across projects, it is more efficient to maintain a single rule than to have duplicate rules that need to be maintained individually.

This obviously needs to be balanced with the fact that global and multi-project rules can only be maintained by users with global Jira administrator permissions and not by project administrators.

Thinking about rule design

Once you have determined how your rules fit in with the overall business and process strategy for your organization, the next thing to focus on is designing the actual automation rules themselves.

One of the key principles of automation is to simplify processes and reduce repeatable work, so you want to try and avoid creating rules that are overly complex and difficult to understand.

Your rules should be atomic and it should be as simple as possible to get the stated task done. Always keep in mind that automation rules usually persist long after the original author has moved on to other endeavors and they should be straightforward enough that others can understand how the rules work and how they work together.

This leads us on to the next point: documenting your rules. It is always good practice to document every rule. You should include in the documentation the business case for the rule, which should align with your existing stated business goals.

The documentation for the rule should also include any dependencies the rule has on other rules or external systems. For example, if the rule can be triggered by the completion of another rule, this should be included in the documentation.

Ensuring your rules are well documented achieves a couple of things:

- It ensures business continuity. When the original rule author moves on, their replacements can quickly understand the purpose behind the rules.

- It promotes visibility. Other project administrators can quickly see whether there are any existing rules that could be utilized in their projects instead of reinventing the wheel.

Lastly, you should keep a copy of your rules in a version control system such as Bitbucket or GitHub. Not only will this ensure you have backups of each rule, but it will also allow you to keep track of the change history of each rule.

You will undoubtedly come across a situation where someone performs a change to a rule that, in the best case, causes some minor errors, or at worst, causes a major incident.

Having the ability to quickly roll back the offending rule to a known working version will enable you to resolve these types of incidents efficiently.

Automation for Jira allows you to export a copy of each rule that can be downloaded in JSON format and that you can then save in your version control system of choice.

In the following screenshot, we can see how clicking on the ellipsis (...) button to the right of an individual rule gives you the option to export the rule:

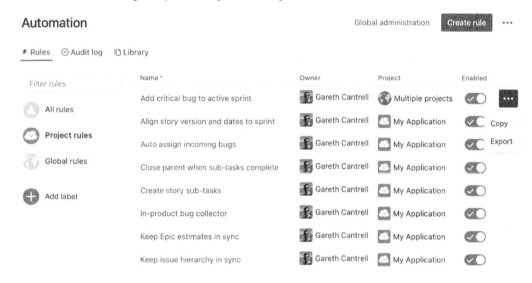

Figure 9.1 – Exporting an individual rule to JSON

Jira administrators also have the option of exporting all the automation rules in the system in a single, downloadable, JSON-formatted file.

Doing this on a scheduled basis and storing the resultant file in version control will allow an administrator to quickly restore all the automation rules across every project in the case of a more widespread incident.

Jira administrators can perform this operation from the global administrative interface by navigating to the **System** menu using the cog icon and then selecting the **Automation rules** tab from the left-hand menu.

You can use the ellipsis (...) button to the right of the **Create rule** button to access the menu option to export all the rules, as can be seen in the following screenshot:

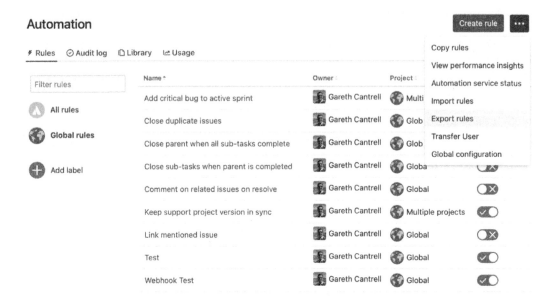

Figure 9.2 – Exporting all rules to JSON

Now that we've understood some of the best practices around planning your rules, let's take a look at an example to illustrate this.

Creating a rule to synchronize high-priority bugs

For this example, we are going to use the following scenario.

We have two software projects in Jira, *My Application* with the project key *MAPP*, which the development team uses to track their development work, and *My Application Support* with the project key *MAPS*, which allows customers to report bugs and raise other requests without inundating the development project with spurious issues.

After speaking with the application support team, we have discovered that manually triaging the highest priority bugs and creating linked development bugs is time-consuming and error-prone. We have also ascertained that there are strict checks in place to limit the creation of the highest priority bugs. The support team can also raise the priority of a bug if required.

Let's use this information to create an automation rule to deal with these particular bugs:

1. We are going to create a global rule as more than one project is involved, so only a Jira administrator can create this rule.

    Click the settings (cog) menu in the top menu bar and select **System**. Then, select the **Automation rules** tab in the left-hand menu and finally, click **Create rule**.

2. The rule needs to work both when the issue is created and when the priority is manually raised, so select the **Multiple issue events** trigger and in the **Issue events** field, select **Issue Created** and **Issue Updated**. Click **Save**.

3. The rule should only apply to bugs in the MAPS project where the priority is highest.

    Select **New condition**, followed by **JQL condition**. Type the following query into the **JQL** field and click **Save**:

    ```
    Project = MAPS AND type = Bug AND priority = Highest
    ```

4. To ensure we don't create multiple bugs in the development project when priorities are changed multiple times, we need to add a further condition to the rule.

    Select **New condition**, and then select **Related issues condition**. Complete the fields as follows and then click **Save**:

    Related issues: `Linked issues`

    Link types: `relates to`

    Condition: `Are not present`

5. Next, we want to create a linked bug in the MAPP project.

    Select **New action**, and then select **Create issue**. From the **Choose fields to set** dropdown, select the `Affects versions`, `Priority`, and `Linked Issues` fields.

    Complete the fields as follows and then click **Save**:

    Project: `My Application (MAPP)`

    Issue type: `Same issue type`

    Summary: Click the ellipsis (…) button and select **Copy from…**

    Description: Click the ellipsis (…) button and select **Copy from…**

    Affects versions: Click the ellipsis (…) button and select **Copy from…**

    Priority: Click the ellipsis (…) button and select **Copy from…**

    Linked Issues: `relates to`

    Issue: `Trigger issue`

The rule should look similar to the following screenshot:

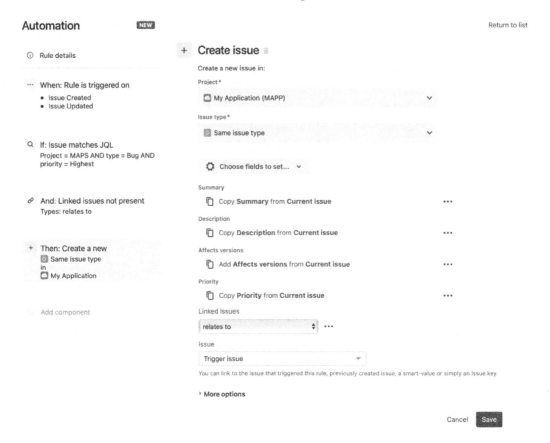

Figure 9.3 – A rule to create linked bugs between projects

6.   Finally, name the rule `Sync highest priority support bugs` and click **Turn it on** to save and enable the rule.

We have learned in this section how planning your rules in advance and ensuring they fit within your overall business and process strategies and are properly documented and controlled will ensure the ultimate success of your automation efforts.

> **Tip**
> Atlassian provides a library of templates that you can use as a starting point for your rules. In addition, an Automation Playground is also provided, which you can use to explore the various rule components and create dummy rules. You can access both of these at `https://www.atlassian.com/software/jira/automation-template-library`.

In the next section, we will take a look at some best practices to follow that will ensure that the rules you write perform efficiently and keep your Jira instance responsive and running smoothly.

Thinking about performance

When planning automation rules for any system, you should ensure that they perform efficiently and do not consume more resources than absolutely necessary. This is essential to maintaining a well-behaved and responsive system.

You are introducing automation to enhance productivity and optimize time-consuming processes. The last thing you want is for the automation themselves to have a negative impact on the system performance.

The automation engine in Jira is designed to maximize performance wherever possible; however, there are some considerations you can take into account when authoring your rules to ensure they perform at their best. We'll take a look at some of these considerations in this section.

Using project-specific rules

The scope of a rule plays an important part when it comes to performance. It determines how many executions are initially queued for a given rule.

If you have 50 projects, for example, and a single global rule that uses the *Create issue* trigger, the rule engine will queue 50 executions when the Create issue event is fired, 1 execution per matching project.

If you add another global rule using the Create issue trigger, 100 executions will be queued, that is, 1 execution per matching trigger per matching project.

As you can see, applying too wide a scope can quickly lead to potential performance issues.

In general, though, the majority of the rules you create will usually be specific to a particular project and the scope should be limited to that project.

Scoping the rule to only the project or projects where it is actually required will ensure that only the minimum number of rule executions will be queued for a given event.

In the next section, we'll look at how choosing the appropriate triggers can lead to the optimized performance of your rules.

Using the appropriate triggers

Another way of ensuring maximum performance is to use an appropriate trigger for your rule. This consideration is particularly useful when your rules are reliant on changes to specific fields.

For example, if you have a rule that should sum all the story points of sub-tasks into the parent task, you could use the **Issue updated** trigger, as can be seen in the following screenshot:

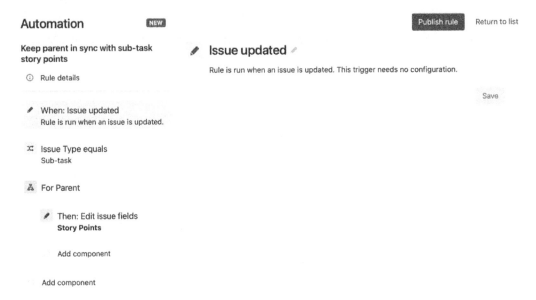

Figure 9.4 – Using an Issue updated trigger for the rule

While this approach is not incorrect and will work perfectly well, a more efficient approach is to use the **Field value changed** trigger and further limit this to the **Edit issue** operation, as can be seen in the following screenshot:

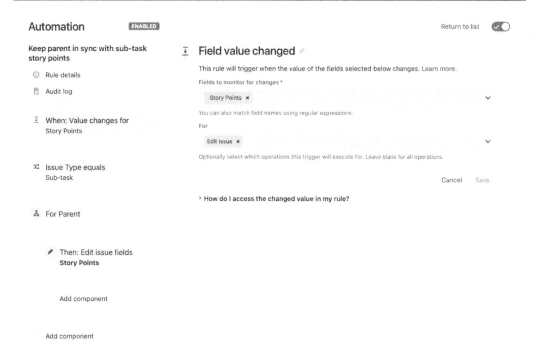

Figure 9.5 – Using the more efficient Field value changed trigger

The reason for this again lies in the fact that when an event is triggered in Jira, the automation engine will queue rule executions that match the trigger.

In the preceding example, using the **Issue updated** trigger will match all the rules that are configured with an **Issue updated** trigger. If, for example, you have 10 rules that use the **Issue updated** trigger, changing the **Story Points** field in a sub-task will result in 10 rule executions to be queued for processing. This is because the rule engine won't know exactly which **Issue updated** rule is relevant.

Changing the rule to use the **Field value changed** trigger and monitoring only the **Story Points** field for the **Edit issue** operation will cause only a single rule execution to be queued, assuming there are no other rules that use this exact same trigger configuration.

Choosing the right conditions

Conditions are used to narrow the scope of the rule by restricting which issues will be affected by further actions in the rule.

The most efficient rules are those that have the least number of issues against which to perform additional actions, so excluding issues that do not need to be processed as early in the rule execution chain as possible will ensure that your rules run as efficiently as possible.

Additionally, not all conditions are created equal. When deciding on which condition to use, the best approach is to consider using the most efficient and performant condition as early as possible.

The conditions listed in order of efficiency, with the highest performance first, are as follows:

- Issue fields condition
- Advanced compare condition
- JQL condition

The **Issue fields** condition works on data already present in the rule at the point where the condition is evaluated and uses simple comparisons to compare the field against a constant value or set of values. As no further processing is required to evaluate, this is the most efficient condition available to your rules.

Where you have multiple fields to compare, you can chain multiple Issue fields conditions together to perform more advanced comparisons and still maintain the overall performance.

The next condition in order of performance is the **Advanced compare** condition. This condition allows the use of smart values and regular expressions and therefore these first need to be resolved before the condition can be evaluated.

Similar to the *Issue fields* condition, you can chain multiple *Advanced compare* conditions together to perform more complex comparisons.

Lastly, the **JQL** condition is the most expensive of these three conditions. It also lets you use the full power of Jira's search facility in your comparisons. The JQL condition can also contain smart values and if used, these first need to be evaluated before the query can be sent to Jira for execution.

Let's re-examine the rule to synchronize the highest priority bugs, which we introduced in the *Planning your rules* section, to see how we can optimize its performance.

Optimizing a rule for performance

In the first iteration of this rule, we created a global rule using the *Multiple issue events* trigger. As we learned, this could potentially have a performance impact on our Jira instance.

This is due to the fact that we used a global scope for the rule as it applies to more than one project. We also used a Multiple issue events trigger to listen for issue creation and update events. Finally, we used a *JQL condition* to narrow the scope of the rule, which we have learned is the least efficient condition available to us.

Let's update the rule to take these performance issues into consideration:

1. As a Jira administrator, click the settings (cog) menu in the top menu bar and select **System**. Then, select the **Automation rules** tab in the left-hand menu and finally, click on the **Sync highest priority support bugs** rule.

2. Firstly, we'll update the trigger to the *Field value changed* trigger.

    Click on the **When: Rule is triggered on** component in the rule-chain view on the left.

    Next, click the pencil icon to the right of **Multiple issue events** to change the trigger.

3. Select the **Field value changed** trigger. Complete the fields as follows and then click **Save**:

    Fields to monitor for changes: `Priority`

    For: `Create issue` and `Edit issue`

4. Next, we are going to switch out the *JQL condition* for the more efficient *Issue fields condition*. We will do this using an *if/else block* to make the rule easier to read.

    Select **New condition** followed by **If/else block**.

5. Click the **Add conditions…** link, then select **Issue fields condition** and complete the fields as follows:

    Field: `Project`

    Condition: `equals`

    Value: `My Application Support (MAPS)`

6. Click the **Add conditions…** link, then select **Issue fields condition** and complete the fields as follows:

    Field: `Issue Type`

    Condition: `equals`

    Value: `Bug`

7. Click the **Add conditions…** link, then select **Issue fields condition** and complete the fields as follows:

   Field: Priority

   Condition: equals

   Value: Highest

8. Click the **Add conditions…** link, then select **Related issues condition** and complete the fields as follows, and then click **Save**:

   Related issues: Linked issues

   Link types: relates to

   Condition: Are not present

9. Delete the **If: Issue matches JQL** condition. You can do this by clicking the **X** in the top-right corner of the component in the rule-chain view, or by selecting the component and clicking the trashcan icon to the right of the name, **JQL condition**.

10. Delete the **If: Linked issues not present** condition by either clicking the **X** in the top-right corner of the component in the rule-chain view or by selecting the component and clicking the trashcan icon to the right of the component name.

11. We then need to move the **Create issue** action into the **If…else block**. This is achieved by clicking and dragging the action in the rule-chain view and dropping it between the **If: all match component** and **Add component** link.

12. The final step is to change the scope of the rule. Click on **Rule details**, complete the following fields, and then click **Save**:

    Scope: Multiple projects

    Restrict to projects: My Application Support (MAPS) and My Application (MAPP)

The rule should now look similar to the following screenshot:

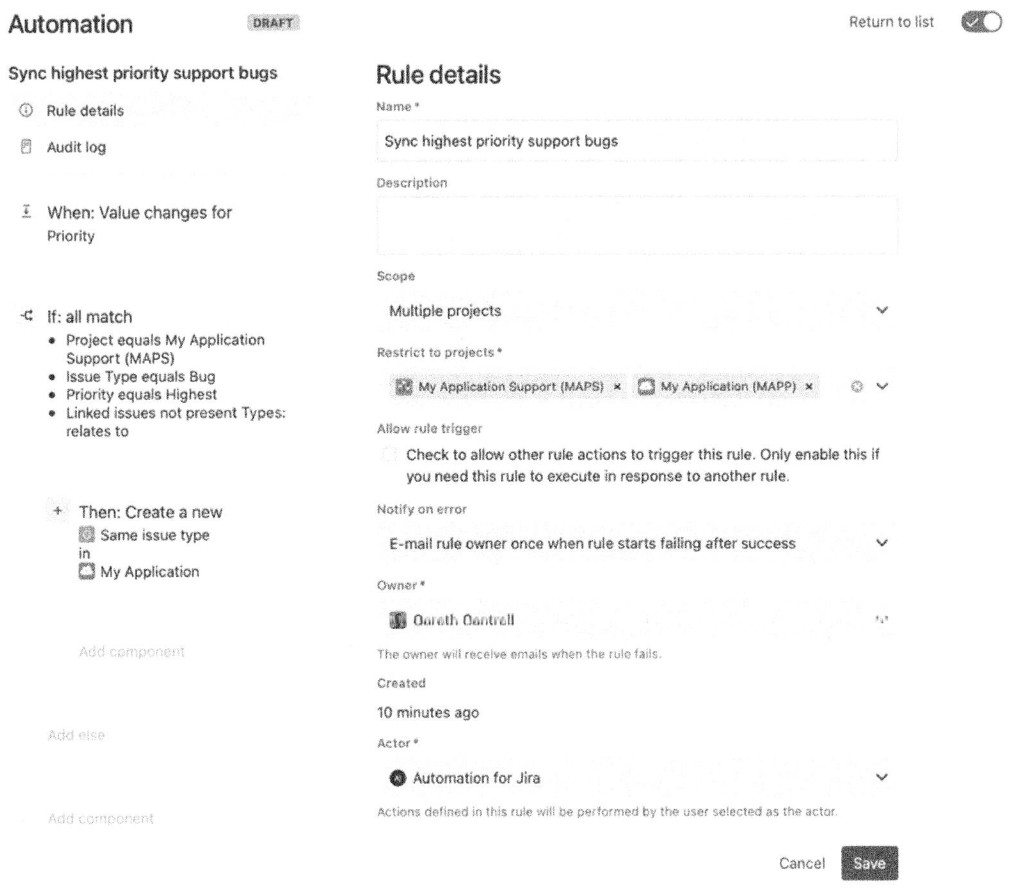

Figure 9.6 – Optimizing the rule for performance

13. Finally, click on **Publish changes** to save the changes we made to the rule.

In this section, we have learned that using the correct scope for your rules can have an impact on performance. We also learned how choosing the appropriate triggers and conditions can keep our rules performing optimally by choosing the most efficient components.

In the next section, we'll take a look at how to organize rules to make them easier to keep track of and manage.

Organizing your rules

Over time, as you automate more and more tasks in more and more of your projects, it is going to become more complex to manage and keep track of all your automation rules.

The best way to deal with an ever-increasing number of automation rules, and configurations in general, is to logically organize each rule.

In this section, we'll look at some best practices to keep your rules optimally organized, which will make them easier to find and manage.

We'll start by looking at what should be a familiar concept to anyone who has had to deal with maintaining large numbers of system configurations: naming conventions.

Using naming conventions

Using a well-defined naming convention allows users to consistently identify rules and allows you to organize your rules in a meaningful way.

A good naming convention needs to be planned in advance, documented, and made visible to everyone who is going to be managing automation rules.

The list of automation rules in Jira is arranged alphabetically and you should make use of this fact when designing your naming convention as it will allow you to group related items together.

> **Note**
> You can sort your automation rules by any of the columns available when working in the list. However, the sort order will always default to alphabetically ascending by name.

For example, your naming convention could state that each rule should be prefixed by the issue type to which it applies. In a software project, this could be something similar to Bug, Epic, Story, Task, and the like. This way, it is immediately apparent what the rule operates on and these rules will always be grouped together when sorted by name.

Apart from establishing naming conventions, it is also good practice to describe in detail what each rule does, using the **Description** field. This will make it immediately clear to anyone looking at the list of rules what in fact is actually happening in the rule without needing to inspect each rule.

In the following screenshot, you can see an example of how using a naming convention will group the rules together:

Figure 9.7 – The rule list with naming conventions applied

Additionally, you can see that by using the rule description to clearly document what the rule is actually doing, it makes it easier to quickly navigate and manage the list of automation rules.

Labeling your rules

In addition to using a naming convention, you can, and should, also define labels to categorize and identify your automation rules.

A **label** in the context of automation rules is a color-coded keyword that you can assign to your automation rules to more easily identify them.

Ideally, you should use short, functional terms for your labels; some examples of functional labels could be the following:

- **Customer notifications**: For rules that send notifications to customers
- **Internal notifications**: For rules that send notifications to team members
- **Support**: For rules that deal with support issues
- **Synchronization**: For rules that deal with keeping issues or other items in sync
- **Software releases**: For rules dealing with versioning in software projects

The preceding list is only a small sample of possible functional label names that you could use in your projects.

Additionally, automation rules can be assigned to multiple labels. For example, a rule that creates a linked bug from a support project into the development project could be labeled with both the **Support** label and the **Synchronization** label.

To create a new label, or to use an existing label that has been previously defined, follow these steps:

1. Click on the **Add label** button in the rule list view on the left.

2. Enter a name for your label in the **Enter label name** field.

3. Optionally, select a color by clicking on the colored block to the right of the field.

    If the label has been previously defined, it will show up in a list below the label name field as you begin typing.

4. To use a previously defined label, simply click on its name.

5. Once you have defined the label name and color, click **Done**.

    You can see how a label is created in the following screenshot:

Figure 9.8 – Adding a new label

Now that you have labels defined, you need to assign your rules to the appropriate labels. You do this by clicking and dragging the rule onto the appropriate label.

Once you have created your labels and assigned your rules accordingly, it becomes much easier to manage large numbers of automation rules by selecting the appropriate label to narrow down the list of rules, as can be seen in the following screenshot:

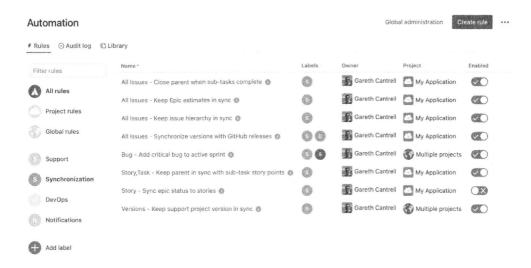

Figure 9.9 – Using labels to quickly find the appropriate rules

Now that we've gained some insight into how we can organize our rules, let's apply this to the rule we optimized in the *Optimizing a rule for performance* section.

Naming and labeling a rule

Let's complete our rule to synchronize the highest priority issues by using a naming convention. We will also use the **Description** field to describe what the rule is doing and then we'll label it appropriately:

1. As a Jira administrator, click the settings (cog) menu in the top menu bar and select **System**. Then, select the **Automation rules** tab in the left-hand menu and finally, click on the **Sync highest priority support bugs** rule.

2. In the **Rule details** view, edit the **Name** and **Description** fields as follows, and then click **Save**:

    Name: `Bug - Sync highest priority support bugs`

    Description: `When a Bug in the MAPS project is created with a priority of Highest or the priority is updated to Highest, create a linked Bug in the MAPP project.`

3. Click **Publish changes** to save the rule, and then click **Return to list** to return to the list of rules.

4. Create two labels, called **Synchronization** and **Support**, and then click and drag the **Bug – Sync highest priority support bugs** rule onto each label in turn.

The rule should now look similar to the following screenshot when listed along with other rules:

Figure 9.10 – Rule organized using naming conventions and labels

We have learned that using a naming convention to organize your rules makes it easier to find and manage them. In addition, using the **Description** field to create a narrative for the rule helps you to quickly identify what the rule is doing. Finally, combining this by applying functional labels will save you both time and frustration when it comes to maintaining your rules in the long term.

Using a checklist

When you are creating your rules, you are not always going to remember all the various points we have discussed in this chapter to ensure that your rules follow best practices.

Having a checklist that you can quickly reference can help in ensuring that you have followed both the best practices we have presented in this chapter and any organizational guidance you have prepared.

We have, therefore, put together a basic checklist that you can use as a starting point to create a checklist in the format that suits you best:

- The rule is correctly scoped to only the project or projects that are affected.

- The rule is documented and includes a business case and implementation approach.

- The rule has been exported and stored in a version control system such as GitHub or Bitbucket.

- An appropriate trigger was used, such as Field value changed rather than Issue updated.

- The rule is using the most efficient conditions, such as the Issue fields condition, and only relies on more expensive conditions later in the rule as necessary.

- The rule is named according to the documented naming conventions.

- The rule description sufficiently describes what the rule is doing.

- The rule is assigned to the appropriate functional labels.

Now that you have a checklist in place, you will be able to use it to quickly identify that your rules follow all the guidelines that you have put in place. In turn, this will ensure that your rules are both manageable and less likely to contribute to performance issues in the long run.

Summary

In this chapter, we learned about some of the best practices to follow when planning, implementing, and organizing your automation rules.

We learned that you should plan your automation strategy upfront to align with your business and process objectives to ensure the ultimate success of your automation efforts in Jira.

We also learned that to ensure business continuity and to avoid unnecessary duplication of effort, your rules should be properly documented in an external system such as Confluence and made visible to the appropriate team members.

Additionally, you should also understand the importance of maintaining external copies of your rules in a version control system such as Bitbucket or GitHub to ensure that any inadvertent breaking changes to rules can be quickly resolved by importing the last known working version of the rule.

Next, we learned how to approach rule writing with performance in mind by using the appropriate project scopes when defining automation rules, and we learned why it is important to use the right triggers and conditions to ensure the optimal performance of automation rules.

Finally, we learned how you could define and use naming conventions to group your rules based on the fact that rules are organized alphabetically by default. We also learned how to use the labeling feature to create labels to organize our rules by functionality.

In the next chapter, we'll look at some tips and techniques to debug your automation rules and how to understand and use service limits and performance insights to monitor the automation rules in your Jira instance.

10
Troubleshooting Tips and Techniques

It is an inevitable fact that at some point, your automation rules will fail with errors or slow down for no apparent reason. Even meticulously planned and implemented rules will eventually be subject to an unforeseen error. In these cases, understanding how to proactively monitor, troubleshoot, and debug your rules will help you solve these issues quicker.

In this chapter, we will introduce you to some tips and techniques to better understand what is happening to your rules and how to debug them. We'll take a look at the audit log and how you can use this to better understand what is going on during your rule executions and how to leverage it for debugging purposes.

We will also learn about the service limits in place to prevent rogue rules from negatively impacting the performance of your instance and how you can proactively monitor your rules to avoid breaching these limits.

Finally, you will learn how to use the performance insight metrics to gain an overview of the performance of the automation rules in your system. This will enable you to identify rules that could potentially cause performance issues, thereby allowing you to maintain and improve the performance of your Jira instance.

In this chapter, we'll cover the following topics:

- Debugging automation rules

- Understanding service limits

- Gaining insights on performance

Technical requirements

The requirements for this chapter are as follows:

- **Jira cloud environment**: If you don't already have access to Jira, you can create a free Jira Cloud account at `https://www.atlassian.com/software/jira/free` and ensure that you have both Jira Software and Jira Service Management selected.

- **Jira Server environment**: If you are using Jira Server (available from `https://www.atlassian.com/software/jira/download`), ensure that you have licenses for both Jira Software and Jira Service Desk. In addition, you will also need to ensure that you install the *Automation for Jira* app available from the Atlassian Marketplace.

In both instances, you will need to have at least **Project Administrator** access to Service Management in order to be able to follow the examples in this chapter. For the examples in this chapter, we have used the *IT Service Management project template* to create the Service Desk project.

You can download the latest code samples for this chapter from this book's official GitHub repository at `https://github.com/PacktPublishing/Automate-Everyday-Tasks-in-Jira`. Please visit the following link to check the CiA videos: `https://bit.ly/2XSttjY`

Debugging automation rules

There are many reasons why automation rules can, and will, fail. These could be due to underlying configuration changes within Jira, or the rule author may not have anticipated an edge case scenario when planning and implementing the rule.

When rules start failing, it is necessary to understand what caused the rule to fail and to either fix the underlying cause or to adjust the automation rule to take into consideration the changes that caused it to fail.

However, debugging is not only about finding and fixing deficiencies in your automation rules or underlying Jira configurations. We can use the same techniques during planning and developing to ensure that we deliver robust rules that are likely to have a higher success rate.

In this section, we will look at how using the audit log for automation rules can help to identify issues and how we can make use of it when debugging our automation rules.

Firstly, let's take a look at the audit log and how it helps us to understand what is happening with our rules.

Understanding the audit log

Every automation rule has an associated audit log containing a list of chronologically ordered items that affect that rule from the time it was created.

These items track not only the creation, modification, and deletion events for the rule, but also every execution of the rule, including the issues affected and the outcomes of every action within the rule.

There are three ways to view the audit log:

- **Global audit log**: The global audit log allows a Jira administrator to see all the audit logs for every project and rule in the system. You can find the global audit log as a Jira administrator by clicking the **settings (cog)** icon in the top menu bar and then selecting **System**. Select the **Automation rules** tab in the left menu and then, in Jira Cloud, select the **Audit log** tab. In *Jira Server* or *Jira Data Center*, click the ellipsis (**…**) button and select **Show audit log**.

- **Project audit log**: The project audit log allows project administrators to see all the audit logs for every rule in that project. To find the project audit log, as a project administrator, navigate to **Project settings**. In *Jira Cloud*, select the **Automation** tab in the left menu and then select the **Audit log** tab. In *Jira Server* or *Jira Data Center*, select the **Project automation** tab in the left menu and then click the ellipsis (**…**) button and select **Show audit log**.

- **Rule audit log**: The rule audit log allows you to see all the log items for that particular rule only. To view the rule audit log, select a rule and then click the **Audit log** item above the **rule-chain** view.

An example of the global audit log can be seen in the following screenshot, showing the audit logs for rules across all projects:

Date	Rule	Projects	Status	Duration	Operations
05/10/20 10:00:40 am (1715017715)	Start-of-week checks	IT Service Desk	SUCCESS	2.95s	Show more
04/10/20 09:37:35 pm (1712809999)	In-product bug collector	My Application	CONFIG CHANGE		Show more
04/10/20 08:59:50 pm (1712722294)	Release issues waiting for deploy	My Application	SUCCESS	9.32s	Show more
04/10/20 08:59:47 pm (1712722250)	Release issues waiting for deploy	My Application	CONFIG CHANGE		Show more
04/10/20 08:59:09 pm (1712721421)	Release issues waiting for deploy	My Application	SOME ERRORS	8.07s	Show more
04/10/20 08:27:37 pm (1712655780)	Release issues waiting for deploy	My Application	SOME ERRORS	6.47s	Show more
04/10/20 08:27:24 pm (1712655426)	Release issues waiting for deploy	My Application	CONFIG CHANGE		Show more
04/10/20 08:26:12 pm (1712653296)	Release issues waiting for deploy	Global	CONFIG CHANGE		Show more
04/10/20 08:22:22 pm (1712645550)	Release issues waiting for deploy	My Application	SUCCESS	7.37s	Show more
04/10/20 08:22:08 pm (1712644596)	Release issues waiting for deploy	Global	CONFIG CHANGE		Show more
04/10/20 08:20:53 pm (1712641125)	Release issues waiting for deploy	My Application	SOME ERRORS	5.57s	Show more
04/10/20 08:20:45 pm (1712640948)	Release issues waiting for deploy	Global	CONFIG CHANGE		Show more
04/10/20 08:19:31 pm (1712637689)	Open issues in sprint notification	My Application	SUCCESS	1.67s	Show more
04/10/20 08:19:14 pm (1712637211)	Release issues waiting for deploy	My Application	SOME ERRORS	5.71s	Show more
04/10/20 08:18:06 pm (1712635908)	Release issues waiting for deploy	Global	CONFIG CHANGE		Show more
04/10/20 08:09:41 pm (1712608586)	Release issues waiting for deploy	My Application	SOME ERRORS	8.42s	Show more
04/10/20 08:09:36 pm (1712608489)	Release issues waiting for deploy	Global	CONFIG CHANGE		Show more
04/10/20 08:08:51 pm (1712607479)	Release issues waiting for deploy	Global	SUCCESS	0.40s	Show more
04/10/20 08:06:43 pm (1712604736)	Sync epic status to stories	My Application	NO ACTIONS PERFORMED	0.15s	Show more
04/10/20 08:06:43 pm (1712604713)	Set user story due date	My Application	NO ACTIONS PERFORMED	1.72s	Show more

Figure 10.1 – The global audit log view in Jira Cloud

Clicking on the name of a rule in the global audit log and project audit log views will take you to the rule audit log view. In each of the rule views, clicking on the **Show more** link in the **Operations** column will expand the audit log details for that particular event.

The following screenshot shows the project audit log view with some of the individual audit items expanded to show the detailed audit log:

Figure 10.2 – The audit log in detail

Let's take a look at each of the items in the audit log:

1. Each audit log has a date and timestamp associated with it that shows precisely when this event occurred, accurate to the second. Audit logs are listed in descending date and time order, with the latest event at the top of the list. The number in brackets next to the date and timestamp is the rule's identification number.

2. This is the name of the rule with which this audit log is associated. In the global audit log and project audit log views, clicking the rule name will take you to the rule audit log for the particular rule. You can also view the audit log history for deleted rules in either the global or project audit log views. Deleted rules are easily identifiable by not having a hyperlink to the rule definition.

3. In this column, you can see whether the rule executed successfully. In addition, it also shows configuration changes to the rule, which help when debugging rule failures.

4. Every time a rule is executed, the time it took to run is recorded and shown in this column.

5. In the case of rule executions, **Associated items** shows which issues were added to the rule execution and by which rule component. Clicking on the component will take you directly to the component configuration responsible for this action. For configuration events, this will show the user who performed the action.

6. All the actions performed by rule execution are listed here, grouped by action. For each action configured in the rule, you will see a list of issues that were successful. If an action was unsuccessful, an error message will be displayed instead. Clicking on any of the actions will take you directly to the action configuration screen.

7. Expanding the **What do the different statuses mean** option will list all the possible status codes and their meanings.

Now that we've learned how to read the audit log, let's take a look at how we can use it to debug our rules.

Using the audit log for debugging

The ability to see what is stored in a smart value or to examine the outcome of a smart value function will give you some insight into what is happening in your rule. This is particularly useful when you are designing a rule or when debugging a rule that is not behaving as expected.

For this purpose, an automation action component, *Log action*, is available to use in your rules. The sole purpose of this component is to inject messages into the audit log, which you can then inspect when debugging a rule.

Let's take a look at an example that utilizes the Log action component.

Logging messages using Log action

The Log action component allows you to inject messages into the audit log so you can add debugging statements to help you understand what is happening when a rule executes.

In this example, we will use the Log action component to add a timestamp to the audit log before and after calling a **Create sub-tasks** action:

1. In your Service Desk project, navigate to **Project settings**, click on the **Automation** tab, and then click on **Create rule**.

2. Select the **Issue created** trigger and then click **Save**.

3. Then select **New condition**, followed by **Issue fields condition**.

    Complete the fields as follows, and then click **Save**:

    Field: Request Type

    Condition: equals

    Value: Onboard new employees

4. Now select **New action**, followed by **Log action**.

    Enter the following message in the **Log message** field and then click **Save**:

    ```
    {{now}} Start create sub-tasks
    ```

5. Next, select **New action** followed by the **Create sub-tasks** action.

    Add two sub-tasks with the following summaries:

    ```
    Provision new laptop by {{issue.duedate.longDate}}
    Setup new desk phone by {{issue.duedate.longDate}}
    ```

6. Again, select **New action** followed by **Log action** and enter the following message in the **Log message** field. Then, click **Save**:

    `{{now}} End create sub-tasks`

7. Next, name your rule `Create onboarding sub-tasks with debug logging` and then click **Turn it on** to save and enable the rule.

    The rule should look similar to the following screenshot:

Figure 10.3 – Creating a rule with debug logging

Now that we have our rule in place, use the **Raise a request** link from your Service Desk project to create a new issue using the *Onboard new employees* request type and then navigate back to the *Create onboarding sub-tasks with debug logging* rule and click on the **Audit log** item.

After expanding the audit log item, you should see something similar to the following screenshot:

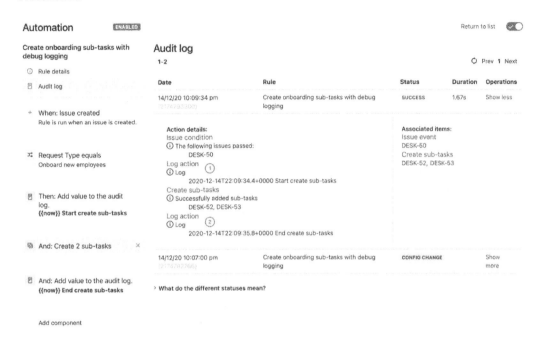

Figure 10.4 – Audit log with debug log messages

You can see in the audit log the messages we inserted around the **Create sub-tasks** action:

1. The first log action message just before the **Create sub-tasks** action is called.

2. The second log action message just after the **Create sub-tasks** action is called.

From this, you can now determine how long the **Create sub-tasks** action is taking to process. In this example, it is taking just over 1 second to complete, which is quite satisfactory. If, however, this was taking minutes, you would probably need to dig deeper into what is causing the delay in creating issues of the Sub-task issue type.

Logging messages using the debug smart value function

Using the Log action to insert messages into the audit log makes debugging your rules a lot easier. However, having too many Log action components to log things such as the output of smart value functions means you have to duplicate your smart values in order to create debug logs.

To get around this, you can use the debug smart value function. This involves surrounding your smart value with the {{#debug}} function.

Let's take a look at an example rule that uses the debug smart value function to achieve this:

1. In your **Service Desk** project, navigate to **Project settings**, click on the **Automation** tab, and then click on **Create rule**.

2. Select the **Issue transitioned** trigger, complete the fields as follows, and then click **Save**:

   From status: Leave blank

   To status: Waiting for customer

3. Now, select **New action** followed by **Comment on issue**. Add the following message to the **Comment** field and then click **Save**:

   Hi {{issue.reporter.displayName}}

   We require some additional information from you to complete your request.

   Please update this issue by {{#debug}}{{now.plusBusinessDays(5).fullDate}}{{/}}.

   Kind regards,

   The Service Desk Team

   Your rule should look similar to the following screenshot:

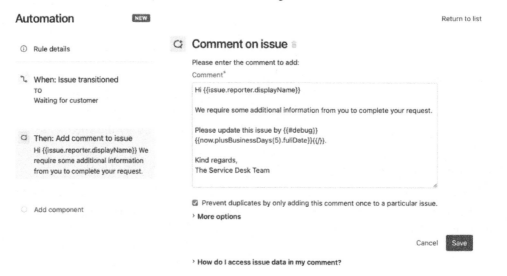

Figure 10.5 – Using the debug smart value function

4. Finally, name the rule `Comment on waiting for customer with debug logging` and then click **Turn it on** to save and enable the rule.

Create an issue of the *Service Request* type, transition it to *Waiting for customer*, and then navigate back to the *Comment on waiting for customer with debug logging* rule and click on the **Audit log** item.

After expanding the top audit log item, your audit log should look similar to the following screenshot:

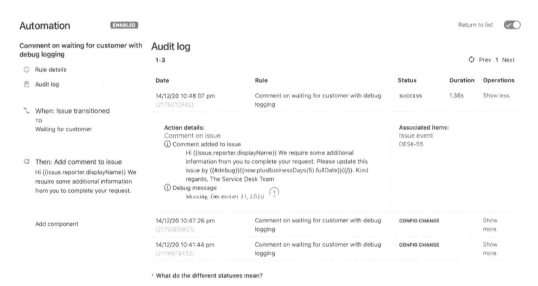

Figure 10.6 – Audit log using the debug smart value function

Using the `{{#debug}}` smart value function has caused a **debug message** to be printed in the audit log, along with the information output by the **Comment on issue** action without needing to add a separate **Log action** component to the rule. You can see this in the item labeled **(1)** in *Figure 10.6*.

We have learned in this section how to understand and use the audit log from a global, project, and rule perspective, and what the various items in the log can tell us.

We have also learned how to send messages to the audit log from our rules to aid in debugging our rules.

In the next section, we will be looking at the service limits that are in place to prevent rules from negatively impacting the performance of your Jira instance.

Understanding service limits

Service limits for automation rules are key to ensuring that automation rules do not have a negative impact on the performance of your Jira instance.

In this section, we'll look at what service limits are in place and how they affect your rules. We'll also look at how to work within these service limits and how we can use automation rules to monitor some of these.

Let's start by looking at what service limits are available.

Getting to know service limits

Service limits are applicable to both the Jira Cloud and Jira Server/Data Center versions of the automation rules.

The service limits that apply to all rules are listed along with a description of how each limit could be breached:

- Components per rule: 65

  Any rule that contains more than 65 conditions, branches, and actions.

- New sub-tasks per action: 100

  A rule that attempts to create more than 100 sub-tasks.

- Issues searched: 1,000

  A JQL search that returns more than 1,000 items will cause this to be breached.

- Concurrent scheduled rule executions: 1

  A rule scheduled to run every 5 minutes, but takes longer than 5 minutes to complete, will cause this limit to be breached as the subsequent execution cannot start while the first execution is still processing.

- Items queued by rule: 5,000 for Jira Cloud, and 25,000 for Jira Server/Data Center

  Any single rule that causes more than the specified number of issues to be queued will breach this limit.

- Items queued globally: 50,000 for Jira Cloud, and 100,000 for Jira Server/Data Center

  The total number of issues queued at any one time cannot exceed the specified limits.

- Daily processing time: 60 minutes per 12 hours

  Any single rule that executes every 5 minutes with a processing time of more than 5 seconds per execution will breach this limit.

- Hourly processing time: 100 minutes

  This limit will only trigger if there are more than 2,000 rule executions per hour on Jira Cloud or 5,000 rule executions per hour on Jira Server/Data Center. This could happen if you perform a bulk operation that causes several rules to fire at the same time.

- Loop detection: 10

  A rule that triggers itself or other rules more than the specified number of times in quick succession.

Dealing with service limit breaches

When rules breach their service limits, the automation engine will throttle the affected rule. The audit log will contain more information and use the *throttled* status to make it easier to identify.

Rules that have been throttled for breaching their service limits will also be disabled so as to prevent any further performance issues.

> **Important note**
> When setting up your rule, you can choose to send the rule owner an email notification when a rule first fails or every time a rule fails. You should be aware that when a notification is sent, the rule will already have been throttled and disabled.

In the case where regularly executing rules are in danger of exceeding their processing time limits, there is a special trigger, the *Service limit breached* trigger, which you can use to monitor your rules. Rather than waiting for the rule to get throttled and disabled, you can set up an automation rule using this trigger to notify you before the breach occurs.

Let's take a quick look at how you can set up an automation rule to watch for and notify you when rules reach 80% of their processing time limit:

1. In your Jira project, navigate to **Project settings**, click on the **Automation** link in the **Project settings** menu, and then click **Create rule**.

2. Select the **Service limit breached** trigger, complete the fields as follows, and then click **Save**:

   When to trigger: `Used more than 80% of the service limit`

   Maximum number of times this rule triggers: `Once per hour`

3. Next, select **New action**, followed by the **Send email** action.

    Complete the fields as follows and then click **Save**:

    To: administrators

    Subject: Rules are about to breach their service limits

    Content:

    There are rules about to breach their 80% processing time limit: {{breachedSummary}}.

    The following rules are about to breach:

    {{breachedRules}}

    The rule should look similar to the following screenshot:

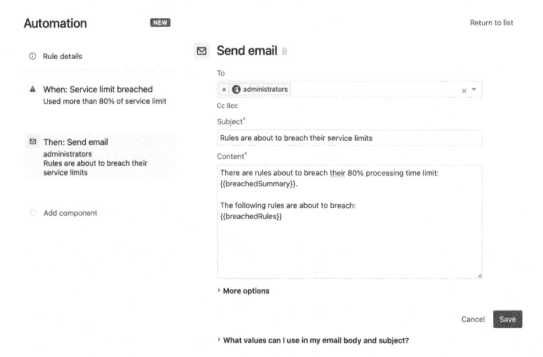

Figure 10.7 – Rule to monitor processing time service limits

4. Finally, name your rule Service limit 80% notification and click **Turn it on** to save and enable the rule.

Now, any time a rule reaches 80% of its processing time limit, an email notification will be sent to the administrators allowing them to take action before the rule gets throttled and disabled.

Working with queued item limits

Automation rules in Jira work by using a rule processing queue. As an example, if you have 50 projects in your Jira instance and a single global automation rule that uses the *Issue updated* trigger, each time a single issue in any project gets updated, 50 rule executions are created and queued.

Adding a second global automation rule that uses the *Issue updated* trigger will cause 100 rule executions to be created and queued; that is, one execution per rule per project.

If, instead, each rule was only specific to a single project, only two rule executions would be created and queued.

As you can imagine, it is quite easy to quickly create a performance bottleneck if you have too many incorrectly scoped rules using non-specific triggers, and this is only one example.

Using JQL searches in a scheduled trigger or in a related issues branch using the *Branch rule / related issues* component can also lead to more issues than the service limits allow being queued per rule.

> **Important note**
> Rules that breach the queued items limit are disabled automatically by the rule engine to prevent any further executions, and the details of the breach are recorded in the audit log.

To prevent your rules from queueing too many items, you should consider the following guidelines:

- Use the narrowest scope possible for your rules. If the rule only needs to operate on a single project or a small group of projects, restrict the scope accordingly.

- Use a trigger such as the *Field value changed* trigger, rather than the *Issue created* or *Issue updated* trigger, when your rule is only interested in changes to a specific field.

- Limit the number of issues returned by JQL queries by making the query as specific as possible.

- Use the *Branch rule / related issues* component sparingly.

In this section, we have learned what the various service limits imposed by the automation rule engine are and how we can use this knowledge to write more efficient rules. In the following section, we'll learn how you can use performance insights to gain an overview of the overall performance of your automation rules.

Gaining insights on performance

To ensure the overall success of your automation rules and that performance is maintained at a satisfactory level requires that you keep an eye out for any issues that could cause problems in the long run.

We have already seen how the audit log can give you insights into whether your rules are running successfully or with errors, or are causing performance issues and being throttled. In addition to this, having the ability to monitor and proactively notify the administrators when rules threaten to breach their service limits helps you to keep an eye on things.

While this does help, it can be time consuming to go through and examine the audit logs, especially when you have a large number of rules executing frequently.

In this section, we'll look at the performance insights feature of automation rules, which will give you a bird's-eye view of the overall performance of your rules.

Performance insights are available to both project administrators and global administrators. Project administrators are able to view the performance of all the rules within their project, while for global administrators, the performance insights give an overview of every automation rule in the system.

To access the performance insights as a project administrator, navigate to **Project settings**, and then select the **Automation** link from the left menu (use the **Project automation** link if you use *Jira Server* or *Jira Data Center*). Then, click the ellipsis (**…**) button and select the **View performance insights** menu item.

To access the global performance insights, click the settings (**cog**) icon in the top menu bar and then select **System**. Click on **Automation rules** in the left menu area and finally, click the ellipsis (**…**) button and select the **View performance insights** menu item.

The performance insights screen is shown in the following screenshot and is similar for both project and global performance insights:

Automation

Return to list

November 14th, 12:00am - December 14th, 6:34pm (Local time)

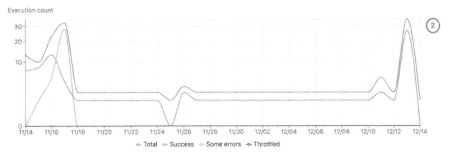

Execution count

○ Total ○ Success ○ Some errors ○ Throttled

Execution count ∨

Rule	Execution count _	Total duration (s)	Average duration (s)	SUCCESS	NO ACTIONS	SOME ERRORS	LOOP	THROTTLED
Commit test	47	29	0.6	13	0	34	0	0
Auto-resolve stale issues	31	14	0.5	0	31	0	0	0
Open issues in sprint notification	30	54	1.8	30	0	0	0	0
Loop test	24	30	1.2	22	0	0	2	0
All Issues - Keep issue hierarchy in sy...	9	20	2.3	4	5	0	0	0
test1	3	6	2.1	3	0	0	0	0
Test	3	1	0.4	1	2	0	0	0
Comment to reporter on issue assign...	3	2	0.5	1	2	0	0	0
Transition to In Progress on commit	2	3	1.4	2	0	0	0	0
Route incoming requests	2	< 1	0.2	0	2	0	0	0
Manage pull request merges	2	5	2.4	2	0	0	0	0
1393252 (deleted rule?)	2	5	2.4	2	0	0	0	0
Reset password bot	2	< 1	0.1	0	2	0	0	0
Sprint - Align story version and dates...	1	9	9.5	1	0	0	0	0
Set user story due date	1	2	1.6	0	1	0	0	0
All Issues - Keep Epic estimates in sync	1	< 1	0.2	0	1	0	0	0
Create story sub-tasks	1	3	2.8	1	0	0	0	0
Send notification to Slack when Sprin...	1	< 1	0.9	0	1	0	0	0
Bug - Auto assign incoming bugs	1	< 1	0.1	0	1	0	0	0

Showing top 20 rules

Figure 10.8 – Viewing performance insights

Let's take a quick look at the various aspects of the performance insights:

1. Use the time resolution options to select whether the graph shows the last hour, day, week, or month's worth of rule executions. Click the circular arrow icon to refresh the data on the screen.

2. For each data point, the graph shows the total number of rule executions, the number of successful rule executions, the number of executions with errors, and the number of executions that were throttled. Hovering over the graph with your mouse will show you the actual number for each of the data points.

3. The drop-down menu directly above the table allows you to select what data is displayed in the rule status columns on the right-hand side of the table. The available options are **Execution count**, **Average duration (s)**, and **Total duration (s)**.

4. The table below the graph shows the top 20 rules that are displayed on the graph. These are sorted by descending execution count by default.

    You can sort the table by **Execution count**, **Total duration**, or **Average duration** in ascending or descending order by clicking on each of the appropriate column headings.

    Clicking on a rule name will take you to the audit log for that particular rule, which will allow you to examine the log in more detail.

As you can see, the performance insights let you quickly see how your rules are performing and allow you to drill down into the problem rules.

Using the performance insights sorted by average duration will allow you to see which rules are taking longer to run per execution. These rules could be prime candidates for further examination to see whether they could benefit from performance enhancements.

Rules with large numbers of executions and slow durations could be candidates for eventually breaching the processing time limits and should be examined for possible improvements. There is no definitive measure about what is considered slow due to how the individual configuration of each Jira instance can vary. You should therefore examine the durations in the context of your other rules, taking into account the specific configurations of your Jira instance.

Summary

In this chapter, we have learned how to approach troubleshooting our automation rules when things go wrong or when our rules start performing sub-optimally.

We have learned how the audit log works and the wealth of information it provides in order to gain insights into what is happening when a rule is executed. In addition, we also learned how to make use of the audit log to output messages, which will help you to debug your rules.

We also learned about the various service limits and how to monitor these using automation rules, giving us the ability to receive an early warning before rules breach their processing limits.

Finally, we looked at the performance insights available to project and global administrators and learned how this gives an overview of the performance of the rules in the system and how we can use this to stay on top of possible performance issues.

By understanding how to use the audit log for debugging, you will be able to write more robust rules and also be able to quickly determine when smart values or functions are causing rules to fail and be able to identify the problem.

Knowing how the service limits work and how you can monitor them using both automation rules and by inspecting the performance insights will enable you to maintain the performance of your Jira instance.

In the next chapter, we'll be looking at another well-known automation app in the Atlassian ecosystem that allows us to perform more advanced automations using Groovy scripting.

11
Beyond Automation; an Introduction to Scripting

In this book, we have focused on automating everyday tasks in Jira using a code-free approach. This automation functionality is native to Jira Cloud and is available in Jira Server and Jira Data Center with the addition of the *Automation for Jira* app.

This approach makes it very easy for Jira administrators to get up and running with automation quickly as they require no specialist coding knowledge. In addition, the ability to create automations can be delegated to project administrators, thereby allowing Jira administrators to focus on other tasks.

However, any book on automation in Jira would not be complete if it did not mention scripting and, in particular, **ScriptRunner for Jira**, which is arguably the most well-known automation app available.

In this chapter, we'll provide a brief introduction to ScriptRunner for Jira and to the Groovy scripting language, which ScriptRunner uses under the hood. In addition, we'll look at the differences between scripting for Jira Cloud and Jira Server.

We will cover the following topics in this chapter:

- Introducing advanced automations with ScriptRunner
- Exploring scripting in Jira Cloud
- Exploring scripting in Jira Server

Technical requirements

The requirements for this chapter are as follows:

- **Jira cloud environment**: If you don't already have access to Jira, you can create a free Jira Cloud account at `https://www.atlassian.com/software/jira/free` and ensure that you have both Jira Software and Jira Service Management selected. You will also need to install *ScriptRunner for Jira* from the Atlassian Marketplace.

- **Jira Server environment**: If you are using Jira Server (available from `https://www.atlassian.com/software/jira/download`), ensure that you have licenses for both Jira Software and Jira Service Desk. In addition, you will also need to ensure that you install the *ScriptRunner for Jira* app available from the Atlassian Marketplace.

You will need to be a global Jira administrator in order to follow the examples in this chapter. In addition, we have used the *IT Service Management project template* to create the Service Desk project that these examples run against.

You can download the latest code samples for this chapter from this book's official GitHub repository at `https://github.com/PacktPublishing/Automate-Everyday-Tasks-in-Jira`. Please visit the following link to check the CiA videos: `https://bit.ly/39L6BIB`

Introducing advanced automations with ScriptRunner

ScriptRunner for Jira allows you to extend the functionality of both Jira Cloud and Jira Server or Jira Data Center using scripts written in the **Groovy** language.

The ability to use the Groovy language in your automations gives you access to the underlying Java platform and the Jira API, as well as providing the full power of the scripting language itself.

As we'll see, in the case of Jira Cloud, access to the Jira API is limited to the interaction with the REST API provided by Jira. In Jira Server, however, your scripts gain access to the entire API that Jira exposes to developers.

We'll begin this section with a quick introduction to the Groovy language, which underpins ScriptRunner, followed by an overview of the ScriptRunner for Jira app.

Introducing Groovy

Groovy, or **Apache Groovy** to give it its full name, is a programming language built on the Java platform. It is both a static language, in that it can be compiled to bytecode, as well as a dynamic language in that it can be interpreted at runtime.

Groovy is syntax-compatible with Java. This means that it integrates and operates seamlessly with Java and, more importantly, with third-party libraries. It also means that you can write Java code in a Groovy script and have it correctly interpreted and executed.

In addition, Groovy supports functional programming and optional typing, meaning it can infer the object type at runtime. It also has a much more concise and expressive syntax than Java and is able to efficiently process both XML and JSON.

Let's take a look at an example that highlights both the differences and similarities between Java and Groovy.

In this example, we will create a list of names and then iterate that list, printing each name out to the console, prepended with the word `"Hello"`, using the following code:

```
List<String> nameList = new ArrayList<>();
nameList.add("Andrew");
nameList.add("Evelyn");
nameList.add("Tony");

for (String name : nameList) {
    System.out.println("Hello " + name);
}
```

Although this code is written in Java, it can run entirely unmodified in Groovy. When writing scripts, an execution context is usually provided by the application. This execution context is essentially an empty method within a class and our script is the method body, so we do not need to declare a surrounding class or method.

Now, let's take a look at the Groovy version of the previous code:

```groovy
def nameList = ["Andrew", "Evelyn", "Tony"]
nameList.each { name ->
    println "Hello ${name}"
}
```

This Groovy script is equivalent to the Java code we saw previously. Let's take a quick look at what is going on in this example line by line:

- `def nameList = ["Andrew", "Evelyn", "Tony"]`: We have used optional typing for the `nameList` variable by declaring it using the `def` keyword. In addition, we have initialized the variable with a list of strings using square brackets.

- `nameList.each { name ->`: Here we are calling the `each` closure on the list, and naming the closure parameter `name`.

  Closures are identified by the use of curly braces, while the arrow (`->`) separates the closure parameters from the code.

  When using a closure with only a single parameter, and where you do not need to reference the parameter in an inner closure, you can omit both the parameter and the separating arrow.

  In this case, the parameter name defaults to the word `it`, as seen in the following example:

  `nameList.each { println "Hello ${it}" }`

- `println "Hello ${name}"`: This line is using string interpolation to print the word `"Hello"` followed by the name currently being iterated.

Additionally, you will notice that the semicolon used in Java to terminate a statement is not required in Groovy.

> **Tip**
> You can learn more about Groovy on the official Apache Groovy website at `https://groovy-lang.org/learn.html`, where there are numerous books, presentations, and courses available to help you learn and get the most out of the Groovy language.

As we have learned, Groovy allows you to write concise, easily readable code in addition to enabling you to write your scripts in Java. Next, let's take a look at how ScriptRunner for Jira leverages this to allow us to create automation scripts in Jira.

Understanding ScriptRunner

Adaptavist's **ScriptRunner** is an app in the Atlassian ecosystem that has been around for over a decade. It incorporates the Groovy scripting engine and configures it in a manner that facilitates scripted access to Jira via the available APIs.

It has been the go-to app for many Jira administrators looking to both automate and extend the base functionality of Jira, and indeed other Atlassian tools, including Confluence, Bitbucket, and Bamboo.

In a nutshell, ScriptRunner gives you access to the Jira application by providing a ready-made framework with all the underlying plumbing already in place, thereby allowing you to concentrate on the business logic of your automations.

> **Important note**
>
> ScriptRunner provides a lot more functionality than just the ability to create scripted automations. It provides the ability to create workflow functions using both built-in and custom Groovy scripts. In addition, it also provides a number of powerful additional JQL features to make searching Jira easier. It also allows you to make customizations to the user interface using script fragments, the complexity of which will vary depending on whether you use Jira Cloud or Jira Server.

Adaptavist provides comprehensive documentation and tutorials for ScriptRunner for both Jira Cloud and Jira Server. You can learn more about *ScriptRunner for Jira Cloud* at `https://scriptrunner-docs.connect.adaptavist.com/jiracloud/quickstart.html`. To learn more about *ScriptRunner for Jira Server*, you can find the documentation at `https://scriptrunner.adaptavist.com/latest/jira/quickstart.html`.

> **Tip**
>
> Adaptavist provides a library of scripts that you can use as is or as a starting point for your own scripts. You can find these at `https://library.adaptavist.com`.

Now that we've had a brief introduction to ScriptRunner and the Groovy scripting language, let's look at how we can create automations using scripts in Jira Cloud.

Exploring scripting in Jira Cloud

ScriptRunner for Jira Cloud enables you to create automations in response to events that occur in Jira, such as when an issue is created or updated, among others. It also has an escalation service, which allows you to perform a scheduled action against a list of issues provided by a JQL query.

ScriptRunner also provides the ability to run scripts at scheduled intervals. This differs from the escalation service in that it does not require a list of issues on which to perform actions, allowing you to perform tasks such as creating issues on a recurring basis.

In this section, we'll take a high-level overview of how the Jira Cloud API works and then recreate the *Incident priority matrix* example from *Chapter 2, Automating Jira Issues*, to understand how to write automations using scripting.

Understanding the Jira Cloud API

In order for an app to integrate with Jira Cloud, it needs to be built using the *Atlassian Connect framework*. This framework allows apps to extend the Jira user interface, access the Jira APIs, and respond to events from Jira Cloud.

An app built using the Connect framework is a web application that operates remotely over the HTTP protocol. This means that when you build a Connect app for Jira, it needs to be hosted on a publicly accessible web server that can receive requests over HTTP from Jira Cloud, and which can send REST API requests to Jira Cloud.

The basic interaction between Jira Cloud and an app built using the Connect framework can be seen in the following diagram. This is a simplified representation as it pertains to automation with ScriptRunner:

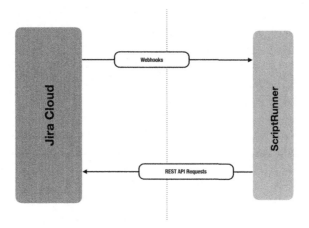

Figure 11.1 – App interaction with the Atlassian Connect framework

When an event occurs in Jira Cloud, a webhook is sent over HTTP to notify the ScriptRunner app that the event has occurred. This prevents the app from needing to poll Jira periodically to determine whether changes have occurred.

In response, ScriptRunner will initiate the execution of any scripts that are configured to listen for the specific events. In turn, these scripts make use of the Jira REST API to retrieve additional information and to update data in Jira.

Scripts that make use of ScriptRunner's scheduled or escalation service will only require access to the Jira REST API to interact with data in Jira.

> Tip
>
> You can learn more about the webhooks available in Jira Cloud at `https://developer.atlassian.com/cloud/jira/platform/webhooks/`, while you can learn about the Jira Cloud REST API at `https://developer.atlassian.com/cloud/jira/platform/rest/v3/intro/`.

Now that we've learned how the Jira Cloud API basically works, let's take a look at how we can use this to create a scripted automation in Jira Cloud.

Creating a scripted automation in Jira Cloud

In this example, we are going to recreate the incident priority matrix automation that we first introduced in the *If/else block* section in *Chapter 2, Automating Jira Issues*. If you have a similar rule using Jira Automation, you should disable it before implementing this rule.

This example will show you how to achieve a similar automation in Jira Cloud utilizing a Groovy script and the Jira Cloud API.

The Groovy script we will use to achieve this is shown in the following screenshot:

```
1    // get custom fields
2    def customFields = get("/rest/api/2/field")              ①
3            .asObject(List)
4            .body
5            .findAll { (it as Map).custom } as List<Map>
6
7    // find the IDs for the Impact and Urgency custom fields
8    def impactCFId = customFields.find { it.name == 'Impact' }?.id    ②
9    def urgencyCFId = customFields.find { it.name == 'Urgency' }?.id
10
11   // get the Impact and Urgency values for this issue
12   def impact = issue.fields[impactCFId]                    ③
13   def urgency = issue.fields[urgencyCFId]
14
15   // set the default priority to 'Lowest'
16   def priority = 'Lowest'
17
18   // work out the correct priority
19 ▼ switch (impact) {                                        ④
20       case 'High':
21           if (urgency == 'High') priority = 'Highest'
22           if (urgency == 'Medium') priority = 'High'
23           if (urgency == 'Low') priority = 'Medium'
24           break
25       case 'Medium':
26           if (urgency == 'High') priority = 'High'
27           if (urgency == 'Medium') priority = 'Medium'
28           if (urgency == 'Low') priority = 'Low'
29           break
30       case 'Low':
31           if (urgency == 'High') priority = 'Medium'
32           if (urgency == 'Medium') priority = 'Low'
33           if (urgency == 'Low') priority = 'Lowest'
34           break
35 ▲ }
36
37   // update the issue with the new priority
38   def resp = put("/rest/api/2/issue/${issue.key}")         ⑤
39           .header('Content-Type', 'application/json')
40           .body([
41           fields: [
42                   priority: [name:"${priority}"]
43           ]
44   ]).asString()
```

Figure 11.2 – The incident priority matrix script in Jira Cloud

Let's take a look at what's going on in this script:

1. The first thing we do is use Jira's REST API to retrieve all the custom fields into a list stored in the `customFields` variable.

2. Using the list of custom fields, we then ascertain the IDs of the `Impact` and `Urgency` fields and save them in the corresponding variables.

3. Now that we have the IDs for the `Impact` and `Urgency` fields, we can use these to extract their respective values from the issue, which is represented as a `Map` object.

4. In this block, we are using the values of the fields to determine the correct priority according to the priority matrix.

   We're making use of the Groovy `switch` statement to make the code more readable than if we had used an if/else block.

5. Finally, we use Jira's REST API to update the issue with the new priority calculated in *step 4*.

Now that we've created the automation script in Groovy, we need to create a script listener in ScriptRunner to actually get the automation working:

1. As a Jira administrator, click on the **Apps** menu in the top menu bar, and then select **Manage your apps**.

2. From the left-hand menu, select the **Script Listeners** tab under the **ScriptRunner** section, and then click the **Add Listener** button.

3. Complete the script listener fields as follows:

   Script Listener called: `Incident priority matrix`

   On these events: `Issue Created` and `Issue Updated`

   In these projects: `IT Service Desk (DESK)`

   As this user: `Current User`

4. We only want this listener to be called if the issue is an incident, so we need to add a condition to the listener, which will evaluate to `true` only if we're dealing with an incident.

   In the **If the following condition evaluates to true** field, add the following condition:

   `issue.issueType.name == 'Incident'`

   This will ensure that this listener only continues to execute if the name of the issue type is `Incident`.

5.   Finally, type the script into the **Code to run** field and then click **Add**. You can also download the script named 11.1 Incident priority matrix - Cloud. groovy from this chapter's GitHub repository and then copy and paste the code into the field.

Your script listener should now look similar to the following screenshot:

Figure 11.3 – Creating a script listener in Jira Cloud

In this section, we have learned how to recreate the incident priority matrix using a Groovy script in a script listener in Jira Cloud. You should now understand how scripting can also be used to automate tasks in Jira.

In the following section, we will take a look at how we can create scripted automations in Jira Server, and we'll reuse the incident priority matrix example so you can see the differences between the platforms.

Exploring scripting in Jira Server

Similar to ScriptRunner for Jira Cloud, ScriptRunner for Jira Server allows you to create automations in response to events within Jira.

Unlike in Jira Cloud, however, you are able to create automations against a much wider range of events in Jira Server due to the fact that you have access to the full Jira API.

In this section, we'll take a look at the API available to scripts on the Jira Server platform. We'll then take another look at the incident priority matrix example so that we can more easily understand the differences between scripting between the platforms.

Understanding the Jira Server API

In contrast to the Jira Cloud API, apps written using the Jira Server API run in the same Java process as the core Jira application and therefore have full access to the underlying application via the public Java-based API.

ScriptRunner for Jira Server is an app built using the Jira **Plugins2 (P2)** framework. This framework allows apps to register as listeners for events within Jira, as well as provide access to the underlying API and public third-party libraries shipped with the application.

The Jira API is vast, and fully understanding every aspect of it could fill a couple of books. For our purposes, however, we will concentrate on the `ComponentAccessor` class, which is documented at `https://docs.atlassian.com/software/ jira/docs/api/latest/com/atlassian/jira/component/ ComponentAccessor.html`.

This class is the entry point to most of the components you will require when writing scripts in ScriptRunner. It gives you a handle of things such as the `IssueService` and `IssueManager` classes, which deal with creating, updating, and modifying issues. You will also use it to get access to the `CustomFieldManager` class, which allows you to manipulate most custom fields you define in Jira.

> **Tip**
>
> You can learn more about how to use `IssueService` and `IssueManager` to interact with issues in Jira in the official *Performing issue operations* tutorial located at `https://developer.atlassian.com/server/jira/platform/performing-issue-operations/`.

To get access to `ComponentAccessor`, you will need to explicitly import the class at the start of your script as follows:

```
import com.atlassian.jira.component.ComponentAccessor
```

As you will see in the example we present in the next section, `ComponentAccessor` is integral to our ability to find and manipulate data in Jira Server.

Now that we've had a brief introduction to the Jira Server API, let's take a look at how we can create an automation script using the API.

Creating a scripted automation in Jira Server

In this example, we are again going to recreate the incident priority matrix using a Groovy script so that we can learn about the differences between scripting in Jira Server and Jira Cloud.

The script we are going to use for this example is presented in the following screenshot:

```
1   import com.atlassian.jira.component.ComponentAccessor    ①
2   import com.atlassian.jira.event.type.EventDispatchOption
3   import com.atlassian.jira.issue.MutableIssue
4
5   // retrieve the issue from the event    ②
6   def issue = event.issue as MutableIssue
7
8   // only continue if the issue type is Incident    ③
9 ▼ if (issue.issueType.name == 'Incident') {
10      // retrieve the Impact and Urgency custom fields
11      def impactCF = ComponentAccessor.customFieldManager.getCustomFieldObjectsByName('Impact')[0]    ④
12      def urgencyCF = ComponentAccessor.customFieldManager.getCustomFieldObjectsByName('Urgency')[0]
13
14      // retrieve the values for the Impact and Urgency fields as Strings
15      def impact = issue.getCustomFieldValue(impactCF).toString()    ⑤
16      def urgency = issue.getCustomFieldValue(urgencyCF).toString()
17
18      // default priority will be 'Lowest'
19      def priority = 'Lowest'
20
21      // work out the correct priority
22 ▼   switch (impact) {    ⑥
23          case 'High':
24              if (urgency == 'High') priority = 'Highest'
25              if (urgency == 'Medium') priority = 'High'
26              if (urgency == 'Low') priority = 'Medium'
27              break
28          case 'Medium':
29              if (urgency == 'High') priority = 'High'
30              if (urgency == 'Medium') priority = 'Medium'
31              if (urgency == 'Low') priority = 'Low'
32              break
33          case 'Low':
34              if (urgency == 'High') priority = 'Medium'
35              if (urgency == 'Medium') priority = 'Low'
36              if (urgency == 'Low') priority = 'Lowest'
37              break
38 ▲   }
39
40      // find the Priority object
41      def newPriority = ComponentAccessor.constantsManager.priorities.find { it.name == priority }    ⑦
42
43      // change the priority of the issue
44      issue.setPriority(newPriority)    ⑧
45
46      // update the issue to persist the changes
47      ComponentAccessor.issueManager.updateIssue(event.user, issue, EventDispatchOption.DO_NOT_DISPATCH, false)    ⑨
48 ▲ }
```

Figure 11.4 – The incident priority matrix script in Jira Server

Let's examine what this script is doing:

1. The first thing we need to do is import the Jira API classes that we'll need for this script. Without these, the script will not compile and will not be able to access the Jira API.

2. Script listeners in ScriptRunner for Jira Server present an event object to the script. The event object contains the underlying issue in the issue field.

   Additionally, we are ensuring that the `issue` variable is cast as a `MutableIssue` type, which will allow us to make changes to the issue.

3. Custom script listeners in ScriptRunner for Jira Server do not have a condition field, so we need to use an `if` statement to ensure that we only continue execution if we're dealing with an incident issue type.

4. Here we are retrieving the custom field objects for the `Impact` and `Urgency` fields by using the `CustomFieldManager` component accessible from `ComponentAccessor`. In this example, I am retrieving the fields by name rather than by ID, but you could use either method.

5. Now that we have the custom field objects for the `Impact` and `Urgency` fields, we can use these to retrieve their respective values from the issue.

    In addition, we are also extracting the string representations of the value so that we can compare them in the next block.

6. In this block, we are using the values of the fields to determine the correct priority according to the priority matrix.

    We're making use of the Groovy `switch` statement to make the code more readable than if we had used an if/else block.

7. In Jira Server, the priority field is an object of the priority type, so we need to find the `Priority` object that corresponds to the string value we calculated in *step 6*.

    We do this by retrieving all the priorities in the system using the `ConstantsManager` class available from `ComponentAccessor`.

    We then use the `find` closure to search for the priority object whose name field matches the priority we have calculated.

8. Once we have found the correct priority object, we can update the issue accordingly.

9. Finally, we need to persist the changes to the database, and we do this by calling the `updateIssue` method on the `IssueManager` object, again obtained from `ComponentAccessor`.

    We do not want this particular update to cause any more update events to fire, so we use the `EventDispatchOption.DO_NOT_DISPATCH` option to indicate this.

    We also do not want any email notifications to be sent when we update the issue, so we set the final parameter to `false`.

As we have learned in this example, scripts written for Jira Server can take advantage of the full Jira API rather than the simpler REST API available to scripts written for Jira Cloud.

> **Note**
> Having access to the complete Jira API is both powerful and dangerous at the same time. You should exercise caution when writing scripts in Jira Server as a badly written script could cause severe performance degradation or worse.

Let's complete this example by attaching the script to a listener so that it executes whenever an incident is created or updated:

1. As a Jira administrator, click on the settings menu (cog) icon and then select **Manage apps**.

2. From the left-hand menu, select the **Listeners** tab under the **ScriptRunner** section, click the **Create Listeners** button, and then select **Custom listener**.

3. Complete the listener fields as follows:

   Note: `Incident priority matrix`

   Project(s): `IT Service Desk`

   Events: `Issue Created` and `Issue Updated`

4. Type the Groovy script into the **Script** field and then click **Add**. You can also download the script named `11.2 Incident priority matrix - Server. groovy` from this chapter's GitHub repository and then copy and paste the code into the field.

The new script listener should now look similar to the following screenshot:

Figure 11.5 – Creating a script listener in Jira Server

Now that we have completed this section, you have learned how to create automations using Groovy scripts in ScriptRunner for Jira Server. You should also now understand some of the core differences in scripting between the Jira Cloud and Jira Server platforms.

Summary

In this chapter, we have introduced ScriptRunner for Jira, an app that allows us to create advanced automations within Jira using scripting.

We have learned about the Groovy language, which ScriptRunner uses to enable scripting within Jira, and how Groovy can execute both Java and Groovy statements, which makes it easier to get started without needing to learn Groovy up front.

To understand how scripts interact with Jira Cloud, we learned about the Atlassian Connect framework, which is used to build apps for Jira Cloud, and how this enables ScriptRunner to provide scripted access to Jira.

We then learned how to create a scripted automation by recreating the incident priority matrix example from *Chapter 2, Automating Jira Issues*, and we learned how the interactions with Jira Cloud are performed by dissecting the script.

Next, we introduced you to scripting on Jira Server and learned how this differs from scripting for Jira Cloud by taking a very brief look at the Jira Server API.

To make it easier to understand the differences between the platforms, we reused the incident priority matrix example script and again, dissected the script to understand how to interact with the Jira Server API.

Understanding how to create advanced automations using Groovy scripts will empower you to create automations beyond the no-code approach, which has been the focus of this book and will enable you to customize your Jira instance to your own specifications.

That brings us to the end of this book, and my hope is that it has both inspired you and given you some ideas on how to take your automations to the next level.

Other Books You May Enjoy

If you enjoyed this book, you may be interested in these other books by Packt:

Scaling Agile with Jira Align

Dean MacNell and Aslam Cader

ISBN: 978-1-80020-321-1

- Understand Jira Align's key factors for success
- Find out how you can connect people, work, time, and outcomes with Jira Align
- Navigate and collaborate in Jira Align
- Scale team agility to the portfolio and enterprise
- Delve into planning and execution, including roadmaps and predictability metrics
- Implement lean portfolio management and OKRs
- Get to grips with handling bimodal and hybrid delivery
- Enable advanced data security and analytics in Jira Align

Jira 8 Essentials - Fifth Edition

Patrick Li

ISBN: 978-1-78980-281-8

- Understand Jira's data hierarchy and how to design and work with projects in Jira
- Use Jira for agile software projects, business process management, customer service support, and more
- Understand issues and work with them
- Design both system and custom fields to behave differently under different contexts
- Create and design your own screens and apply them to different project and issue types
- Gain an understanding of the workflow and its various components
- Set up both incoming and outgoing mail servers to work with e-mails

Leave a review - let other readers know what you think

Please share your thoughts on this book with others by leaving a review on the site that you bought it from. If you purchased the book from Amazon, please leave us an honest review on this book's Amazon page. This is vital so that other potential readers can see and use your unbiased opinion to make purchasing decisions, we can understand what our customers think about our products, and our authors can see your feedback on the title that they have worked with Packt to create. It will only take a few minutes of your time, but is valuable to other potential customers, our authors, and Packt. Thank you!

Index

debug smart value function
  used, for logging messages 253, 255
deployment build
  starting, via automation rule 216-220
deployments
  synchronizing, with sprint
      completion 216
DevOps triggers 11, 12
dot notation 139

E

edit issues fields
  about 52
  rule creating, to align user
      story due dates 52, 53
  rule creating, to align user
      story fix versions 52, 53
email notifications
  sending, with automation 102-104
email requests
  triaging, by rule creation 155-157
epics
  aligning 185
  synchronizing, via automation
      rule 186-190
event payload
  URL 212
external systems
  requests, sending 129-132

F

functional labels, examples
  customer notifications 239
  internal notifications 239
  software releases 239

support issues 239
synchronization 239

G

Git commits
  synchronizing 199
GitHub
  used, for releasing versions
      automatically 211
GitHub webhooks and events
  reference link 212
global audit log 247
Groovy
  about 266, 267
  script 268
  URL 268

H

high-priority bugs synchronization
  automation rules, creating for 228-230

I

if/else block
  about 30, 43
  rule creating, to define incident
      priority matrix 43-46
incoming requests
  processing 155
  rule, creating to route requests 158-160
  rule, creating to triage email
      requests 155-157
incoming webhooks
  data, working with 147
  used, for receiving requests 142-145

S

Printed in Great Britain
by Amazon

43625007R00176